D1209449

The Age of Louis XV

FRENCH PAINTING 1710–1774

Under the High Patronage of M. Valéry Giscard d'Estaing
President of the French Republic

The Age of Louis XV

FRENCH PAINTING 1710-1774

PIERRE ROSENBERG

1975–1976

The Toledo Museum of Art
October 26–December 7

The Art Institute of Chicago
January 10–February 22

The National Gallery of Canada
March 21–May 2

Library of Congress Cataloging in Publication Data 75–21037

French Painting
The Age of Louis XV.

Ohio	The Toledo Museum of Art
1975	June 1975

CONTENTS

COVER: Ranc, *Vertumne et Pomone,* detail

LENDERS TO THE EXHIBITION

AMIENS
Musée de Picardie

ANGERS
Musée d'Angers

AUTUN
Musée Rolin

AUXERRE
Musée d'Art et d'Histoire

BALTIMORE, MARYLAND
The Walters Art Gallery

BERLIN, WEST GERMANY
Gemäldegalerie — Dahlem

BIRMINGHAM
City Museum and Art Gallery

BOSTON, MASSACHUSETTS
The Museum of Fine Arts

BREST
Musée des Beaux-Arts

CAEN
Musée des Beaux-Arts

CHICAGO, ILLINOIS
The Art Institute of Chicago
The David and Alfred Smart Gallery, The University of Chicago

CLERMONT-FERRAND
Musée Bargoin

CLEVELAND, OHIO
The Cleveland Museum of Art

DETROIT, MICHIGAN
The Detroit Institute of Arts

DIJON
Musée des Beaux-Arts

DOUAI
Musée de la Chartreuse

DUNKERQUE
Musée de Dunkerque

FONTAINEBLEAU
Musée National du Château de Fontainebleau

HARTFORD, CONNECTICUT
The Wadsworth Atheneum

INDIANAPOLIS, INDIANA
The Indianapolis Museum of Art

KANSAS CITY, MISSOURI
The Nelson Gallery-Atkins Museum

LE HAVRE
Musée des Beaux-Arts

LE MANS
Musée de Tessé

LE PUY-EN-VELAY
Musée Crozatier

LILLE
Musée des Beaux-Arts

Lenders to the Exhibition

LONDON
Private Collection

MACON
Musée Municipal des Ursulines

MADRID
Museo del Prado

MARSEILLES
Musée des Beaux-Arts

MILWAUKEE, WISCONSIN
Dr. Alfred Bader

MINNEAPOLIS, MINNESOTA
The Minneapolis Institute of Arts

MONTPELLIER
Musée Fabre

MUNICH
Bayerische Staatsgemäldesammlungen

NEW ORLEANS, LOUISIANA
New Orleans Museum of Art

NEW YORK
The Metropolitan Museum of Art
Private Collection

NÎMES
Musée des Beaux-Arts

ORLEANS
Musée des Beaux-Arts

OTTAWA
The National Gallery of Canada

PARIS
Musée du Louvre
Musée du Petit Palais
Musée Carnavalet
Musée de la Chasse et da la Nature
Collection Beytout
Three Private Collections

PAU
Musée des Beaux-Arts

PERPIGNAN
Musée Rigaud

PHILADELPHIA, PENNSYLVANIA
Private Collection

PIEGUT-PLUVIERS
Private Collection

PONCE, PUERTO RICO
Museo de Arte de Ponce

RICHMOND, VIRGINIA
The Virginia Museum of Fine Arts

ROME
Galleria Nazionale d'Arte Antica Palazzo Corsini
Museo di Roma, Palazzo Braschi

ROUEN
Musée des Beaux-Arts

SAINT-OMER
Musée de l'Hôtel Sandelin

SAN FRANCISCO, CALIFORNIA
The Fine Arts Museums of San Francisco (M.H.de Young Memorial Museum)

SEVRES
Manufacture Nationale de Sèvres

STOCKHOLM
Nationalmuseum

STRASBOURG
Private Collection

TOLEDO, OHIO
The Toledo Museum of Art

TOULOUSE
Musée des Augustins

TOURS
Musée des Beaux-Arts

VERSAILLES
Musée National du Château de Versailles

WASHINGTON, D.C.
The National Gallery of Art

WORCESTER, MASSACHUSETTS
The Worcester Art Museum

PREFACE

WHY AN EXHIBITION of French painting of the 18th century, limited to the lifetime of Louis XV (1710–1774)? Surely this must be familiar ground to most of us. We know the great names of Watteau, Boucher, Fragonard, Chardin and perhaps a few others. But do we really know the depth and breadth of French painting of the Age of Enlightenment; and how many artists respected and successful in their own lifetime are now forgotten or almost unknown?

American collecting in our century has tended to emphasize the familiar names endorsed by the Goncourts, plus a handful of others. However, it is worth remembering that a certain number of religious paintings were brought to Canada from France in the 18th century. Later, but still at an early date, two pictures in this exhibition, *L'enlèvement d'Europe* by Noël-Nicolas Coypel, and Natoire's *La toilette de Psyché,* came to America in 1815 with the brother of Napoleon, Joseph Bonaparte, who lived here until 1841.

It is the purpose of this exhibition to present the 18th century in France in its own terms; to consider the work of artists successful and well-known in their own day; and to examine not only art made for the court which is best known to us today, but also the considerable body of work for the Church, for public buildings and for the newly-wealthy middle class. The exhibition in this sense is exploratory and adventurous. It presents many artists whose very names are now unfamiliar.

It is one of the remarkable qualities of this exhibition to redirect our attention toward the history and religious painting so esteemed by the 18th century. It has been the intimate, charming and sensual aspects of French painting that we have prized, but here we may see other facets of it, ones with strong roots in Renaissance and Baroque France and Italy. To this must be added the revelation of many paintings from French museums, churches and private collections that are little known even in France itself.

Among these pictures one can find relationships with French art of the 17th century, especially in some religious and allegorical works. But generally, the art of 18th century France is an expression of the broad new developments in French life and culture under Louis XV.

Louis XV, the great grandson of Louis XIV, was born in 1710 and came to the throne when only five years old. His long reign was marked by French participation in a series of inconclusive but costly wars. More important in characterizing the period were the powerful political and cultural influences of the king's two most famous mistresses, Madame de Pompadour, who influenced political policies for almost 20 years until her death in 1764, and Madame du Barry, who was powerful at court until her banishment at the death of Louis XV in 1774. Most important, however, was the growing intellectual freedom and economic rise of the middle classes, so evident in the *philosophes* and *encyclopédistes* who sought "universal knowledge" as they expanded their studies of science, literature, music and architecture.

Much of Paris as we know it today was built during the reign of Louis XV. Louis XIV had centered his reign at Versailles for political reasons. The resulting expansion of a hunting lodge into Europe's most magnificent palace was at the expense of 17th century Paris, which only dimly reflected the brilliance and grandeur of the Sun King's palace at Versailles.

However, although Louis XV continued to embellish Versailles with such exquisite additions as the Petit Trianon and the Opera, it was also during his reign that such glories of Paris architecture as the Ecole Militaire and Sainte-Geneviève (the largest and most important neoclassical building in France, now known as the Pantheon) were constructed; the Louvre was completed; and those great landmarks of city planning, the Place de la Concorde (then the Place Louis XV) and the Champs Elysées were laid out.

The new architecture, whose chief exponents were Ange-Jacques Gabriel and Soufflot, was characterized by a new classicism of clear and simple forms derived from Greek rather than Roman precedents. Not only Paris, but also many cities in the provinces, benefited from the enormous increase in public buildings, town halls, planned streets and quarters built throughout France during the second half of the reign of Louis XV.

The Age of Louis XV (1710–1774) was also the age of Voltaire (1694–1778), Jean Jacques Rousseau (1712–1778) and Diderot (1713–1784), three of France's greatest philosophers and writers. In their political philosophy, primarily expressed in Diderot's *Encyclopédie,* lay the advanced intellectual theories in which are the seeds of the French Revolution that came so soon after the death of Louis XV. It is Louis XV to whom is attributed the famous phrase "After us, the deluge" which predicted the close of a relatively prosperous and stable era in French history and the beginning of a new period of dynamic revolution which radically changed the political and social order of the West.

Plans for this exhibition were initiated four years ago when Pierre Rosenberg, Curator of Paintings at the Louvre, was invited by Toledo, Chicago and Ottawa to assist in the organization of a joint exhibition and to prepare this catalogue. We are principally indebted to him for his collaboration in this international effort, for his scholarly research, his guidance, his assistance in so many ways and his continuous and enthusiastic support of the concept of the exhibition. To the many generous museums and private collectors in France, the United States, Canada and other countries who have lent precious works of art to this exhibition, we are deeply grateful. To the staff members of our museums and many others who have given of their knowledge and time we express our appreciation and thanks.

Financial support and encouragement has come principally from funds administered by the trustees of our three institutions, generously augmented by grants from the National Endowment for the Arts of the United States, the Ohio Arts Council, the bequest of William E. Levis of Toledo, The Plough Foundation of Memphis and other special funds.

Finally, we are honored that the President of the French Republic, M. Valéry Giscard d'Estaing, agreed to place the exhibit under his high patronage, thus lending support and encouragement to the project. We are grateful to His Excellency Jacques Kosciusko-Morizet, Ambassador of France to the United States, who first proposed this patronage to his President, as well as to His Excellency Jacques Viot, Ambassador of France to Canada for his gracious encouragement of the exhibition at The National Gallery of Canada.

As in any great international cultural undertaking, many are involved with its presentation and success. To all who participated in this exhibition we express our gratitude and appreciation for their efforts which have expanded and deepened our understanding of a significant aspect of the history of French art.

JEAN S. BOGGS
Director, The National Gallery of Canada

JOHN MAXON
Vice President for Collections and Exhibitions, The Art Institute of Chicago

OTTO WITTMANN
Director, The Toledo Museum of Art

The English edition of the catalogue has been translated from the French and edited by J. Patrice Marandel and Susan Wise.

INTRODUCTION

ANOTHER EXHIBITION of French art! How different from others is the one presented today to the American and Canadian public? What about it is new? What is its organizer's point?

Without repeating what appears in our essay, let us only say that it seemed necessary for us to present a panorama, as wide as possible, of French painting during the era of Louis XV. Strange as it may sound, the many exhibitions on this subject and the books, even the most recent ones, on this period have shown or discussed those works brought into favor during the nineteenth century, rather than those considered important and appreciated during the eighteenth century.

By regrouping the paintings of about ninety different artists,[1] we have attempted to give, without pretending to be exhaustive, a more exact image of the opposite tendencies, of the varied movements, of the innovating or archaizing currents of three quarters of a century of French painting. Therefore, we have presented, without much consideration of their fame today, the works of those artists who were particularly famous during their lifetimes.

We have often chosen works shown at the Salons, regretting that occasionally we have been able to

[1] Almost twenty of these ninety artists are not represented in the collections of the Louvre! We are giving below a partial list of the artists not included in this exhibition: G. Allegrain, Arnulphy, Aubry, Berthélemy, Blanchet, Bonaventure de Bar, Bon Boullongne, Callet, Casanova, Châtelet, Clérisseau, Collin de Vermont, Demachy, Dieu, Ducreux, Dulin, Dumont le Romain, Dupont, Favray, Frontier, Gamelin, Houel, Huilliot, Hutin, the Jeaurats, Jollain, J. J. Lagrenée, Le Barbier, Lenoir, A. Loir, Lonsing, Manglard, Marot, Ménageot, Ollivier, Oudry *fils,* Octavien, Pécheux, Peyron, Pillement, Quillard, Raoux, Renou, Santerre, M. Serre, Silvestre, Suvée, Taraval, Tiersonnier, Trinquesse, Valade, Vestier, Voiriot, Watteau de Lille.

Certain dynasties of painters are represented only by one member of the family: the Belles by Alexis-Simon, the Parrocels by Pierre (and not by Charles!), the Van Loos by Jean-Baptiste, Louis-Michel and Carle, but not by Amédée and César.

exhibit only the sketch for a large composition while the artist actually considered his completed work far more important. We have also tried to reach an equitable representation among the different genres by showing as many portraits as still lifes and as many history paintings as landscapes or genre scenes. We have deliberately chosen works dated no later than 1774, the year Louis XV died; however, some were executed prior to 1710, his year of birth. It seemed crucial to consider the roots of a style, the origin of which is to be found among the best pupils of Le Brun and Mignard.[2]

Only a few of the paintings exhibited are unknown (although those by Vincent, no. 116, and Bertin, no. 7, have never been reproduced), but our hope is that we will not be reproached for either this, or the fact that only in a few instances paintings bear an attribution contrary to that which they have had until now (Allegrain, no. 1, Deshays, no. 27, Duplessis, no. 33, and Jean-Bernard Restout, no. 123).

Does this panorama, which we have attempted to make as complete as possible, correspond to the ideal exhibition about which we have dreamed? For the most part, yes. Without establishing a list of missing artists, one will regret the absence of a Hallé from Leningrad, a Lemoine from Sao Paolo, and a Pierre from the Musée Nissim de Camondo or another from the Church of Saint-Sulpice in Paris. Some will reproach us for not having shown any pastels: one knows, however, how fragile these works are and how carefully their loans must be handled.

[2] On the subject of the transformation of French painting during the second part of the reign of Louis XIV and the *Régence,* one should consult Pierre Marcel's *La Peinture française au début du XVIIIème siècle, 1690–1721,* Paris, 1906, and above all Antoine Schnapper's monograph on Jean Jouvenet (1974). We thank Antoine Schnapper for his constant and friendly help throughout the preparation of this exhibition, the choice of the pictures, and the redaction of the entries.

Perhaps a more serious criticism would be this: major personalities, such as Pierre, have been represented with only one painting, especially in those cases where the artist treated many subject types. But how is it possible either to present an exhibition, of hardly more than a hundred paintings, which is complete, or to do justice to these first-rate artists, by showing them at their best, when so much remains to be known about them? We will be satisfied, after this exhibition, if the visitor understands that painting of this period was varied and richly inspired,[3] and if puzzled by one of these pictures, this visitor reconsiders the ideas he may have received concerning a century which is simultaneously charming, solemn and moving. Our satisfaction will be still greater if this exhibition offers him the *"delectation"*, which Poussin considered the goal of art, an gives him impetus to know better those painters who have been seriously underestimated.

Let us add a few words concerning the catalogue itself. The entries are listed alphabetically. In each biography we have mentioned one or two bibliographical references which should indicate the present state of research on these artists. In the entry itself, we have greatly condensed the information concerning the provenance of the works; we have also given only one or two bibliographical references—the most important or the most recent ones, when they summarize that which has been written until now about the painting. The plates are in chronological order. When the painting was dated, we had no problem. When it was exhibited at the Salon, the task was not much more difficult, since the paintings were usually (but not always, see no. 45) executed shortly before their exhibition. However, in certain cases, the date was difficult to estab-

[3] The exhibition *Louis XV. Un moment de perfection de l'art français,* Paris, 1974–1975, is a magnificent synthesis of the arts during the period. In the sumptuous catalogue, we have given a first version of the essay below.

lish, and we know that new research will correct, or make more precise, those dates which are hypothetical.

One has recently proved that French painting in 1830 no longer was and could not be what it was in 1774.[4] Is this also true for the period about which we are concerned? During Louis XV's sixty-four years of life, were changes as importable, were currents as contradictory as those which occurred during the fifty-six years from the beginning of Louis XVI's reign to the Restorations? If between 1690, Le Brun's death, and 1721, Watteau's death, French painting changed direction, one cannot say, however, that it went through considerable changes during Louis XV's reign. If one looks through the plates of this catalogue, one witnesses the slow maturation of a certain style. Even more, one is sensible to a series of artists who do not feel the need to constantly change their style, or to rebel against the teachings of the former generation: they affirm themselves through continuity and faithfulness more often than through opposition and questioning. Perhaps this is the lesson of this "moment of perfection" recently celebrated in Paris.

We must now thank those who have helped us in this work; we are certain, however, that many have been forgotten here and beg their forgiveness: Mesdames and Misses A. Caubet, I. Compin, L. Duclaux, R. Erbslöh, J. Held, M. Henraux, I. Julia, R. Loche, M. A. Joué, J. Montagu, O. Picard, A. Pingeot, O. Popovitch, M. Roland-Michel, M. C. Sahut, M. Stuffmann, E. Walter; Messieurs A. Brejon, G. Brunel, B. Chesnais, Ph. Comte, J. P. Cuzin, M. Eidelberg, J. Foucart, J. R. Gaborit, Th. Gaehtgens, B. Hercenberg, J. Lacambre, M. Laclotte, G. de Lastic, S. Laveissiere, J. Lugand, E. Magnien, J. F. Méjanès, E. Munhall, D. Ojalvo, H. N. Opperman, J. P. Samoyault, A. Schnapper, J. Vilain.

Our gratitude goes, above all, to the lenders from Italy, Spain, Germany, Sweden, England, Canada, the United States and France, from Paris as well as from provincial towns. Without them, this exhibition would have been impossible.

We would particularly like to thank three people: Mr. Otto Wittman, Director of The Toledo Museum of Art, who initiated this exhibition; Dr. John Maxon and Miss Jean Boggs, Directors of The Art Institute of Chicago and of The National Gallery of Canada respectively, who have continuously supported this project. Without the friendly and generous help of J. Patrice Marandel, Curator of Painting, Susan Wise, Assistant Curator of Painting, Richard Born and Valerie Tvrdik, all of The Art Institute of Chicago, this exhibition would not have been realized.

PIERRE ROSENBERG

[4] *De David à Delacroix, La peinture française de 1774 à 1830.* This exhibition, the product of a friendly Franco-American collaboration, opened in Paris before being presented in Detroit and New York.

The Age of Louis XV

FRENCH PAINTING 1710–1774

FRENCH PAINTING DURING THE REIGN OF LOUIS XV, 1715–1774

IS IT PARADOXICAL to suggest that French painting in the age of Louis XV (1710–1774) is particularly misunderstood today? In spite of the considerable strides art history has made in the last half century to reveal information about Caravaggism outside Italy or about French painting during the reign of Louis XIII (to cite just two striking examples), or to continually revise or dust off our notions concerning periods always in vogue, art history has not touched upon this great moment in French art. Certainly one might argue that Boucher and Fragonard are popular, or that Chardin and Watteau are looked upon with much admiration. Indeed, no art history textbook omits them, and all museums dream of owning a few of their works which bring record prices in major sales. Luckily, sketches left by some of these masters "foreshadow" Impressionism! But, is it right, regarding one of the longest reigns in the history of France, that only a small number of painters are known at all, and that the art-world politics of an epoch, admired today for its elegance, refinement and *savoir vivre,* is remembered only by one or two improper anecdotes concerning the Marquise de Pompadour or Madame du Barry? Art history surely makes other demands, not the least of which is the respect for historical accuracy. In the following pages, we will attempt two things: to give, on the one hand, a brief, general outline of French artistic life during the age of Louis XV, a King who is still frequently and unjustly decried or at least too rapidly judged; and, on the other hand, to indicate how successive generations of artists borrowed from their elders while, on various grounds, distinguishing themselves from them.

It is generally known that eighteenth-century painting fell into relative oblivion at the end of the century; the so-called Neoclassical reaction was, to some extent, responsible for this development. But one must modify this judgement if only to recall that in 1794 David, at the summit of his career and notwithstanding the intolerance of which he was wrongly accused, summoned some of the painters he is said to have disdained, to assist in the formation of the Musée du Louvre: one of them was Fragonard of whom David remarked "à la fois connaisseur et grand artiste, il consacrera ses vieux ans à la garde des chefs d'oeuvres dont il a concouru dans sa jeunesse à augmenter le nombre." Additionally, one can recall that Denon, Director of the Musée Napoléon and effectually Minister of Fine Arts to Napoleon, distributor of official commissions, and supporter *par excellence* of modern art at that time, bought for his personal collection Watteau's *Gilles*. It is true that the price he paid for it, 150 francs (at the sale after his death in 1826, it brought 650 francs!) gives some indication of the discredit, at least commercially speaking, into which eighteenth-century art had fallen. In buying for 218 francs at the Bruzard sale in June 1839, three pastels by Chardin, two self-portraits and the *Portrait de Madame Chardin,* the Louvre proved itself most daring. Again, the price shows that the number of amateurs who bought the work of this artist was highly restricted.

It is often said that painting of the eighteenth century was restored to honor by the Goncourts. They are, in reality, only the most celebrated among others who were, above all, collectors. We must remember, within France alone, the Lavallard brothers who gave their paintings to the Museum of Amiens, Hippolyte Walferdin and the Marcilles brothers, Ernest and Olympe, as well as others, without forgetting the most remarkable of them all, Doctor La Caze, who bequeathed, upon his death in 1869, some 600 paintings to the museums of France. Without La Caze, the Louvre would be impoverished in the works of Chardin; fourteen of thirty-two Chardins in national collections and nine of twenty-three Fragonards came from his collection. Dealers and scholars followed the example of collectors. Studies, occasionally very well documented, frequently of literary, sentimental or licentious overtones, multiplied; the prices obtained at public sales indicate the amateur's new infatuation for this period: a Fragonard brought 35,000 francs in 1865 at the sale of the Duc de Morny; a Greuze surpassed the 100,000 gold francs at the San Donato sale in 1870—126,000 francs for *Les oeufs cassés!*

But who were the artists restored to honor? Their names are among those painters of the century still celebrated today: Watteau, Boucher and Chardin, born within four years of one another; Fragonard and Hubert Robert, born one year apart; and, to a lesser extent, illustrators and draftsmen of *vignettes galantes*—Gravelot, Cochin, Eisen, Debucourt, Moreau le Jeune, and the greatest of them all, Gabriel de Saint-Aubin, who in the words of Greuze, "avait un priapisme du dessin." If one adds the names Maurice Quentin de la Tour, who was a pastellist, and Greuze and Prud'hon, who continued to paint into the nineteenth century but in an eighteenth-century style, and if one omits from this list of honors the name Hubert Robert, one has a most accurate list of artists—painters, but also draftsmen and engravers—contained in Jules and Edmond de Goncourt's basic work *L'Art du XVIIIème siècle* published beginning in 1859. If we completed this list of painters with the names of Watteau's satellites—the painters of *fêtes galantes,* Lancret and Pater, and a few portraitists, especially Nattier but also Tocqué or Perronneau—would the list correspond to one that would have been compiled by a well-informed amateur of the eighteenth century? In other words, would these be the painters celebrated in their time? If, on the one hand, it is impossible to compile a list contrary to that of the Goncourts and which reflects a certain historical accuracy, it is, on the other hand, certain that the artists whom we have named were far from occupying, during their lives, the first rank or at least they were not the only ones to do so. The Goncourts' courageous effort to undertake the restoration of a century, of which they had considered only one aspect, was never followed up. It remains that, in spite of the various views imposed by different periods, opinions and criteria, by official recognition as well as by the monetary value of the works during the lifetimes of the artists or the international reputation they obtained, the eighteenth century admired in its own time is not the one we have learned to like.

One knows the official organization of artistic life during this period. One institution, the Académie, occupied the place of supremacy; the *Surintendant des Bâtiments* directed it; and one doctrine, the hierarchy of genres, in effect, epitomized it. Artistic life found its expression in the Salon.

During the reign of Louis XV, four notable men occupied the position of *Surintendant des Bâtiments:*

the mediocre Duc d'Antin, the legitimized son of Madame de Montespan from 1709 to 1736; the *Contrôleur général,* Philippe Orry, more competent in financial than in artistic matters, from 1736 to 1746; and from 1746 to 1751, the remarkable Lenormant de Tournehem, uncle by marriage of the Marquise de Pompadour. The Marquis de Vandières (1727–1781; no. 104)[1] succeeded him until 1774; Marigny was replaced briefly by the Abbé Terray, before the long and influential direction by the Comte d'Angiviller during the reign of Louis XVI. The mark left by these men on the artistic life of their time was profound. Obeyed in their choices, distributors of pensions and commissions, themselves informed collectors, they played a rôle which, again, has been wrongly studied, but the impact of which was to be frequently evidenced.[2] To mention only a few examples indicating the importance of this position, in 1727 the *Surintendant* wished to restore history painting; it was no longer possible for artists to publicly exhibit their work; only one Salon had been held since 1704. D'Antin decreed a competition with prizes between painters he considered the best at that time. Although Jean-François de Troy and Lemoine, great rivals of the day, shared the victory,[3] the critics unanimously preferred canvases by Charles-Antoine Coypel, *Persée délivrant Andromède* (Louvre; no. 20) and by Noël-Nicolas Coypel, his uncle and junior by four years, *L'enlèvement d'Europe* (Philadelphia, Private collection; no. 22). To cite another example, before he was appointed *Surintendant,* Madame de Pompadour had the Marquis de Marigny make the indispensable journey to Italy (from 1749 to 1751). The indolent and irascible Marigny visited the most famous monuments of Rome, of course, and also those of Naples and of Venice. He was accompanied by Soufflot, the Panthéon's future architect, Cochin, the erudite draftsman who was to become the *éminence grise* of the Académie, and the Abbé Le Blanc,[4] an art critic. Apart from the fact that this journey was itself important, it shows how seriously the office of *Surintendant* was taken.

It was the responsibility of the *Surintendant* to recommend to the King those artists who should be named *Premier Peintre.* This position, first and gloriously held by Charles Le Brun (d. 1690), and then by Pierre Mignard (d. 1695), was not filled for the rest of Louis XIV's reign. In 1716 the Regent appointed Antoine Coypel. At his death in 1722 it remained vacant for three years before going to Louis de Boullongne, who held it until he died in 1733. Lemoine had to wait until 1736, and the completion of his grandiose ceiling in the *Salon d'Hercule* at Versailles, to become the next *Premier Peintre* a few months before he took his own life. There was another vacancy, for the ten years from 1737 to 1747, before Charles-Antoine Coypel, Antoine's son, assumed these duties. He performed them so conscientiously that, until his death in 1752, he was able to exert considerable influence on the artistic life of the time. He was succeeded by Carle Van Loo. At Van Loo's death in 1760, Boucher became *Premier Peintre;* he was himself followed by Jean-Baptiste-Marie Pierre who held this office from 1770 on, during the entirety of Louis XVI's reign. Vien held this position only for a few months at the beginning of the Revolution.

It may seem surprising today that Boucher's name should appear between those of Van Loo and Pierre, especially since Van Loo was younger than Boucher. In the eighteenth century, however, this seemed a very natural choice, because all three painters enjoyed equal reputations.

THE ACADEMIE, founded by Colbert, and over which the *Surintendant* had authority, experienced a good many crises during the reign of Louis XV. Nonetheless, it continued to be a living institution which performed its many functions to perfection: it was a public art school for the most gifted young artists, selected according to merit and talent; it assisted the social promotion of artists; and it protected their interests. Foreign rulers passing through Paris never

[1] Younger brother of the Marquise de Pompadour, he was amusingly nicknamed the 'marquis d'avant hier', but was better known as the Marquis de Marigny, and at the end of his life, the Marquis de Ménars.

[2] Locquin, *La peinture d'histoire . . . ,* 1912; this irreplaceable and authoritative work concerns itself with only the second part of the reign of Louis XV, when Tournehem and Marigny held the office of *Surintendant.*

[3] Both pictures are now in Nancy.

[4] Le Blanc, 1970; his letters, published at the time of their trip to Italy, attracted considerable attention.

failed to visit it, to admire its collections, and to borrow ideas for academies that were being established throughout Europe. To be sure, the old Académie de Saint-Luc survived, but the Académie Royale was wise enough to admit talented artists, such as Chardin, who had not received their training there.[5]

How did one become a member? The long training was divided into three essential stages: the *Grand Prix,* the *agrément* and the *réception à l'Académie.*

The *Grand Prix* was obtainable only after careful instruction, which consisted of both practical courses and lessons in general culture. The young student was accepted only if he could present a *billet de protection* signed by the *académicien* who was sponsoring him and certifying that he had been trained in the rudiments of drawing.[6] He began by copying academic drawings by the professors.[7] He continued, studying casts from antiquity in the Académie's extensive collection before beginning the study of live models (who were exclusively male). There was a hierarchical order governing the position where one sat in the studio of the Académie to sketch the model, a respected man who was privileged to wear a sword and the King's livery. Deschamps was a famous model who, according to Wâtelet, held the position of model "pendant plus quarante ans". Theoretical studies were no less exacting: courses in geometry, perspective, anatomy, classes in poetry, and ancient or religious history and geography. Lectures by *académiciens* on a particular master (especially Poussin) or a particular problem in aesthetics followed. This training was intended to make the student an *honnête homme.* Blondel said about this type of education:

> L'Académie royale de peinture a pour objet de former des peintres, des sculpteurs et des graveurs d'un mérite éminent. Elle a pour base l'école du modèle, qui se tient tous les jours de l'année à l'exception des dimanches et fêtes, pendant deux heures. Cette école est conduite par un professeur, qui change chaque mois, et par l'un des recteurs, qui sert par quartier. Le premier moyen d'émulation dont on use dans cette école est de faire travailler pour les places. Le second, de faire couronner, tous les trois mois, trois des meilleurs desseins ou bas-reliefs faits d'après le modèle. C'est ce qu'on appelle les petits prix . . . Au reste, ce sont les grands prix qui excitent aux plus grands efforts . . . Le concours des grands prix s'ouvre quelques jours avant le premier samedi du mois d'avril. Ceux des étudiants en l'école qui se croient assez forts pour pouvoir en être se présentent au jour marqué en l'une des salles de l'Académie. Le professeur en mois s'y enferme avec eux. Il leur propose un sujet, qui est ordinairement tiré de la Bible. Ils composent sur ce sujet donné sans se déplacer. Leurs esquisses sont présentées dans l'assemblée la plus prochaine. L'Académie retient alors les meilleures, au nombre de huit au plus. Ensuite les esquisses sont exécutées en grand, dans des loges pratiquées dans l'intérieur de l'Académie, afin d'éviter toute aide étrangere. Ce jugement se fait le dernier samedi du mois d'août et est formé par le suffrage de tous les académiciens assemblés.[8]

In principle, the *Grand Prix* made it possible to live at the Académie de France à Rome, located in the Palazzo Mancini, and directed during Louis XV's reign by a succession of eminent painters. From 1724 to 1737 the excellent Nicolas Vleughels was in charge. He, indeed, revived this institution which, like the Académie, had been created under Louis XIV. From 1737 to 1752 it was directed by Jean-François de Troy, and then by Charles Natoire until

[5] See Montaiglon, 1875–1892, V.

[6] It should be noted that often a student was related to a painter, thus the dynasties of artists so prevalent in the seventeenth and eighteenth centuries.

[7] Examples by Jouvenet are still at the Ecole des Beaux-Arts.

[8] Blondel, book 6, p. 37, n. f; "The aim of the Académie Royale de Peinture is . . . to educate painters, sculptors and engravers of outstanding merit. It is based on the study of the model which is held every day of the year for two hours except Sundays and holidays. This class is conducted by a professor who is changed every month, and by one of the *recteurs,* who serves on a quarterly basis . . . The best means to stimulate emulation is to make the students compete for the best seats in the room; the second way is to award prizes every three months to the best three drawings or reliefs made from the model. These prizes are called *petits Prix* . . . However, the *Grands Prix* are the awards that call forth the greatest efforts . . . Competition for the *Grand Prix* begins a few days prior to the first Saturday in April. Students at the school who feel that they are good enough to take part go to one of the rooms in the Académie on the appointed day and present themselves as candidates. The professor for that month locks himself in with them. He suggests a theme, usually taken from the Bible. They execute a composition on this theme without leaving the room. Their sketches are presented at the very next assembly. The Académie then sets the best ones aside, no more than eight at most. These sketches are then enlarged, in separate rooms or studio cells that have been set up within the Académie to prevent outside help from being given. Judging takes place on the last Saturday in August and a decision is reached by vote of all assembled *académiciens.*"

1774, three years before his death at Castel Gandolfo.

The detailed letters exchanged between the King's *Surintendants des Bâtiments* and the directors of the Académie de France à Rome constitute a well-documented account of the picturesque style of life enjoyed in Rome.[9] To the gossip concerning the health of this or that *pensionnaire,* or the escapades and extravagance of another (including those sometimes lodged at the Académie de France without being *Grand Prix* winners, such as Barbault, who had "la sottice [*sic*] de se marier secrètement avec de la misère"), is added much valuable information on artistic life in eighteenth-century Rome—still the capital of modern art—on the works which the *pensionnaires* were copying for the King (mostly Raphael and the Bolognese, but also Caravaggio) and on the progress of one student, the difficulties of another, or the talent for landscape painting of a third. From 1754 the *pensionnaires* were required to send to Paris an *académie peinte* [a painted academic study of the nude] (no. 12) and a *tête de caractère* [a painted character study portraying a particular emotion or expression], as well as two or three drawings after Old Masters. In addition, they were advised not to confine their curiosity solely to Rome and its monuments, but also to visit Florence, Bologna and Venice. In 1747 it was felt that only fully-trained *Grand Prix* winners should be sent to Rome. The Ecole Royale des Elèves Protégés, a school for sponsored students, was created for this purpose, and directed by Carle Van Loo from 1749 to 1765 with the assistance, for literature, of the painter Michel-François Dandré-Bardon.[10] These three years of free education (there were about sixty students in all) delayed the departure for Rome of the Académie de France's future *pensionnaires* for that time and helped to correct any deficiencies in their early training.

After the most gifted young artists had returned from Rome, or when the others had completed their studies at the Académie, they all had to be approved by their seniors by submitting one of their works to the assembled *académiciens.* After being *agréé,* they were required to present a *morceau de réception* [reception piece] on a given subject within a set period of time—one year, as a rule. If the artist had chosen to become a history painter, he was required to submit one picture; if he had chosen either to become a portraitist or painter of still lifes, he had to present two. Chardin was remarkable in being *agréé* [approved] and *reçu* [received] by the Académie on the same day, with *La raie* and *Le buffet,* both now in the Louvre.[11] The reception pieces belonged to the Académie, and with a few exceptions (Ecole des Beaux-Arts, and the museums in Tours and Montpellier) are now divided between the Louvre and Versailles. Certain artists, such as Fragonard, were only *agréés.* He had won the *Grand Prix* in 1752 with his *Jéroboam sacrifiant aux idoles* (Ecole des Beaux-Arts). He was approved by unanimous decision in 1765 with his huge *Corésus et Callirhoé* (Louvre) but refused to submit a reception piece. A number of others who wanted to be admitted as history painters were admitted only as genre painters. This was the case of Greuze whose *Caracalla* (Louvre) was submitted in 1769. As a result he was so embittered that he refused to exhibit in the Salon again. But from then on, of the painters whose reputations still survive, there were none who did not want to be recognized by the Académie, not even Gabriel de Saint-Aubin who had tried to gain admission to the Ecole Royale des Elèves Protégés with his *Laban cherchant ses dieux,* recently given to the Louvre.[12] The Académie was a living institution, and although its decisions were often challenged, its rôle and importance were not.

The number of *académiciens* was variable. At the death of Louis XV the Académie had one hundred members, some forty *agréés* artists who were painters, sculptors, engravers or architects, and *associés libres* who were generally art critics or collectors, or sometimes dealers: La Live de Jully, Mariette, Caylus, the Chevalier de Valory, Wâtelet, Bergeret de Grandcour, and the Abbé Gougenot were among them.

[9] Montaiglon and Guiffrey, 1887–1912.

[10] Courajod, 1874; the Ecole Royale des Elèves Protégés is the subject of this excellent book.

[11] Fontaine, 1910 and Vitet, 1861; the Académie regulations, which were as unclear on these points as they were disregarded in practice, have been carefully examined in these two works.

[12] The sketch is in The Cleveland Museum of Art.

There was a significant separation between the common *académicien* and the *Premier Peintre,* on whom the King conferred the *Cordon de Saint-Michel* and sometimes a title of nobility. Restout, for example, one of the greatest religious painters of the century, was born in 1692; the career of this nephew of Jouvenet follows a straight progression. He was *agréé* in 1717 and was received by the Académie later. In 1730 he became an assistant professor, and professor four years later; in 1746 he was named *recteur assistant* and *recteur* in 1752; by 1760 he was director, and the following year he was made *chancelier.*

TODAY THE DOCTRINE of the hierarchy of genres is badly misunderstood, although in the eighteenth century it was still universally accepted and respected. For contemporaries it was the only scale of values by which to judge a work of art. Paintings were divided into categories according to their subject, and this classification survived until the middle of the nineteenth century. History painting, the *grand genre,* was supreme: the subjects of these paintings were taken from sacred or ancient history. Modern history, which meant Medieval French history, did not really make its appearance until the time of Louis XVI. Glorification of the King and portrayal of important events of his reign, however, did not end with the death of Louis XIV and belonged to history painting. Next in order of importance was portraiture, followed by genre scenes and, finally, still life and landscape painting. Why this hierarchy? How was it justified, and what were its consequences? It should be noted that the basic criterion was Man, and that in the eighteenth century the quality most prized in an artist was his *imagination.* Is it not more difficult to portray this saintly miracle or that heroic deed of antiquity (which the artist had obviously not been able to witness), or to record with his brush this Biblical episode or that passage from Ovid, than it is to paint a few apples or a dead jack rabbit? These objects could be arranged by the artist as he wished; he then copied them. The portraitist who not only tries to capture a likeness, but who also seeks to analyze the psychology of his model, ranks higher. This argument is supported by La Font de Saint-Yenne, the greatest French art critic before Diderot, in a frequently quoted phrase: "Le Peintre Historien est le seul peintre de l'âme, les autres ne peignent que pour les yeux."[13] Nothing explains this doctrine, accepted by everyone without reservations, better than these few lines written by the all-powerful *Premier Peintre,* Pierre, in a letter to Chardin. The subject at stake was a royal pension. Pierre wrote to the old artist, respected by all and who was on the verge of dying: "Vous devez convenir qu'à travail égal, vos études [Chardin's still lifes, genre scenes and pastels] n'ont jamais comporté de frais aussi dispendieux ni des pertes de temps aussi considérables que celles de Messieurs vos confrères qui ont suivi les grands genres."[14] One might wonder if Chardin accepted this kind of discrimination. There is every indication that he suffered his entire life from the fact that the *grand genre* was inaccessible to him. At the beginning of his career he was singled out as a still life painter by Largillierre, and without hesitation abandoned the Académie de Saint-Luc to enter the Académie Royale. He thus exhibited only at the Salon. When he introduced the human figure into his canvases—those admirable silent and contemplative genre scenes—he advanced a step within the domain of the hierarchy of genres, and yet another when he took up portraiture (which does not constitute the best of his work, except for the moving pastels from the end of his career). However, in order to deal with the *grands sujets,* he lacked the necessary and lengthy period of instruction by the professors. Further, he had not competed for the highly coveted *Prix de Rome,* or lived in Rome. Unable to realize this ambition, he wanted to do so through another. By his first wife, Marguerite Saintard, he had a son, Pierre-Jean, who in truth, had little talent for painting. By dint of skillful intrigue and playing upon the esteem in which he was held by his fellow *académiciens* who were more influential than he, Chardin was able to assure that in 1754 his son

[13] La Font de Saint-Yenne, 1752, p. 195.

[14] Paris, Archives Nationales, O[1] 1925.B, Letter from J.-B.-M. Pierre to J.-B.-S. Chardin, July 21, 1778; see also, G. Wildenstein, 1933, p. 139: "You must agree that for equal work your studies were never as costly in terms of time and money as those of your colleagues who worked in the *grand genre.*"

was awarded a *Grand Prix* for his *Mathatias* (now lost). This award was compensation for the one Chardin had never obtained. The story ended unhappily. It takes more than study to make a great painter, and in the opinion of Charles Natoire, Director of the Académie de France à Rome, Pierre-Jean was "un des plus faibles sujets de tous;" he lacked the one essential quality, talent. He committed suicide, it seems, by drowning himself in a canal in Venice, and not one of his paintings remains by which to judge his ability. Chardin found no solace in respect to his son's failure. Perhaps it would not be too "literary" to suggest that it was Diderot who was to profit, some years later, from the lessons that Chardin had tried unsuccessfully to instill in Pierre-Jean. Chardin, who had been responsible since 1755 for hanging the pictures in the Salon, also served as Diderot's guide there. Diderot was not without gratitude; he devoted some of his finest pages to Chardin's work.

THE SALON WAS the highlight of the year. Strange as it may seem, its history has never been the subject of extensive study.[15] The term "Salon" derives from the *Salon Carré* of the Louvre where exhibitions were held from 1737 onwards. The most important artists also had their studios in the Louvre. The first Salon (with a catalogue) was held in 1673, but it was not until 1737 that it became a more or less regular event—first annually, then every other year from 1755 onwards.

During the reign of Louis XV twenty-six Salons were held. Opening day was August 25, the Feast of St. Louis and the King's nameday; the exhibition lasted about 20 days. Occasionally the period of exhibition was extended so that certain pictures could be shown; this was the case in 1750 when Jean-François de Troy's paintings had not yet arrived from Rome. Also, after the scheduled closing, the exhibition occasionally remained open so that certain large-scale works commissioned by the King and which had been hung very high on the walls could be seen at a more reasonable height. Only *académiciens* and *membres agréés* were entitled to have their work shown. The number of works, including paintings, sculptures, and engravings, increased constantly throughout Louis XV's reign. There were sometimes as many as four hundred and fifty, and the exhibition often overflowed into the *Grande Galerie* and the *Galerie d'Apollon*.

In 1748 at the request of the Abbé Le Blanc, whose name has been mentioned earlier, a jury was appointed, apparently by Lenormant de Tournehem, to review, before opening day, works intended for the exhibition; though it seems that very few paintings were ever rejected. In any case, this formality did not apply to canvases submitted by Académie officials. If in 1763 a canvas by Baudouin depicting a priest teaching young girls catechism was refused, the cause was a complaint by the Archbishop of Paris. A *livret* (the first one dates from 1673), the ancestor of our catalogues, made the public's visits to the Salon easier. It listed all exhibited works, not in alphabetical order, but in order of the hierarchical importance of the *académiciens,* from the *Premier Peintre du Roi* to those painters most recently *agréés,* separating painting, sculpture and engraving. This *livret,* which occasionally appeared in a succession of updated versions, was originally compiled by the treasurer of the Académie, then by its secretary, and then in turn by Lépicié (the engraver, and father of Nicolas-Bernard), by the influential Cochin, and lastly by Renou. Receipts from its sale (it cost twelve sous in 1783) constituted a considerable profit for the Académie. Hanging the paintings was the domain of the *décorateur,* or *tapissier;* first this was Stiémart, then the draftsman Portail, who was replaced, unofficially, then officially, by Chardin. Numerous complaints were launched toward those who accepted this inglorious task, but hanging the pictures according to the hierarchical rank of the artist excluded preferential treatment toward this painting or that friend. The Salon was visited by the King, usually before the official opening. The exhibition gave rise to numerous comments, published rather promptly and semi-officially and the reading of which is often tedious but occasionally quite fascinating. Those who frequent the Cabinet des Estampes of the Bibliothèque Nationale are familiar

[15] Guiffrey, Table génerale . . . , 1873; although this was written a century ago and few use it as a reference, it still remains the best effort in this direction. See also, Zmijewska, 1970.

with the volumes in which Mariette, Cochin and Deloynes, *auditeur à la Cour des comptes,* grouped in chronological order most of these critiques, of which there are hundreds.[16]

Two figures give an indication of the Salon's importance: in 1755, 8000 *livrets* were sold; in 1783 sales were up to 20,000. In 1763 Mathon de La Cour estimated that the Salon received eight hundred visitors a day, a good attendance even today. Naturally there was a reason for the Salon's success: apart from the churches (the part they played is especially evident before the Salon was permanently re-established in 1737) it was the only place where an artist could gain wide public recognition and establish his reputation. Seldom would painters stand aloof from it, as did Fragonard. Although Greuze refused to exhibit his work there after 1769, he opened his studio freely to all visitors who wished to come; in any case, his reputation was such by then that he no longer needed the Salon to become known.

One might wonder if those painters honored in their day were also the most famous ones, and if their paintings brought the highest prices?[17] First let us consider the subject of royal commissions.[18]

Few purchases were made during the Duc d'Antin's administration. In 1736, for example, the year Lemoine received 30,000 livres in payment for his ceiling of the *Salon d'Hercule,* commissions were given for a series of hunting scenes intended for the King's *petits appartements* (Amiens, Musée de Picardie). All of the artists chosen—Lancret, Charles Parrocel, Pater, Jean-François de Troy, the young Boucher, Carle Van Loo—received the same amount, 3400 livres, for their respective pictures. The following year 500 livres were paid for each of Lancret's *Saisons.* Often the best paid commissions were tapestry cartoons by Oudry, as well as by Restout and Carle Van Loo. In 1751 Chardin was paid 1500 livres for *La serinette.* This was the only picture he sold to the King, apart from overdoor paintings for Choisy and Bellevue. Only Sébastien Le Clerc, who was paid 1200 livres, received less. Tocqué was paid 1650 livres for his *Portrait du Surintendant Lenormant de Tournehem.* Silvestre, Carle Van Loo, Restout, Oudry and Charles-Antoine Coypel received between 1600 and 8000 livres, surpassed by the 15,900 livres received by Nattier for his portraits of the royal family. Under Marigny in 1767, Boucher, then *Premier Peintre du Roi,* received 7200 livres for six pictures; Noël Hallé earned 9000 livres for his *Justice de Trajan* (Marseilles) and his *Hippomène et Atalante* (Saint-Etienne); and Hubert Robert earned 800 livres for a canvas of *Ruines.*

Actually, the price of a work was determined on the basis of its size and the category (history, portrait, and so forth) to which it belonged. During the eighteenth century the *Surintendant* and the *Premier Peintre du Roi* used their influence on numerous occasions to have the price of portraits lowered and that of history pictures raised in order to encourage painters who practiced the *grand genre.* On May 13, 1747, Tournehem wrote as follows: "Je n'entends payer dorénavant les portraits en grands . . . que 4000 livres, ceux coupés aux genoux 2500 livres et ceux en buste 1500 livres." A few days later Charles-Antoine Coypel, successful in obtaining an increase in the rates paid for cartoons for the Manufacture des Gobelins, that is, for large scale history paintings, said, "Je croirais qu'il vaudrait mieux distribuer moins d'ouvrages aux peintres et les payer plus noblement." In 1756 Cochin in turn managed to get a new scale of fees, even more favorable to history painting, "qui exige de plus grands talents."

More objective criteria are the public auctions, but they did not really come into their own until the middle of the century. Thus in 1769 at the sale of La Live de Jully, "ancien introducteur des ambassadeurs et honoraire de l'Académie de peinture," two of Boucher's pictures brought 1021 and 750 livres, and two Chardins brought, together, 720 livres. A Carle Van Loo brought 1200 livres, a Jean-François de Troy 950 livres; *La belle Stras-*

[16] Duplessis, 1881 and Zmijewska, 1970; these two works should be consulted for their treatment of the fifty-six volumes compiled by Deloynes, and on the Salon critiques.

[17] This is a poorly studied domain, and one regrets that no book has been written for French art, such as Francis Haskell's Patrons and Painters (London, 1963), devoted to Baroque Italy.

[18] Engerand, 1901; this work is a detailed study of royal commissions and is the source of our present knowledge of the subject.

bourgeoise by Largillierre brought 500 livres, and a painting by Hubert Robert sold for 360 livres. Two Greuzes brought the highest prices (2350 and 4750 livres) and a Lemoine sold for 9050 livres. In 1774 at the Vassal de Saint-Hubert sale, Chardin's *Aveugle des Quinze-Vingt,* and its pendant, Fragonard's *Joueur de vielle,* sold for 1700 livres; a Lemoine brought 900 livres, and a Carle Van Loo religious subject, 1600; and, lastly, Boucher's *Le sacrifice de Gédéon* sold for 1400 livres, while an oil sketch by the same brought only 75 livres; these prices are evidence of the contempt in which art lovers of the eighteenth century, unlike today, held this category of work.

A last word on the European fame of these artists: on October 1, 1757, Grimm wrote, "Le roi de Prusse a commandé, avant le commencement de la guerre présente, trois grands tableaux aux trois premiers peintres de l'école française."[19] It should be remembered that in 1757 Boucher was fifty-four, Chardin was four years older, Greuze was thirty-two and Fragonard twenty-five. These three *Premiers Peintres* were Carle Van Loo (born 1705, who became not only *Premier Peintre du Roi* but also, in the words of Diderot after his death, *"Premier Peintre de la Nation"*), Restout (b. 1692) and Pierre (b. 1714). These paintings decorate the *Prunksaal* of the Neues Palast in Potsdam. To conclude, let us consider a quotation which did not escape Locquin. Lagrenée *l'aîné,* who had succeeded Vien as head of the Palazzo Mancini, wrote in 1781 to d'Angiviller, the *Surintendant des Bâtiments*: "on ne commande point au talent . . . On est né peintre, comme on est né poète; en vain, par des règlements on exigera pour l'avancement de la peinture que l'on se lève à telle heure, que l'on se mette à telle ou telle autre heure à tel au tel autre ouvrage; tous les ordres, fussent-ils émanés du Père Eternel . . . tout cela et rien c'est la même chose. Les Arts ont toujours été et seront toujours enfants de la Liberté. La Peinture ainsi que la Poésie, est un beau feu qui nous anime et qui ne s'allume au commandement de personne, mais quand nos organes sont disposés à en recevoir la divine étincelle. . . ."[20] Thus, there was no mistake about this; it was not meant to produce painters forcibly but to support promising young artists and to help them affirm their talents. If the Académie was respected throughout the eighteenth century, it was because it was not an end in itself, but rather, a means, an instrument.

Has there ever been a century as seriously mistaken about itself? After reading Grimm and Diderot, or examining the list of artists awarded official commissions or appointed *Premier Peintre du Roi,* or after leafing through the sales catalogues of the day, one would be tempted to ask, what do we know about the period or these artists, so celebrated in their lifetimes? On the one hand there are monographs, often obsolete but occasionally excellent (such as the exhaustive studies of Watteau's followers or the eighteenth-century portraitists) which deal with painters who are particularly difficult to study because they were less famous during their lifetimes. On the other hand, there are the artists who are now merely names; their works, generally large in size, are neglected in the storerooms of French museums or lost in the depths of gloomy churches. Thus, not a single *Premier Peintre,* not even Boucher, has merited an accurate monograph accompanied by an indispensable illustrated *catalogue raisonné,* however respectable the works of Louis Dimier, Charles Saunier, Louis Réau or André Michel.

The stress has been put on only one aspect (the most seductive) of this period, but we lack an understanding of its institutions, of their real significance and of their ideals; in our ignorance we are contemptuous of artists greatly celebrated in their day. Is it surprising, then, that this period should have fewer and fewer champions and attract less and less attention? How can we relinquish this

[19] Grimm, Diderot . . . , 1877–1882, II (1813), October 1, 1757.

[20] Montaiglon and Guiffrey, 1887–1907, XIV (1905), p. 146; "No one can order talent . . . One is born a painter or a poet; vainly some will formulate regulations to make painting progress: they will ask to get up at a certain hour, to work on such or such painting at a precise time; even if these regulations came from the Eternal Father . . . they would amount to nothing. Arts have always been and will always be children of Liberty. Painting, as well as Poetry, is like a great fire that burns within us; no one else can start it; it burns only when our organs are ready to accept this divine spark. . . ."

image of monotony, with its frozen, smiling façade? And yet, what variety of inspiration, what diversity of talent, what originality one sees in the treatment of widely differing themes! We make no attempt here to give a comprehensive account of painting under Louis XV.[21] Let us try, however, to recall briefly the great moments of the period and the slow, but profound changes in painting under Louis XV. The purpose of the exhibition is to illustrate these changes. Most of the painters whose names appear below are represented in it, and the catalogue illustrations, which have been arranged in approximately chronological order of execution, are, in a sense, a visual commentary accompanying our text.

When Louis XIV died in 1715, France's most famous painters did not include Watteau, who was not to be admitted into the Académie until two years later as a painter of *fêtes galantes,* a category created especially for his *Pèlerinage à l'île de Cythère*. Instead, it included Charles de La Fosse, who survived the King only a year, Jean Jouvenet (d. 1717), Louis de Boullongne *le jeune,* who was to live until 1733, and Antoine Coypel, named *Premier Peintre* by the Régent, who had commissioned him to decorate the *Galerie d'Enée* in the Palais-Royal. One might add to this list of artists representing the *grand genre* the names Cazes, Sébastien Le Clerc II, and Galloche; in the field of portraiture, besides François de Troy, the list would include Tournières or Alexis-Simon Belle, and Largillierre or Rigaud, both of whom were already famous. The best known landscape artists were Etienne Allegrain and Domenchin de Chavannes; still life painting with hunting subjects was best represented by Desportes; the finest examples of genre painting were executed by Ranc (of provincial background like Antoine Rivalz), Bertin (one of the countless eighteenth-century Frenchmen who worked outside France), Favanne, Courtin, Grimou, and many others. An important observation should be made: these artists did not restrict themselves to a single style. Rigaud, a painter from the south of France and great admirer of Rembrandt, offered his *Présentation au Temple* (no. 87) as a gift to the King in 1743. Largillierre, trained in Antwerp, was another who painted religious pictures, landscapes and delectable still lifes (nos. 58 and 60), which helps to explain his admiration for Chardin. Desportes left a series of studies (no. 28) of landscapes or animals (mainly birds) which were painted from life and the spontaneity of which is worthy of the Barbizon school.[22] Jouvenet painted a few portraits characterized by austere grandeur. The life styles of these painters were also dissimilar: Jouvenet lived a sedentary life, ignored Italy and painted for the Church; La Fosse spent time in Venice, tried to establish himself in London and decorated Montagu House; and Antoine Coypel was interested in the theory of expressions (perhaps excessively so for our present taste). Countless other examples could be cited.

Can these artists be considered in terms of a *"style Régence"?* Although it is true that Watteau (who, it should be remembered, was born in 1684, and was just as isolated in that generation as he would have been in the following one) had some followers and was able to create a style distinctively his own, it seems more difficult to determine that which other artists of this period have in common. Le Brun's tyranny has often been referred to. Judging by the very different approaches taken by his emulators, associates and followers, from La Fosse, the Rubeniste champion of color, to Jouvenet, who was a Poussiniste and, according to cliché, established the pre-eminence of line, one may doubt whether this tyranny did, in fact, exist.

THIS GENERATION was rapidly opposed by a new one dominated by four outstanding personalities, all quite different: Jean Restout (1692–1768) who, generally speaking, can be said to have continued the tradition of his uncle, Jouvenet, whose clientele he inherited, especially the religious orders and the church commissions. Charles-Antoine Coypel (1694–1752), an artist, both ambitious and difficult to understand, who attempted to transcribe on can-

[21] This has been tried quite recently in England within the boundaries of a large exhibition, and even more recently in a book, although of high quality, the conceptions of which seem old-fashioned to us.

[22] These studies are now divided between Compiègne, Gien, Sèvres and the Musée de la Chasse et de la Nature in Paris.

vas the passions and emotions of the theatre and to portray the psychological tension inherent in the tragedies of Racine. Jean-François de Troy (1679–1752) with his bold and robust style, for which he was appropriately nicknamed the "Jordaens français", was a prolific and light-hearted, though sometimes rather flashy, painter; and Francois Lemoine (1688–1737), his rival, whose sensuality was more refined and introverted, wanted to prove, with his ceiling in the *Salon d'Hercule* at Versailles, that the French were as capable as the Italians of painting large mural surfaces in the *à ciel ouvert* technique. Lemoine was never satisfied with himself, and took his own life when still young. As can be seen in this exhibition, all these artists painted portraits as well. It was a field in which many specialized, for example, Nattier (although he was admitted to the Académie as a history painter; no. 73), Tocqué, and Delyen, as well as a host of others now forgotten. Their art was in a constant state of evolution, and not one of them can be described in terms of a narrow formula; a study of each would hold some delightful surprises, such as Restout's charming *Portrait de Jean-Bernard Restout* of 1736 (Stockholm). Behind these great names is concealed a host of artists who have been too quickly labeled minor, such as Nicholas Vleughels (1668–1737), Director of the Académie de France à Rome, who was fond of working on a small scale in a doubtless pastiche of Veronese. He also executed remarkable studies in oil (Louvre) with complete technical mastery. Others are Noël-Nicolas Coypel (1690–1734), Antoine Coypel's nephew, and Antoine Pesne (1683–1757) who successfully pursued his career in Berlin. There was also the mysterious Paul-Ponce-Antoine Robert de Séry (1686–1733) whose only popular work, *Portrait de femme* (no. 91), now at Lille, has saved him from complete oblivion. Michel-Ange Houasse (1680–1730), who painted an amazing series of views of Spanish towns and palaces (no. 47) was yet another, as well as Watteau's followers, Pater and Lancret, also Lajoue and Mercier. Finally, there was Oudry, whose marvelous series of *Bois de cerf* (no. 76) is at Fontainebleau.[23]

[23] Publication of N. H. Opperman's eagerly awaited monograph on Oudry's immense *oeuvre* will make it possible to judge the artist's talent.

Better known today is the generation of painters born around 1700. Of these, two names dominate: Chardin and Boucher. There are others, however, who should not be overlooked: Subleyras and Jeaurat who, like Chardin, were born in 1699; Dandré-Bardon and Natoire were born the following year; Frontier and Dumont le Romain, born in 1701; and Aved, born one year before Trémolières and Boucher, and who is represented here by his very fine *Portrait de Jean Gabriel de la Porte duTheil* (no. 2). Finally one might mention Blanchet and Carle Van Loo, born in 1705. Many of these painters were from the provinces, especially the south of France: Natoire, future Director of the Académie de France à Rome, was from Nîmes; Carle Van Loo, already mentioned several times, was born in Nice despite his name; Dandré-Bardon, the peerless draftsman and painter who is sometimes confused with Piazzetta and occasionally with the Austrian masters of the eighteenth century, was a native of Aix-en-Provence; Subleyras was born, not in Uzès, but in Saint-Gilles du Gard; Nonnotte came from Besançon; and Liotard, a great traveller, was born in neighboring Geneva. Last, there was Françoise Duparc, a woman painter who has been included in our exhibition, and who is known only by her pictures at Marseilles, probably her native city.

Practically all these painters went to Italy for more or less extended stays—Italy, with not only its Roman antiquities, but also its great Baroque painters (the Romans, of course), but also the painters of the Bolognese school, the Caravaggists and the sixteenth-century Venetian masters, whom Vleughels urged them to study. And, last, modern Italy, with its customs, the costumes of its people, its celebrations and the famous countryside around Rome. One of these artists never returned to France, Subleyras, whose training in Toulouse had left him with a taste for restrained and rigorously-controlled compositions. Italy was to teach him subtle juxtapositions of colors—blacks, whites, and pinks, which he placed side by side to rare advantage (as did his delightful rival, Jean Barbault (1718–1762), who also worked with Piranesi). When he died in 1749, Subleyras was one of the most famous painters in Rome. His *Messe de saint Basile,* painted two years before for San Pietro, established his reputation (with Vouet, Valentin and Poussin, he was one of the few Frenchmen ever to have the honor of a commission for the Basilica). But when the oil sketch for this painting (Louvre) was acquired for the King by Pierre in 1777, the artist's fame became even greater: was this picture, and his work in general, not considered one of the sources of the "*nouveau style*"?

Chardin was born the same year as Subleyras. Unlike the southerner, he never went to Italy; indeed, he scarcely ventured beyond the gates of Paris. Nonetheless, in spite of their different themes, (though Subleyras, too, painted a few still lifes and genre scenes, and even a nude (no. 95) that falls between similar works by Velasquez and Manet), these two painters have points in common: the same love of a silent world, and the same liking for the arrested gesture and for a solidly constructed universe in which emotion, although controlled, is ever present. Boucher and Carle Van Loo both were *Premiers Peintres du Roi;* both painted Mme de Pompadour and tried to make mythology pleasant and graceful; and both are misunderstood today. Boucher's copious work has been encumbered with drawings and sketches which have nothing to do with his sensual, animated, gay and alert style. Van Loo's work, more earnest, less easily approached than Boucher's, less brilliant, occasionally bland or even insipid, has been totally ignored in spite of its seductiveness.

The reaction to this group of painters, the most important of whom developed a luminous style, a lyrical art that was glowing and full of life, and which today might be called Baroque if the term had not become debased from over-use, was soon to be felt. The works of recognized painters of the new period, such as Noël Hallé (1711–1781), Jean-Baptiste-Marie Pierre (1714–1789), Joseph-Marie Vien (1716–1809) or Louis Lagrenée *l'aîné* (1725–1805), shared several elements which separated their artistic ideal from that of their elders. This new ideal appears again in the portraits by Perronneau (1715–1783), Drouais (1727–1775), Louis-Michel Van Loo (1707–1771), the Swedish artist Roslin (1718–1793), and Joseph-Siffred Duplessis (1727–1802). It is equally apparent in the works of the still life painter Bachelier (1724–1806) and Roland de la Porte (1724–1793) and the landscapists Joseph Vernet (1714–1789) and Lallemand (1716–1803), as well as the work of Gabriel de Saint-Aubin (1724–1780) and Jean-Baptiste Greuze (1725–1805), the two greatest artists of the era. This new restraint and control mark the efforts of a whole group of artists who were anxious to return to a less "artificial" style of painting, to a style that tended more toward an accurate rendering of facial characteristics or realism of landscape sites. Although it is impossible to summarize his career in a few words, it is Greuze who more or less epitomizes this movement. Even today he is still one of the most misunderstood and disdained artists in the entire history of painting, and it seems that there is to be no important exhibition to mark the 250th anniversary of his birth. In *La malédiction paternelle,* Greuze wished to paint a scene from everyday life; he apparently also wished to render the great themes of all times such as the story of the rejected son turned from his home. By the example he presents, he touches, rouses, and gives us cause for reflection, thus conveying to us a higher virtue. Supported by Lenormant de Tournehem, the history painters endeavored similarly to express these ideas. They were triumphant with David.

Fragonard and Hubert Robert were born a year apart, in 1732 and 1733. When Louis XV died they were over forty. Fragonard, by this time, had painted his principal masterpieces. He produced his *Figures de fantaisie* in 1769 (no. 38). But are they portraits in a traditional sense? Do they try, like those of Perroneau or Drouais, to render the features of the sitters or are they not, rather, costumed sketches, each of which represents a different character, like those described in La Bruyère's book? Fragonard was the most gifted of an entire group of artists closely associated with him. At the outset of their careers such painters as Brenet (1728–1792), Deshays, Boucher's son-in-law (1729–1765), Durameau (1733–1796), or Vincent (1746–1816) would use a face, a landscape or a genre scene as an implement for expressing themselves with lyrical enthusiasm and complete freedom. The artist is not overshadowed by his subject; contrarily, the model, no longer principally important, is merely a pretext for executing a picture, the subject of which is actually the painter himself. This thoroughly modern attitude did not become the essential element of a work of art until the end of the nineteenth century, when artists consciously exploited it, and it was accepted by everyone. However, to judge eighteenth-century French paintings from this single point of view, using the only criterion familiar to us today, and to talk about "pure painting" when the subject was still an integral and indissociable part of the work, is to limit oneself to the accidental and exceptional case of Fragonard, and to only a few of his pictures at that. To remember only one aspect of eighteenth-century art, one which was little understood even at the time, is tantamount to committing a serious interpretive error.

Hubert Robert was first influenced by Panini's pictures of architecture and ruins which he had admired during his years in Italy (1754 to 1765). Looking to the relics of antiquity for inspiration, he participated in the formation of a new aesthetic. French travellers and collectors began to decorate their houses with more or less imaginary paintings of Roman ruins, while English tourists preferred Venetian canal scenes by Canaletto or Guardi.

AFTER LOUIS XV's death, French painting assumed a new orientation. The most obvious outward evidence of this was Marigny's replacement as *Surintendant* by d'Angiviller, the choice of Pierre to fill the position of *Premier Peintre du Roi* after Boucher's death, and Vien's appointment replacing Natoire as Director of the Académie de France à Rome. Although Madame du Barry had commissioned Fragonard to paint panels for Louveciennes (New York, Frick Collection), she preferred Vien's compositions because his style was more severe and his execution more restrained. The change was certainly not a brutal one, and many artists continued to paint as before; within a few years, however, the atmosphere had changed. Fragonard, the painter of genius that he was, understood this perfectly and in *Le verrou* adapted brilliantly to the new aesthetic without repudiating his own.

Nothing could be more revealing in this regard than the Salon *livrets*. More space was given to painting concerning France's history and the heroic deeds of her soldiers. Serious subjects and *exempla virtutis* became increasingly numerous. As early as the Salon of 1771, Beaufort (1721–1784) showed a *Serment des Horaces* (no. 5), fourteen years before David's triumph with a picture of the same subject at the Salon of 1785. In the year the King died, Jacques-Louis David (1743–1825) finally, on his fourth attempt, won the *Premier Prix de Rome*. The year before the jury had rejected his *Mort de Sénèque* (sketch, no. 25; finished picture, Petit Palais), preferring Peyron's (1744–1818) painting of the same subject.

PAINTING DURING the reign of Louis XV has often been considered facile, charming, light, frivolous, and superficial. Everyone wanted this and considered it completely effortless and unambitious, or at least unpretentious; but the effort was hidden behind a smile. Conceived to delight the eye, eighteenth-century art was thought to evade the disagreeable and uninviting aspects of everyday life. It was not a case of prudishness—indeed, far from it—but rather, a case of good manners. Suffering was concealed, not because it did not exist, but because of a distaste for making others feel uncomfortable through an indecent display of it. We should be careful not to exchange this stereotype, which is far from being totally false, for another, which would limit art at that time to a single *grand genre*. Religious painting was certainly important during this century—a century not so irreligious as is generally believed. But still life played an important rôle, and the same collector who would commission Greuze to paint edifying themes would ask Fragonard for licentious ones. To be sure, the huge "machines" with obscure themes were the focus of every commentary, and were universally admired; but the artists who painted them acknowledged and appreciated the work of their less ambitious rivals. Hence works by Chardin were to be found in the collections of artists such as Dandré-Bardon or Jean-François de Troy. The most famous painters did not consider it beneath their dignity to descend from their pedestals: de Troy did so with *La moissonneuse endormie* (Nîmes; no. 103) or Pierre with his charming *Mauvaise nouvelle* (Paris, Musée Nissim de Camondo); there was also

François Lemoine with his *Partie de chasse* (Sao Paolo) and even Vien, who painted and sketched his fellow students at the Académie de France à Rome. It would take several pages to list all these delightful, surprising, and enchanting works.

French painting at the time of Louis XV is most varied. Profoundly tolerant and perhaps ambitious —hence its greatness—it is less easily understood than one thinks. Only a conscious effort toward comprehension—which many learned minds still do not make because of preconceived notions inherited from the nineteenth century, a daring but partial epoch—will permit us to appreciate its richness and to enjoy its unique and distinguishing qualities. This time, we believe, has come.

1. Jouvenet, *La déposition de croix,* 1709

II. Desportes, *Etude de nauges éclairés par le soleil couchant*

III. Desportes, *Etude de paysage: coin d'étang dans lequel se reflète le ciel et les coteaux*

IV. Watteau, *Le mezzetin*

v. N.-N. Coypel, *L'enlèvement d'Europe*, 1727

VI. Chardin, *La gouvernante,* 1738

VII. Boucher, *Le déjeuner*, 1739

VIII. Oudry, "*Teste bizarre d'un Cerf pris par le Roy le 3 juillet 1741*", 1741

IX. Subleyras, *Le bienheureux Jean d'Avila*

x. Bachelier, "*Tête bizarre d'un cerf attaqué par le roi le 2 juin 1764 dans les taillis d'Épernon*", 1764

XI. L.-M. Van Loo, *Portrait de Diderot*, 1767

XII. Duplessis, *Portrait de Mme Freret-Déricour*, 1769

XIII. Fragonard, *Portrait de Marie-Madeleine Guimard*, 1769

CATALOGUE

Height precedes width in the listing of all dimensions.

Due to the severe time limitations under which the English edition of the catalogue was prepared, the author was unable to read the translated entries which follow. *The Editors*

ÉTIENNE ALLEGRAIN
Paris 1644–Paris 1736

Académicien in 1677, Allegrain devoted his entire career to landscape painting. He worked for the Trianon and for the Ménagerie at Versailles. His abundant work is, still today, absorbed by that of Poussin, his evident model, and the work of Millet, Dughet, Glauber, and Van Bloemen. A classical artist, he constructs his landscapes with successive and rigorous geometric levels, and adorns them with figures and architectural ruins. Allegrain likes pale hues, foggy mountainous backgrounds and dusty atmospheres which he renders meticulously, foreshadowing the "Neoclassical" landscape painters. His work should not be confused with that of his son, Gabriel (1679–1748), whose paintings are less structured, freer in execution, and warmer. The clearly cut personality of Etienne Allegrain has not yet been fully reconstructed.

Antoine Schnapper has devoted a few pages to him in the catalogue of the exhibition, *Au temps du Roi Soleil . . .* (1968). One expects much from the exhibition of French landscape painting at the time of Louis XIV which will take place in Dijon in 1976.

1 *Paysage au Lac* PL. 10

Oil on canvas, 56.5 x 78 cm / 22¼ x 30¾ in.

Considered until now as a work by Francisque Millet (1642–1679) and exhibited twice with this attribution, this painting is without doubt by Etienne Allegrain. A comparison with two paintings at the Louvre, *Paysage à la rivière* and *Paysage au troupeau,* is sufficient proof of this. The two Louvre paintings were executed in 1700 for the *antichambre* of the *appartement d'été* in the Ménagerie at Versailles (Rosenberg, Reynaud, Compin, *Musée du Louvre,* 1974, pp. 12, 13; nos. 2, 3). Similarly to the *Paysage à la rivière,* the artist has enlivened his landscape, where water and mountains are brought together, with figures clad in classical garments. In addition, Allegrain uses, almost exactly, the same composition: the trees to the right of his canvas; and the tree which is reflected in the water at the center of the composition.

This painting gives one a feeling of silence and rest, and of quiet magnitude; it is this feeling which shows the artist's ties with the classical landscape formulated by Poussin.

Collection of Dr. Alfred Bader

JACQUES ANDRÉ JOSEPH AVED
Douai (?) 1702–Paris 1766

Aved, a pupil of the French engraver Bernard Picard in Amsterdam, arrived in Paris in 1721. He then frequented the studio of Alexis-Simon Belle and met Boucher, Carle Van Loo and Chardin, who portrayed him as his *Souffleur* (1734, Louvre). He was received in 1734 at the Académie with his portraits of Cazes and Jean-François de Troy (Versailles), and showed regularly at the Salon between 1737 and 1759. Aved remained influenced by his formative years in Holland. He received the nickname "Batave" and was a collector of Dutch paintings. A straightforward portraitist, one of the best of his generation, Aved moved away from formal renderings and researched a kind of "truth". His models were painted with frankness and he found his clientele principally among the bourgeoisie. George Wildenstein's monograph on Aved (1922) is exemplary (see also, G. Wildenstein, 1935).

2 *Portrait of Jean-Gabriel de La Porte du Theil,* 1740 PL. 58

Oil on canvas, 125 x 97 cm / 49 x 36¼ in.

PROVENANCE: Salon of 1740, no. 85 — Edouard Kann, Paris, in 1922 — Delaney, Paris — sale, Paris, Hôtel Drouot, December 10, 1956, no. J with plate — Wildenstein — acquired in 1963.

BIBLIOGRAPHY: G. Wildenstein, 1922: I, pp. 51, 53–55, 66, 72, 118, 121; II, no. 47, plate opposite p. 66.

Jean-Gabriel de la Porte du Theil (1683–1755) was *premier commis* at the Affaires Etrangères; when this portrait was painted, he had just played a prominent part in the signing of the 1738 treaty of Vienna which gave Lorraine to France. The document on the table alludes to this. In this portrait, the "masterpiece of the painter" (G. Wildenstein, 1922, p. 55), Monsieur du Theil holds in his hand the seal with which he has just stamped the treaty. The smoke of the candle used to melt the wax shows clearly that the act was recently consummated. Jean-Gabriel du Theil wears a sumptuous purple and gold costume with the *Ordre de Saint-Lazare.* He turns himself toward the viewer with an expression of satisfaction mixed with anxiety. Aved never went further in showing his concern to serve his model as scrupulously as possible.

The Cleveland Museum of Art,
John L. Severance Collection

JEAN-JACQUES BACHELIER

Paris 1724–Paris 1806

Pupil of Pierre, Bachelier was *agréé* in 1750. He was received in 1752 at the Académie as a painter of flowers and later, in 1763, as a history painter as well with his *Mort d'Abel* (Auxerre?) for which he substituted in 1764 a *Caritas Romana* (Paris, Ecole des Beaux-Arts). This painting appears in the background of the portrait of the artist by Wertmüller (Paris, Institut Tessin). Bachelier exhibited regularly at the Salons between 1751 and 1767 and again in 1791. In 1752 he was made Artistic Director of the Manufacture de Vincennes before its transfer to Sèvres (he eventually became Director of the Manufacture de Sèvres). Bachelier received important commissions (Choisy among others) and was a beneficiary of the Marquise de Pompadour. With the Comte de Caylus he played an important part in the invention of a new technique involving burned wax *(inustion),* called "peinture à l'encaustique". In 1765 he opened a free drawing school in Paris which met with great success. In 1786, Bachelier became the Director *ad vitam* of the Académie de Marseille. Bachelier is mainly known as a painter of flowers. However, he also executed hunting scenes, *trompe-l'oeil,* and figures of animals in the style of Oudry. Bachelier, not successful as the history painter he wanted to be, was one of the best painters of a "minor" genre which he treated without affectation. M. Faré's few pages devoted to this artist (1962) summarize our knowledge of this yet underrated painter.

3 *"Tête bizarre d'un cerf attaqué par le roi le 2 juin 1764 dans les taillis d'Épernon"*, 1764 — PL. 100

Oil on canvas, 79 x 98 cm / 31⅛ x 38½ in.

Signed and dated lower left: *Bachelier 1764 / Tête bizarre d'un cerf attaqué par le roi le 2 juin 1764 dans les taillis d'Épernon*

PROVENANCE: Louis XV, the painting once decorated the semi-circular staircase leading to the *petits appartements* of Louis XV at Versailles; it was at Fontainebleau between 1833 and 1837 and again in 1845 when it decorated the *passage* of the *appartements de chasses* of the Ducs d'Aumale and de Montpensier.

BIBLIOGRAPHY: "Louis XV à la chasse. . .", pp. 110–15.

After Oudry's death in 1755, it remained the custom to commission paintings of which the subject matter was the oddly-shaped antlers of stags killed at the royal hunts. This painting commemorates the hunt which took place on June 2, 1764 in the forest of Rambouillet and the brushwoods of Epernon where this large and old stag was eventually killed. Bachelier has placed the animal's head on the corner of a stone balustrade, against a cloudy blue sky. While meticulously rendering the antlers, the painter creates an original and unusual composition accentuated by the blue Magrittesque sky and the sun rays.

Musée National du Château de Fontainebleau

JEAN BARBAULT

Viarmes 1718–Rome 1762

Barbault, possibly Restout's pupil, arrived in Rome in 1747 where he spent his entire career. In 1748, Jean-François de Troy, Director of the Académie de France à Rome, asked him to execute twenty small, full-length portraits (eleven have since reappeared) of the *pensionnaires* of the Palazzo Mancini in Turkish costumes: "La caravane du Sultan à La Mecque" had been, that year, the theme chosen by the French for participants to the Carnival, and de Troy wanted to keep a painted record of the event (see no. 112). His first landscapes were done in 1750; the same year, the Marquis de Vandières, then in Rome, commissioned him to do twelve pictures representing "Italian costumes", a subject the artist was often to repeat.

Barbault was married secretly in 1753. A few months later, he was asked to leave the Palazzo Mancini. Henceforth, it seems he lived more often from the sale of his engravings than from the sale of his paintings. He executed over five hundred prints — mostly views of Rome in the style of Piranesi with whom he worked. Barbault is not only one of the witnesses of Rome in the eighteenth century, but also a delightful and enjoyable painter, exhibiting occasionally a touch of humor. His strange landscapes may have influenced those of Hubert Robert. He is an outstanding colorist who delights himself in mixing golds and purples, olive greens and blacks, with the refinement of a great artist.

We have tried in collaboration with Nathalie Volle, in our catalogue of the Barbault exhibition (Rosenberg and Volle, 1974–75), to indicate this artist's true position in eighteenth-century art, and to establish a catalogue of his work.

4a *"Chevau-léger"* — PL. 80

Oil on canvas, 27.5 x 18.5 cm / 11 x 7¼ in.

PROVENANCE: Comte Léon Vandalin Mniszech — sale, Paris, March 10, 1926, no. 31 — Mr. and Mrs. Henry R. Luce, New York — sale, New York, October 22, 1970, no. 75 — acquired in 1971.

BIBLIOGRAPHY: Rosenberg and Volle, 1974–1975, no. 33, pl. LIV.

4b *"Fille dotée"* PL. 79

Oil on canvas, 24 x 18 cm / 9½ x 7 in.

PROVENANCE: See provenance for no. 4a.

BIBLIOGRAPHY: Rosenberg and Volle, 1974–1975, no. 25, pl. XLIX.

During his visit to Rome in 1749–51, the Marquis de Vandières commissioned Barbault (perhaps through Jean-François de Troy) to paint twelve (or fourteen) "Italian costumes". According to old sales catalogues and engravings done after pictures of this kind, Barbault must have frequently repeated, and occasionally altered, these compositions until his death in 1762. For this reason it is impossible to prove that these paintings belonged to the series commissioned by Vandières. Set upon a hillock, the *"chevau-léger"* is profiled against a distant architectural background inspired by the Quirinal in Rome. The dusty light of the sunset makes his dark red, blue and gold apparel and his feathered hat shine. His elongated silhouette, with its tiny face, as if seen from below, fills the canvas. In this painting, Barbault attempts primarily to demonstrate his refinement as a colorist, his taste for a porcelain-like texture — enameled and creamy — and his very personal touch of humor. As for the *Fille dotée,* veiled in white, her particular charm comes from the strange appeal of this dream-like apparition.

Orléans, Musée des Beaux-Arts

JACQUES-ANTOINE BEAUFORT
Paris 1721–Rueil 1784

Beaufort, who was *agréé* by the Académie in 1766, is known today only through his reception piece executed in 1771 (no. 5). He had, however, exhibited regularly at the Salon between 1767 and 1783. He also received important official commissions for the *Salle de la Compagnie des Indes de Pondichéry* as well as for the chapel of the Ecole Militaire in Paris — an enterprise in which some of the better painters of his generation participated. The Surintendance des Bâtiments du Roi commissioned him to paint successively a *Mort de Calanus,* a *Mort de Bayard* and a *Duc de Guise chez le Président de Harlay.* If his *Brutus* has been well studied, clearly because of the famous picture by David (1784), the other works of this artist, which indeed received little attention when they were exhibited in the eighteenth century, are quite ignored. Perhaps they would reveal surprises: one would perhaps realize that Beaufort is more than one of the first painters to treat an heroic subject and to react against the rococo aesthetic, then much in favor.

5 *Brutus, Lucretius, père de Lucrèce et Collatinus, son mari, jurent sur le poignard dont elle s'est tuée, de venger sa mort et de chasser les Tarquins de Rome,* 1771 PL. 119

PROVENANCE: Barnett Hollander, London — Private collection, London.

BIBLIOGRAPHY: Rosenblum, 1970, pp. 269–73 — Rosenberg and Schnapper, 1970, p. 760.

This painting is a study (the sketch is in a Private collection in Rouen) for the artist's reception piece at the Académie, exhibited at the Salon in 1771 (no. 152) and today at the Museum in Nevers. The subject, *Brutus, Lucretius, père de Lucrèce et Collatinus, son mari, jurent sur le poignard dont elle s'est tuée, de venger sa mort et de chasser les Tarquins de Rome,* had already been treated, as is often the case with those subjects in favor during the "Neoclassical" period, by Gavin Hamilton, before David gave the story its immortal interpretation with *Le serment des Horaces* (1784, the year of Beaufort's death). One easily understands the reasons why this picture was well received at the Salon except, curiously, by Diderot. Seldom until then had artists tried to show so clearly an heroic subject composed so "nobly"; seldom had they tried to present it with this "terrible" simplicity where each gesture is meaningful. David, far from being insensitive to it, copied the painting (denuding the figures) and also copied the engraving by Domenico Cunego after the painting by Hamilton.

Private collection

ALEXIS-SIMON BELLE
Paris 1674–Paris 1734

Pupil of his father, Jean (a painter of Scottish origin), and and of François de Troy, *Grand Prix* in 1700, *agréé* by the Académie in 1701, received as portraitist two years later, Alexis-Simon Belle settled early in Saint-Germain-en-Laye where he worked for the exiled Kings of England, James II and James III, from 1701 on. Belle is one of the good portraitists of his generation, at his best when representing children (Versailles, *Mlle de Béthisy et son frère*). "Painter of three courts, that of the French, that of King Stanislas of Poland, and that of James III of England," Belle, to quote an eighteenth-century source (Dussieux, Soulié. . . , eds., II (1854), pp. 232–35), "excelled in portraits and through the delicacy of his brush added to the softness of his strokes a perfect likeness." Belle is the father and grandfather of two history painters of the eighteenth century, Clément (1722–1806) and Augustin (1757–1841).

J. Messelet has written some pages on the artist and outlined the catalogue of his work (in Dimier, II, 1930).

6 *Mme de la Sablonnière (?) et sa fille*, 1724 PL. 30

Oil on canvas, 137 x 105 cm / 54 x 41¼ in.

Signed and dated on the foot of the table, to the left, in capitals: *Peint par AS* (interwoven) *Belle 1724*.

PROVENANCE: Given to the Louvre through the Récupération Artistique par l'office des Biens Privés, 1950–1957 — transferred by the Louvre to the Musée des Beaux-Arts, Pau, in 1952 (M.N.R. 87).

Two other pictures are from the same year, 1724: the *Portrait de la princesse de Bouillon* (Baltimore, Walters Art Gallery), proudly signed *S. Belle pictor regis britain.;* and the portrait of *Louis XV en costume de sacre* recently found by F. Watson (1974, pp. 534–37, fig. 36), bought from the painter in 1724. The Pau picture — a mother giving her daughter a singing lesson (on the music sheet she holds, one reads, *"L'apologie de la Voix 1723")* — summarizes the qualities of the painter: beginning with the formulas established by Rigaud, and under the influence of his teacher, François de Troy, Belle wants above all — more than his two great rivals Rigaud and Largillierre — to bring attention to his models rather than to his own artistic expression.

Pau, Musée des Beaux-Arts

NICOLAS BERTIN
Paris 1667 (?)–Paris 1736

A pupil of Vernansal, Jouvenet and Bon Boullongne, Bertin went to Rome for four years after having won the *Grand Prix*. *Académicien* in 1703, professor twelve years later, Bertin refused the directorship of the Académie de France à Rome which was offered to him by the Duc d'Antin. He had previously refused to go into the service of the Kurfürst von Mainz who, like the Kurfürst von Bayern, collected his work. Painter of religious subjects (ceiling of the chapel in the Château of Plessis-Saint-Pair, 1718; sketch for it in Houston, Museum of Fine Arts; pictures in the church of Bury and at Saint-Germain-des-Prés in Paris; reduction of the Saint-Germain picture in the Louvre), he also worked at Meudon, at the Ménagerie at Versailles and at the Trianon. Bertin is at his best in small charming and acidulated works, refined in composition and sharply colored. Antoine Schnapper has written two articles on this prolific artist (1972; and *Bulletin of the Museum of Fine Arts*, Houston, to be published), whose work is well reprsented in German museums.

7 *Anacréon et l'Amour* PL. 22

Oil on canvas, 46 x 37 cm / 18 x 14½ in.

PROVENANCE: Acquired by the Musée des Beaux-Arts, Autun, at the public sale, Paris, Hôtel Drouot, May 23, 1973, salle 6, with its pendant representing *Vénus et l'Amour*.

One night, Eros knocked at Anacreon's door and asked for shelter; he was cold and wet; he dried himself at the fire. He then wanted to know if his bow was rusted and by testing it hit Anacreon with an arrow. This small, unpublished picture of a rare subject can be compared to the *Apollon percé par une flèche* (Baltimore, Walters Art Gallery), probably slightly earlier. Both are typical of Nicolas Bertin: the same taste for elongated figures, sophisticated colors, unwieldy attitudes, and heads thrown back. A curious chiaroscuro effect is obtained here by the double source of light — the fire in the fireplace, in front of which two chairs are silhouetted, the oil lamp casting its light on Anacreon. In front of the poet rests a book, titled in Greek, of one of his most famous works. This refined painting with its delicate touch of humor is indeed the work of a *petit maître*, but it is executed with perfect taste and devoid of vulgarity and facile effects.

Autun, Musée Rolin

FRANÇOIS BOUCHER
Paris 1703–Paris 1770

François Boucher first studied with his father and later with François Lemoine. He started working for the engraver, Laurent Cars, before working with Julienne, mostly on the engraving of the *Figures de différents caractères* after Watteau. He received the *Grand Prix* in 1724 and left for Italy in the company of Carle Van Loo in 1727. Upon his return in 1731, he became *agréé* and was received as a history painter (Louvre, *Renaud et Armide*). In 1735, he obtained his first commission for Versailles. From that point on, he took part in the most important decorations and remodelings of the royal residences (the *chambre de la reine* and the *petite galerie du roi* at Versailles; the *petits appartements, salle à manger,* and *salle du conseil* at Fontainebleau; the Bibliothèque du roi (today Bibliothèque Nationale); Marly and Choisy). He worked on various hôtels (for example, the Hôtel de Soubise, today the Archives Nationales), created sets for the Opera, and executed cartoons for tapestries (such as the famous suite of the *Amours des Dieux*). After Oudry's death, Boucher actually became *Surinspecteur* at the Manufacture des Gobelins. Yet, he did not abandon drawings, easel paintings, portraits, landscapes, pastoral and genre scenes, religious subjects, and *chinoiseries* as well as, of course, mythological paintings. After Carle Van Loo's death, Boucher was made *Premier Peintre du Roi.*

Boucher's total *oeuvre* is immense and uneven, especially that of his later years, which was severely criticized during his life, notably by Diderot, when the artist's style was about to become unfashionable. His studio, his numerous imitators, and his indulgent critics have contributed to the increase in the amount of the works that bear his name. One should regret (but the task is, indeed, colossal) that no one, in a recent publication, has tried to compile a strict and chronological *catalogue raisonné* that would enable us to study the transformations of his style and which would consider this *oeuvre*, today wrongly isolated, in its context. (One should, however, mention the book by A. Michel, L. Soulié and C. Masson (n.d.), and the exhibition catalogues of C. Sterling (1932), Paris, Galerie Cailleux (1964), R. S. Slatkin (1973), and P. Jean-Richard (1971).) Then only would it be possible to judge this artist: he was an outstanding decorator, passionate toward painting, and an unremitting formal innovator who wanted always to please and to seduce, yet never became vulgar.

8 *Vénus demandant à Vulcain des armes pour Enée,* 1732 — PL. 46

Oil on canvas, 252 x 175 cm / 99¼ x 69 in.

Signed and dated lower right: *f. Boucher 1732*

PROVENANCE: Musée du Louvre since the Revolution.

BIBLIOGRAPHY: Michel, Soulié and Masson, n.d., no. 315.

Vénus demandant à Vulcain des armes pour Enée was one of Boucher's favorite subjects. The Louvre picture, executed just after his trip to Italy (1727–1731), is one of the most accomplished versions of the subject. If something remains of the cold elegance of Boucher's teacher, Lemoine, and if there is still some clumsiness in the composition, in contrast, then, the freshness of the colors, the spontaneous execution, the flexibility of the naked bodies, opposed to the straight line of the sword which cuts the scene, show the artist's admirable rhythmic sense and talent for organization of the canvas. Boucher sometimes tires one by repeating his compositions too often. If his facility is disturbing, while making the mythology as pleasant and attractive as possible in this picture, he, nevertheless, affirms himself as the great painter later rewarded with the position of *Premier Peintre du Roi.*

Paris, Musée du Louvre

9 *Le déjeuner,* 1739 — PL. 57

Oil on canvas, 81 x 65 cm / 32 x 25½ in.

Signed and dated lower right: *f. Boucher 1739*

PROVENANCE: Anonymous sale, March 26, 1749, no. 50 — Prousteau sale, June 5, 1769, no. 51 — Gueting sale, February 19, 1848, no. 11 — Marcille sale, January 12–13, 1857, no. 6 — anonymous sale, April 13–15, 1881, no. 1 — bequeathed to the Louvre in 1894 by Dr. Achille Malécot; accessioned a year later.

BIBLIOGRAPHY: Michel, Soulié and Masson, n.d., no. 1157 — Rosenberg, Compin and Guilmard, 1974–1975, no. 92, pl. p. 119.

Several preparatory drawings for this famous picture (engraved by Lépicié in 1744) are known, notably one, at the Art Institute of Chicago, of the young man pouring chocolate (rather than coffee, in spite of the lettering under the engraving and the oldest sale catalogue where this picture is featured). Does this painting represent, as has often been advanced, the family of the artist: his wife, Marie-Jeanne Busseaux then twenty-three; and her first two children, Jeanne-Elizabeth Victoire (who married the painter Deshays) and Juste-Nathan, who in 1739 were respectively four and three? This is an assumption that goes back only to the nineteenth century. One very fascinating aspect of the picture is the depiction of the furniture of a contemporary bourgeois apartment: paneling, brackets, rococo clock, chocolate pot and the magot on a shelf, which is evidence of the period's taste for Chinese objects.

Boucher, however, does not describe only an interior and the rich dresses of his models. In this delicate genre scene, so close and yet so different from Dutch renditions of the same subject a century before, Boucher also shows his qualities and ability to use colors daringly; he also shows his ability to manipulate the spatial composition — he enlarges the room by using two devices, the window which brings light from the left, and the mirror (with its painted trumeau) in which the door is reflected.

Paris, Musée du Louvre

10 *Le moulin dit de Charenton,* 1758 PL. 89

Oil on canvas, 113 x 146 cm / 44½ x 57½ in.

Signed and dated to the right: *f. Boucher 1758*

PROVENANCE: Madame Veuve Lenoir — sale, Paris, May 18, 1874, no. 3 — Baron Anselm de Rothschild — Albert, then Louis de Rothschild, Vienna — Maurice de Rothschild, Château de Prégny — acquired in 1954.

BIBLIOGRAPHY: Michel, Soulié and Masson, n.d., no. 1763.

Boucher painted several versions of this so-called mill of Charenton, named after one of the favorite locations outside Paris where artists liked to stroll. The most famous versions are the picture in the Museum in Orléans, and the canvas recently acquired by the National Gallery of London (dated 1755: see Michel, Soulié and Masson, no. 1762). Neither of them, however, is as large as the Toledo picture, one of the masterpieces of landscape in Boucher's *oeuvre:* never was Boucher able to mix with such skill, fantasy and reality; starting from an actual location with its mill, its real trees, with washerwomen and a fisherman observed from nature, Boucher creates an idyllic landscape where imagination and invention play an essential part. Boucher alters nature, magnifies it, transforms it into something perhaps slightly artificial, but shows, at the same time, his qualities of invention and poetry.

The Toledo Museum of Art, Gift of Edward Drummond Libbey

LOUIS DE BOULLONGNE LE JEUNE
Paris 1654–Paris 1733

Pupil of his father, and brother of the painter Bon Boullongne (1649–1717), Louis lived between 1675 and 1680 in Rome where he copied Raphael and admired the works of the Bolognese painters. He worked at Versailles, the Trianon, Meudon, Fontainebleau, the Church of the Invalides in Paris (see Schnapper, 1970, no. 9), the Chapel at Versailles, and devoted himself almost entirely to mythological and religious painting. Ennobled in 1724, *Premier Peintre du Roi* the following year, Boullongne had a busy and brilliant career, which made him a respected and rich painter.

An outstanding draftsman (the Louvre owns a superb series of drawings executed in black chalk, heightened with white, on blue paper), Boullongne, in spite of his vast culture, is less original than his great rivals, Antoine Coypel or Charles de la Fosse. Boullongne *le jeune* deserves study additional to that by Caix de Saint-Aymour in his 1919 monograph. A pleasant painter, tasteful although lacking in boldness, Louis de Boullongne, even if one is not moved by him, compels respect for the correctness of his drawing, and the care with which he executed his paintings.

11 *Diane et ses compagnes se reposant après la chasse,* 1707 PL. 3

Oil on canvas, 106 x 163 cm / 41¾ x 64¼ in.

Signed and dated lower right: *L. Boulogne le Jeune 1707*

PROVENANCE: Painted for the *grand cabinet du roi* at the Château de Rambouillet which belonged to the Comte de Toulouse. When the Duc de Penthièvre sold the Château to Louis XVI in 1783, he kept some of the paintings which he put in his château at Chanteloup. They were seized there during the Revolution, in 1794, and given to the Museum in Tours.

BIBLIOGRAPHY: Caix de Saint-Aymour, 1919, cat. no. 403, p. 271 — Lossky, 1962, no. 17 with plate — Schnapper, Lille, 1968, pp. 49–50, no. 60, color plate.

Three preparatory drawings for this painting (could it be the one, of the same subject, exhibited at the Salon of 1740?) are known today: two at the Louvre and one in a private collection, Paris. Influenced by Domenichino's famous composition of the same subject (Rome, Galleria Borghese), the Tours picture also inspired Watteau, who borrowed the figure of the nymph drying her foot in a picture engraved (1729) by P. Aveline (the picture is known today through a different version in the Groult collection, Paris).

Pleasant and elegant, learned without being a pastiche, this picture falls at the beginning of a most important trend in eighteenth-century French painting — the *mythologie galante* — of which Boucher was to be the most distinguished representative.

Tours, Musée des Beaux-Arts

NICOLAS-GUY BRENET
Paris 1728–Paris 1792

Brenet, like the best painters of his generation, went to the Ecole Royale des Elèves Protégés, the director of which was Carle Van Loo. In 1756, he went to Rome for three years where he copied Caravaggio. From 1763 on he exhibited regularly at the Salon and, in 1769, was received by the Académie. Brenet worked above all for the Church, primarily outside Paris (Lyons, Versailles, and Douai, where he also painted the decoration of the *Grand'Chambre du Parlement,* Bayonne, Compiègne, and particularly for the Jura area, Pont-de-Vaux, Dôle, Salins, Chamblay, Ounans). From 1773 on, instigated by d'Angiviller, Brenet painted scenes from Roman history as well as from French history. Brenet occupies a prominent position in the movement to "renovate" history painting. His style, easily recognizable, owes something to his teacher, Boucher, primarily for the plastic as well as intellectual "readability" of the scenes he paints; these scenes show a concern for monumentality, with nobility and lack of movement, typical of his time.

Since the study by Marc Sandoz (1961), various articles (Mirimonde, 1968 and Pérez, 1974) have been devoted to Brenet. He does, however, deserve a complete monograph.

12 *Endymion endormi,* 1756 PL. 86

Oil on canvas, 80.5 x 101.5 cm / 31¾ x 39⅞ in.
Signed and dated: lower left: *Brenet/1756*

PROVENANCE: Private collection, Toulouse — private collection, Paris — acquired from Herner-Wengraf Ltd., London, 1973.

BIBLIOGRAPHY: Welu, 1974, pp. 5–7, with plate.

This work is one of the earliest paintings we know by Brenet: in 1753, Brenet had painted for the Concours, open to the pupils of the Académie for a position at the Ecole Royale des Elèves Protégés, a *Laban cherchant ses idoles* (lost today: see Pérez, pp. 199–212; the sketch for the picture is in an English private collection, see Marandel, 1973–1975, p. 15, no. 5 with figure) which had won the competition over the painting by Gabriel de Saint-Aubin (today at the Louvre; sketch in Cleveland). From Rome, where he lived between 1756 and 1759, he sent (as was the custom; see also no. 123), in addition to a copy of the *Entombment* by Caravaggio, a *Silence* and an *Académie d'homme* which Marigny (Montaiglon and Guiffrey, XI, p. 216) "blames for its olive-like hues. . . ." These pictures were sent only in 1758, and we can hardly believe that this *Académie d'homme* is in fact the Worcester picture dated 1756 (one should remember, however, that Brenet had been seriously ill in 1757). The technically confident Brenet — in his pursuit of a cold, nocturnal light, as well as in his care to achieve flat impasto — wished to treat his nudes differently from those of Boucher, which were painted with a broad technique and vivid coloration.

Worcester Art Museum, Sarah C. Garver Fund

PIERRE-JACQUES CAZES
Paris 1676–Paris 1754

Pupil of Bon Boullongne, *Grand Prix de Rome* in 1699 (his picture is now at the Ecole des Beaux-Arts, Paris), and *académicien* in 1703, Cazes had an official career: *recteur* of the Académie in 1743 and director the year following, he was made *chancelier* in 1746. He took part in the Concours of 1727 (*Naissance de Vénus*; several versions are known, the best of which is available on the current Italian art market) and of 1747 (*Enlèvement d'Europe)*, and in the Salon of 1737. Cazes, however, painted principally for the Church. In spite of this success during his life, Cazes is not particularly well known today, except for having been Chardin's teacher, probably around 1718–1720. Of his numerous surviving pictures, which are to be found in different locations and attributed to various hands (Amigoni in Sacramento; Natoire in Caen; Conca at the National Gallery of London until this painting was returned to the Victoria & Albert Museum under its actual authorship).

His style is rather distinct: he is fond of "draperies larges bien jetées", of oval and small heads lacking expression, and of colors "d'une fraîcheur admirable", to quote his eighteenth-century biographers, Dézallier d'Argenville (1762) and the Marquis d'Argens (1752) who also said that he "faisait les doigts des mains trop longs pour leur donner plus de grâce. . . ."

Isabelle Julia is currently working on a monograph with a *catalogue raisonné* of the artist. Her work will enable us to judge his talent and will place him deservedly among the good painters of the first half of the eighteenth century.

13 *La balançoire*, 1732 PL. 43

Oil on canvas, oval, 97 x 88 cm / 38¼ x 34½ in.

PROVENANCE: Painted in 1732 for the *petits cabinets du roi* at Versailles — Musée du Louvre since the Revolution.

BIBLIOGRAPHY: Engerand, 1901, pp. 77–78.

This painting and its pendant, *Danse de villageois* (recently returned to the Louvre), were executed for the *petits cabinets du roi* at Versailles. The 1732 date borne by the *Danse de villageois* confirms its being one of the two paintings commissioned that year. In 1732 three artists, Galloche [see no. 39], Domenchin de Chavannes and Cazes, shared a commission by contributing two pictures: each artist then, for the two works, received 600 livres. The Louvre picture is evidence that Cazes, particularly devoted to mythological and religious paintings, also executed genre pictures with ease. The heads, small like the hands and feet of the figures, are without expression; the colors are bright and the composition, characterized by the spruceness of its agreeable rhythm, is very different from the spirit and technique of Fragonard's *Escarpolette* (London, Wallace Collection). These things give to this work charm and a very personal character.

Paris, Musée du Louvre

JEAN-BAPTISTE-SIMEON CHARDIN
Paris 1699–Paris 1779

Pupil of Cazes and of Noël-Nicolas Coypel, member of the Académie de Saint-Luc, Chardin was "discovered" by Largillierre who helped him become, on the same day, both *agréé* and received by the Académie in 1728 with two paintings: *La raie* and *Le buffet* (Louvre). In 1731 he married Marguerite Stainard. Two years later he began painting genre scenes in the Dutch tradition. In 1740 he gave Louis XV the *Mère laborieuse* and the *Bénédicité* (Louvre). Unofficially, from 1755 on, and officially beginning in 1760, Chardin was charged with the hanging of the Salon. This difficult task brought him in contact with Diderot who wrote some of his best pages on this artist ("Vous revoilà donc, grand magicien. . . ."). Chardin's fame, as a still life as well as genre painter, remained until agout 1770. At that time, his style became unfashionable. Furthermore, his sight dimmed and, in order to rest his eyes, the artist turned to pastels. Some of his most beautiful portraits (self-portraits and portraits of his second wife, Marguerite Pouget, at the Louvre) are done in this technique. The facts of Chardin's career seem opposed to the official organization of artistic life in the eighteenth century. He was not trained at the Académie, did not receive any *prix*, never went to Italy, did not attempt to become a history painter and received only a few official commissions. This, however, is somewhat misleading. Chardin was never a marginal artist: he was a conscientious *académicien* who accepted, without criticism on his part, the hierarchy of genres. Chardin, never having himself secured an official position, attempted to make his unsuccessful son a great official artist. A poet of the silent life, painter of restrained emotions (he said: "One uses colors but one paints with one's heart"). Chardin knows admirably how to construct a canvas and use colors. G. Wildenstein's monograph (the 1933 version is better than the one republished in 1963) has not been replaced.

14 *La gouvernante*, 1738 PL. 56

Oil on canvas, 46.5 x 37.5 cm / 18⅜ x 14¾ in.

Signed and dated left of center: *Chardin 1738*

PROVENANCE: Salon of 1739, n.n. — Chevalier Despuechs, Paris, 1739 — acquired by Prince Joseph-Wenzel von Liechtenstein during his ambassadorship, 1737–1741, in Paris — the Liechtenstein Princes, Vienna — acquired by the National Gallery of Canada, 1956.

BIBLIOGRAPHY: G. Wildenstein, 1933, no. 87, fig. 19 — G. Wildenstein, 1963, no. 191, pl. 29 .

"What completed his fame was the picture called

La gouvernante which was thought to have been painted for M. de Jullienne, who seemed to have wanted it but, which having, in fact, been acquired by a banker named Despuechs, was in turn bought for 1800 livres by the Prince of Liechtenstein during his ambassadorship in France" (Mariette, 1851–1860, I (1851–1853), p. 358). This picture (its pendant, *La pourvoyeuse,* dated 1738, is also in The National Gallery of Canada) was engraved in 1739 by Lépicié. It ranks, in this particular genre, among the masterpieces of Chardin. The half-open door, in front of which the young boy is silhouetted, allows the artist to open the background of his rigorously constructed canvas; this device also gives it a depth which the lines of the parquet reinforce. This work is animated by picturesque details — the playing cards, the shuttlecock, the work basket on the floor — all of which defray any excessive harshness without distracting the viewer. If in the eighteenth century one saw in this kind of painting a precise significance, in the nineteenth century everyone (the brothers Goncourt first) saw in it the truthful representation of the hard-working bourgeoisie; this is opposed to the description of the leisurely upper class witnessed by Boucher and Fragonard. In our century this type of composition is often analyzed in cubist terms. Malraux calls Chardin "[du] Braque habillé". Is it a better view? Doesn't the greatness of this work reside in its success to move each period differently? One can see in the creamy white of the wide skirt, against which the tricorn of the young student is set, an harmonious accompaniment to the meditative and moving dialogue of the pupil with his governess.

Ottawa, The National Gallery of Canada

15 *Un dessert, ou la brioche,* 1763 PL. 99

Oil on canvas, 47 x 56 cm / 18½ x 22 in.

Signed and dated lower left: *Chardin 1763*

PROVENANCE: (?) Salon of 1763, no. 59; would then have belonged to Phélippeaux de la Vrillière, Comte de Saint-Florentin — (?) de Livois in 1791 — Gamba sale, December 17, 1811, no. 55 — Dr. La Caze — bequeathed to the Louvre in 1869.

BIBLIOGRAPHY: G. Wildenstein, 1933, no. 1090, fig. 161 — G. Wildenstein, 1963, no. 323, pl. 49.

Among the thirty-two paintings by Chardin in the Louvre, fourteen came from the collection of Dr. La Caze, to whom the Louvre owes its eighteenth-century masterpieces. *Le dessert* (more so than its pendant, *Raisins et grenades,* Louvre) is one of the most accomplished works of the artist, done at a time when he reached perfection. On a stone table is a brioche topped by a twig of orange blossom; around it are a porcelain sugar bowl, two peaches, cookies, cherries and a small gilded glass decanter filled with liqueur. The pyramidal composition they describe is all but systematic. It is for Chardin the pretext for creating a discreet work of feeling and silence—one of the artist's secrets. The Salon of 1763, where Chardin possibly exhibited this painting, is of great importance for the artist. Diderot noticed him then and wrote enthusiastically: "He is the one who understands the harmony of colors and reflections. O Chardin! it is not red, white and black you mix on your palette: it is the very substance of objects, it is the air and the light you take with the tip of your brush and fix on your canvas. . . One doesn't understand this magic. These are heavy coats of colors, applied on top of each other, whose effect goes from bottom to top . . . get closer, everything blurs, flattens and disappears; get farther away, everything becomes real and appears" (Seznec and Adhémar, I (1957), pp. 222–23).

Paris, Musée du Louvre

16 *Les Attributs des Arts,* 1766 PL. 103

Oil on canvas, 113 x 145 cm / 44¼ x 57¼ in.

Signed and dated, lower left: *J. B. Chardin 1766*

PROVENANCE: Salon of 1769, no. 31—Abbé Pommier in 1769 — Wille sale, December 6, 1784, no. 64 — Mme Devisme, née Pigalle; sale, March 17, 1888, no. 37 — C. Groult — Wildenstein — acquired in 1952.

BIBLIOGRAPHY: G. Wildenstein, 1933, no. 1132, fig. 169 — G. Wildenstein 1963, no. 344, pl. 531.

Chardin exhibited nine pictures at the Salon of 1769. The catalogue entry of the picture, now in Minneapolis, reads as follows: "Les Attributs des Arts et les Récompenses qui leur sont accordées. This picture, another version (with some changes) of the painting done for the Empress of Russia, belongs to the Abbé Pommyer, Conseiller en la Grand'Chambre du Parlement, Honoraire Associé libre de l'Académie. . . ." This is, indeed, the replica (with no considerable variations) of the painting now in the Hermitage. It was well received at the Salon. Saint-Aubin sketched it in the margins of his catalogue. Diderot wrote a long comment about it: "The way the objects reflect in one another . . . makes it . . . sensitive as a whole and secret in each part. . . Chardin is an old wizard whom age has not deprived of his magic stick." The painting shows the Attributes of the Arts (Sculpture is symbolized by a plaster version of Pigalles' *Mercure* (1742) and the *Cordon de Saint-Michel*, the highest award any artist then could have desired. For Chardin it is also the occasion to render the texture of paper, silk and metal, as well as the pure colors of the palette. The composition, apparently more encumbered than usual for the artist, is very simple with its skillful play of curves and lines, its perfect counterpoint of volumes, and its harmony of soft colors. Beyond its hidden virtuosity and poetic refinement, this painting—so different from Van Loo's *Allégorie de la Peinture* (no. 107)—seems intended primarily to please and satisfy the eye.

The Minneapolis Institute of Arts, William Hood Dunwoody Fund

JEAN-FRANÇOIS GILLES, *dit* COLSON
Dijon 1733–Paris 1803

Jean-François Gilles, called Colson, was the son of the miniaturist Jean-Baptiste Gilles, and seems to have been the pupil of, successively, Brother Imbert in Avignon, Nonnotte in Lyons and Despax in Toulouse. He probably settled in Paris in 1759 and quickly specialized in portraits, working for a varied clientele of musicians, comedians, military men, and so forth. Colson was, above all, the "*directeur et ordonnateur des Bâtiments*" for Charles-Godefroy de la Tour d'Auvergne, the Duc de Bouillon and for Godefroy-Charles-Henry de Bouillon, the Prince de Turenne. This position forced him to become engineer, architect, and even sculptor at the splendid residence of the Bouillons near Evreux, the Château de Navarre (destroyed in 1834). Colson also wrote treatises on perspective, and among other things, an account of the 1775 Salon.

Colson exhibited at the Salons of 1793, 1795, 1797 and, shortly before his death, was elected, in An XI, a member of the Académie des Sciences, and elected a member of Arts et Lettres de Dijon, his hometown. A charming and able artist, Colson was studied at the time of the exhibition in Dijon (Quarré, 1969). P. Quarré has devoted several articles to this artist.

17 *Le repos*, 1759 PL. 91

Oil on canvas, 93 x 73 cm / 36½ x 28¾ in.

Inscribed and dated on the back: *Colson 1759*

PROVENANCE: (?) Château de Navarre, near Evreux — belonged to the Musée Spécial de l'Ecole Française at Versailles, 1802 — entered the Musée des Beaux-Arts, Dijon, between 1815 and 1818.

BIBLIOGRAPHY: Quarré and others, 1969, no. 2, pl. 11.

This picture—Colson's most famous—had the *Action* as a pendant (on the English art market some years ago). Both paintings were engraved by Nicholas-Gabriel Dupuis (1698–1771), Colson's uncle. A painted copy of the Dijon picture is at the Musée Cognacq-Jay in Paris, and a drawn copy (?) is at the Fogg Art Museum. The subject—a young girl asleep in an armchair, holding a ribbon attached to a canary which is under the watchful eye of a tomcat—is somewhere between those of Chardin and Greuze. Like both of these artists, Colson delights himself in painting childhood but, unlike Greuze, a coquettish, still innocent one. Chardin's world is also more concentrated and solemn. Colson, however, was able to create, in the depiction of this imminent little drama, an image of just observation and of delicate analysis of emotion.

Dijon, Musée des Beaux-Arts

JACQUES-FRANÇOIS COURTIN
Sens (?) 1672 (?)–Paris 1752

Like many good painters of his generation, Courtin was the pupil of Louis de Boullongne. Courtin painted the last *May* for Notre-Dame (*Résurrection d'Eutyque*, 1707, Cathedral of Saint-Etienne de Toulouse) and several other mythological and religious subjects (for example, the *Pietà* in Brussels), and quickly specialized in genre pictures which were occasionally somewhat naughty (*Le billet-doux*; *Le couple amoureux*; *Jeune fille au masque*). These compositions became famous through engravings. Courtin, however, did not forfeit an official career: elected to the Académie in 1710 (*Loth et ses filles*, Paris, Ecole des Beaux-Arts), he took part in the important Concours of 1727 (*Pan et Syrinx*, now lost, but known through the engraving by Jean Haussard) and all the Salons between 1737 and 1751. His life and work, until now much neglected, have been studied in an article by Michel Faré (1966).

18 *Le jeu de bilboquet* PL. 24

Oil on canvas, 97 x 78 cm / 38¼ x 30¾ in.

PROVENANCE: On the reverse, "certificate" by Gault de Saint-Germain (1754–1842), who rightly identifies the painting, yet attributes the engraving after it to Louis Surugue.

BIBLIOGRAPHY: Faré, 1966, p. 302, and notes 41 and 42, fig. 8, p. 305.

The attribution of this painting does not present a great problem: it has been engraved by François de Poilly, probably shortly before he died in 1723. Beyond the ambiguous expression of the sitter—preoccupied with smiling at the viewer rather than watching her clearly symbolical game—what strikes one most in this painting is the acid quality of the colors: the contrast between the yellow dress and the blue ribbon that closes the blouse; the green chair on which she rests; and the red of her stole. Courtin liked this kind of leaning figure, these deep *décolletés*, the "galant" subjects—all the elements of this confused world which foreshadow the still more perverse world of Greuze. His very personal way of draping his sitters and the abundance of folds in their dresses make his pictures easily recognizable.

France, Private collection

ANTOINE COYPEL
Paris 1661–Paris 1722

Son of Noël Coypel, Antoine followed his father, who became Director of the Académie de France (1673–1675), to Rome. According to tradition, Antoine would then have received the advice of both Maratta and Bernini; he also had the chance to admire the works of Correggio in Parma. *Académicien* at twenty, Antoine Coypel had, thanks to the patronage of the Orléans family, one of the most brilliant official careers of his time. He painted religious compositions and mythological representations, such as *Bacchus et Ariane* (1693) or the *Triomphe de Galatée* (1695) (lost today, but known through numerous copies which prove their popularity). Coypel worked for Meudon, painted the ceilings of the *Galerie d'Enée* at the Palais Royal (1702–1705; see Schnapper, 1969) and of the chapel at Versailles (1709); he also completed the decoration of the *Galerie d'Enée*. *Premier Peintre du Roi* in 1716, he was ennobled in 1717 but, because of illness, stopped painting at a time when his two major rivals, La Fosse and Jouvenet, disappeared one after the other. Misunderstood and little appreciated today, this admirer of Correggio, Rubens and Le Brun—whose research on the theory of passions he investigated further—has a refined sense for colors: he particularly likes harmonies of rare hues. His compositions are smooth and elegant. An ambitious artist (like his two seniors, he worked on large decorations), experimenting to the point of becoming strange and "bizarre", Antoine Coypel is today considered insipid in his pleasant compositions and too "literary" in his religious paintings. His drawings, many of which are at the Louvre, are better understood. A thorough study of this very great artist (Louis Dimier's poorly illustrated study was published in 1928!) should allow for a more equitable judgement of his work.

19 *Adam et Eve sous le regard de Dieu après le péché*, 1704 PL. 2

Oil on canvas, 117.5 x 91 cm / 46¼ x 35¾ in.

PROVENANCE: Marquis de Bute, England — sale, London, Sotheby's, November 16, 1960, no. 30; as Gérard de Lairesse — acquired in 1961 as Le Brun.

BIBLIOGRAPHY: Held, 1965, pp. 43–44, fig. 92.

The attribution of this painting to Antoine Coypel, first proposed by Julius S. Held, is beyond doubt. The picture was engraved between 1724 and 1726 by Pierre-Imbert Drevet (1697–1739; see Didot, 1876, pp. 91–92; and D. Wildenstein, 1964, p. 142, no. 4, fig. 4). Should one go any further, to identify this work with the *Adam et Eve qui, après leur faute cherchent à éviter la présence de Dieu* exhibited at the 1704 Salon? If so, this work would represent a very important step in the still poorly established chronology of the painter. It would also date from the time when Coypel worked on the *Galerie d'Enée* at the Palais-Royal; this was one of Coypel's major works which, admired and copied throughout the entire eighteenth century, was destroyed in 1784. The Ponce picture summarizes well the aesthetics of Antoine Coypel: softness of line, declamatory gestures and attitudes, rare and searching colors. Annoying and irritating as it may be, this style is, nevertheless, not without its own perverse, yet attractive, charm.

Museo de Arte de Ponce, Puerto Rico, The Luis A. Ferré Foundatión

This picture will be shown only in Toledo and Chicago.

CHARLES-ANTOINE COYPEL
Paris 1694–Paris 1752

The grandson of Noël Coypel and son of Antoine Coypel, Charles-Antoine was received by the Académie as early as 1715. Charles-Antoine Coypel led three careers simultaneously: a dramatist, an art critic and a painter. *Premier Peintre du Roi* in 1747, he also had the task, along with the *Surintendant*, Lenormant de Tournehem, to reorganize the Académie and to increase its power and rôle. Starting in 1716, Charles-Antoine worked on a *Suite de Don Quichotte* for the Manufacture des Gobelins and exhibited regularly at the Salon, after its reestablishment in 1737. Most of the work he produced was inspired by the opera or the theater, Racine's plays above all. Coypel wanted to bring to an extreme the *théorie des modes* of Poussin and the *traité des passions* of Le Brun. His deliberate departure from "nature"—for which Mariette already reproached him—and his attempt to translate on to canvas the actors' emotions, as well as the beauty of the theater, were directed toward a complete lack of realism. His daring attempt—"the craziest attempt ever made to bring together literature and painting"—deserves respect and is not, because of its intellectual refinement, without charm.

I. Jamieson's work on Charles-Antoine Coypel (1930) concerns itself mostly with the dramatist. The few articles of Florence Ingersoll-Smouse (1920) and Antoine Schnapper (1968) make one bitterly regret the lack of a thorough study on this misunderstood painter, whose ambition should seduce people of our time, who are taken with the cerebral aspects of painting.

20 *Persée délivrant Andromède, 1727* PL. 36

Oil on canvas, 131 x 196 cm / 51½ x 77¼ in.

PROVENANCE: Louis XV; acquired by the King for 2000 livres at the 1727 Concours, organized among the *académiciens* by the Direction des Bâtiments du roi.

The 5000 livres grant, given by the King to reward the winner of the 1727 Concours, was shared by Jean-François de Troy and Lemoine (both pictures in Nancy); the Duc d'Antin also persuaded the King to purchase the much admired painting by Coypel (see also no. 22), the engraving of which was done by L. Surugue in 1732. If one notes in it the strong influence of Rubens' *Vie de Marie de Médicis,* much admired by the artist (especially in the Nereid group), one should also remark that the painter has already found the formulas which established his reputation: the colors are arbitrarily precious, harsh and even out of tune; the expressions are similar to those of the actors on stage. The whole scene somehow resembles the final scene of a spectacular opera performance, with the sudden appearance of a winged Perseus falling from the sky to fight the monster; the monster, which spits water through his nostrils, is like those one sees in the fountains at Versailles. In its own way, the Coypel picture is close to the "*bizarrerie inexplicable*" of Ingres' *Roger et Angélique* (Louvre).

Paris, Musée du Louvre

21 *Portrait de Philippe Coypel, frère du peintre,* 1732 PL. 47

Oil on canvas, 75 x 61 cm / 29½ x 24 in.

Inscribed upper left: *Peint en 1732 par Charles Coypel, son frère*

PROVENANCE: Given by Jean Cailleux and Mme Denise Cailleux in 1968.

BIBLIOGRAPHY: Compin, 1969, pp. 93–97.

Charles-Antoine Coypel was an excellent portrait painter, in oil as well as pastels, who rendered mellow and velvety surfaces in this picture. In the Louvre portrait of his brother "as well as friend", Philippe (born in 1703), executed the year of his brother's wedding (perhaps one should see there a wedding gift: this could be confirmed by the existence of a pendant, *Madame Copyel,* also dated 1732; New York, Finch College Museum of Art), Charles-Antoine proves to be a fine colorist. For instance, to the red of the jacket and the gold and white of the laces, he opposes the changing lustre of the velvet on the shoulder, the bluish shadows of the mousseline folds and the glistening of the black bow. The large pupils at the edge of the eyelids are the trademark of the artist.

Paris, Musée du Louvre

NÖEL-NICOLAS COYPEL

Paris 1690–Paris 1734

Noël-Nicolas, half-brother of Antoine Coypel (born in 1661), belongs to the generation of Antoine's son, Charles-Antoine. *Agréé* in 1716 and *académicien* in 1720, he participated, like the best painters of his generation, in the decoration of the Hôtel du Grand Maître at Versailles, and was one of the contestants at the 1727 Concours. His major work, the painted cupola of the *chapelle de la Vierge* in the Church of Saint-Sauveur, Paris (1731), was already destroyed at the end of the eighteenth century. He died still young in 1734 and "as his fame was increasing each day" (Dézallier d'Argenville, ed., IV, p. 446). An elegant draftsman, a graceful and voluptuous painter, Noël-Nicolas foreshadows, in his clear mythological compositions with less refinement but more luminosity than Lemoine (who died in 1737), the most seducing works of Natoire and Boucher. The excellent pages by Jean Messelet (in Dimier, II), devoted to this artist, deserve to be updated.

22 *L'enlèvement d'Europe*, 1727 PL. 37

Oil on canvas, 129.5 x 194.5 cm / 51 x 76½ in.

Signed and dated lower right: *Noël Coypel 1727*

PROVENANCE: Acquired after the 1727 Concours by the Comte de Morville — Joseph Bonaparte, 1768–1844, Napoleon's older brother — given by him in 1839 to General Thomas Cadwalader — John Cadwalader, Philadelphia.

BIBLIOGRAPHY: Benisovich, 1956, p. 298, fig. 6.

"The King ordered the Concours in 1727 and encouraged the painters of the Académie by offering a prize of 5000 livres in addition to the usual 1500 livres for the winning picture; among the twelve pictures, all of the same size, exhibited in Paris in the Salon at the Louvre, the one by Noël-Nicolas Coypel, which represented the *Triomphe d'Amphitrite* [*sic*: it is, of course, an easily understandable lapsus; the picture, in fact, represents the *Enlèvement d'Europe*] was thought to be so beautiful, its color seemed so fresh and so soft that it was given preference by the public. To enjoy a triumph one needs, however, a victory: the court did not agree with this and awarded the prize to two painters [Lemoine and J.-F. de Troy; see no. 20] who had the most credit. One *secrétaire d'état* [Dézallier d'Argenville notes his name, the Comte de Morville] aware of the injustice done to Noël-Nicolas, gave him the 1500 livres promised by the King for the winning picture" (Dézallier d'Argenville, IV, pp. 442–43). Unknown to Messelet, this picture is certainly the artist's masterpiece, and one of the most elegant and luminous realizations of French eighteenth-century painting. A comparison of the Cleveland picture, *Saint Jacques guérissant un malade* (1726), with the pictures in Geneva (1726), at the Louvre (1727), in Stockholm (1728), and at the Ponce art museum (1729), is evidence that it is by Noël-Nicolas and not by Charles-Antoine as is sometimes advanced.

Anonymous loan

MICHEL-FRANÇOIS DANDRÉ-BARDON

Aix-en-Provence 1700–Paris 1783

As early as 1720 in Paris, where he entered the studios of his compatriot, J.-B. Van Loo, and of J.-F. de Troy, Dandré-Bardon received the second *Grand Prix* in 1725 and left for Rome, at his own expense, after a stop in his native city where he executed an important commission for the Chambre des Comptes de Provence. He stayed in Italy five years and returned to France after a stay of six months in Venice. Dandré-Bardon was received by the Académie in 1735 with *Tullie faisant passer son char sur le corps de son père* (Montpellier, Musée Fabre; sketch in Châteauroux). Thenceforth, Dandré-Bardon hesitated between a first rank in his native area (founder of the Académie de Marseille, he became director of it in 1754) and a good position in Paris: he occupied a prominent position at the Ecole Royale des Elèves Protégés. From 1750 on, Dandré-Bardon tried a literary career: he wrote poems, treatises on painting or art history—especially an excellent *Eloge de Carle Van Loo* (1765). In 1770, an attack of apoplexy left him partially paralyzed, but he did continue, if not to paint, at least to draw. A "prolific, impetuous and vigorous draftsman" —to use Mariette's terms—(we have studied him as a draftsman; see Rosenberg, 1974), Dandré-Bardon treats, as a painter, every possible genre. He compensates the obvious clumsiness of parts of his composition with a great taste for glaucous colors, a "manière libre. . . plus heurtée que fondue;" and a dynamism in the organization of his canvas explains why his works are sometimes given to Austrian painters. Nothing essential after the eighteenth century (sale after death; see Ageville) has been written on this multifaceted artist, presently studied by Daniel Chol.

23 *L'adoration des crânes* PL. 44

Oil on canvas, 53 x 63.5 cm / 20¾ x 25⅛ in.

PROVENANCE: Lewis Einstein, Paris—given to the National Gallery, 1956.

BIBLIOGRAPHY: Rosenberg, 1974, p. 140, no. 5, fig. 14.

This painting, formerly attributed to the French eighteenth-century school, now has a definite ascription: we actually know, because of various figures in this painting and its pendant (Paris, private collection), a group of preparatory drawings, some of which come from the collection of Mariette, his contemporary.

There is, in particular for the Washington painting, a drawing of the whole composition (not reproduced in our article, 1974) which is typical of the artist. The exact significance of the subject, members of a mendicant order praying before skulls, is more difficult to determine. Also difficult to establish is the date of this composition; the chronology of the artist's work remains to be done.

Strongly influenced by Italy (could this work have been painted there?), this strange picture, lusciously painted, with its counterpoint between the vertical of the columns and the ample and enveloping robes of the monks, is noteworthy for its fantasy and humor, which are comparable to that of Magnasco.

Washington, National Gallery of Art, Gift of Lewis Einstein, 1956

JACQUES-LOUIS DAVID
Paris 1748–Brussels 1825

Pupil of Vien, to whom he had been recommended by Boucher (a relative by marriage), David received the *Grand Prix* only after his fourth attempt in 1774. Both Suvée in 1771 and Peyron in 1773 (see no. 25) were chosen over him. David found his own way during his first stay in Rome, between 1775 and 1780, and established himself as the leading painter of his generation with his *Académies* in Cherbourg and Montpellier, his *Funérailles de Patrocle* (1778–1779, Dublin), his *Saint Roch* (1780, Marseilles), his *Portrait de Potocki* (1780, Warsaw), and his *Bélisaire* (1781, Lille). David's career, after these works, does not belong to our subject any longer: everybody knows the great masterpieces of the artist (for example, *Le serment des Horaces* and *Brutus*), his importance during the Revolution (*Député* at the *Convention*; he voted for the King's death), and his rôle in organizing, with Denon, the artistic life under the Empire. David has regained his place among the greatest French painters only recently and often with reservations, justified for some of his early works, but less so for the production of the last ten years he spent in exile in Brussels. The catalogue of the David exhibition (Paris, Orangerie des Tuileries, 1948), the books of J.L.J. David (1880), R. Cantinelli (1930), L. Hautecoeur (1954), and the texts edited by D. and G. Wildenstein (1973) enable us to know the life and the work of this fascinating artist. There is, however, no *catalogue raisonné* of the paintings and drawings of this artist, who, along with Goya, dominated European artistic life during the last quarter of the eighteenth and the first quarter of the nineteenth centuries.

24 *Madame Buron, 1769* PL. 114

Oil on canvas, 65 x 54.5 cm / 25⅝ x 21½ in.

Signed lower right: *J. L. David 1769*

PROVENANCE: Baudry, descendant of both the artist and the model, until 1903 — Regnault; sale, June 22, 1905; bought back — Regnault until 1913 — Wildenstein — acquired by Chicago in 1963.

BIBLIOGRAPHY: Florisoone in Paris, Orangerie des Tuileries, 1948, no. M. O. 1 — Hautecoeur, 1954, p. 25.

Mme Buron was David's aunt on his mother's side. When the artist portrayed her, as well as her husband, a master-mason (portrait sold with the Victor Gay collection, April 23, 1909, no. 27 with plate), and perhaps their daughter (Algiers), he no longer lived with them. Instead he was staying with the architect Michel Sedaine (1719–1797), a poet and playwright who, as a young orphan, had himself been a beneficiary of the hospitality of the Burons.

The Chicago portrait ranks among the first known works by David. It shows an artist more responsible to the style of Aved or Duplessis than to that of Vien, to whom the young artist had been recommended by Boucher. Mme Buron, elegantly dressed, interrupts her reading to look at her nephew. It is above all a realistic and simple image that David has left in remembrance of his aunt, whom he held in affection throughout his life. This affection was reinforced by the fact that she was the one who persuaded her husband to let the young David become a painter.

The Art Institute of Chicago, Gift of Mrs. Albert J. Beveridge, in memory of her mother, Abby Louise Spencer Eddy

25 *La mort de Sénèque,* 1773 PL. 121

Oil on canvas, 43 x 53 cm / 17 x 21 in.

PROVENANCE: In the family of Sedaine, according to Charles Saunier — M. de Brisay de l'Isle Adam, according to inscription on stretcher — Baron Bethmann as early as 1913; sale, June 21–22, 1923, no. 149 with plate — acquired by the Petit Palais at the R. Kieffer sale, May 29, 1969, no. 84.

BIBLIOGRAPHY: Saunier, 1905, pp. 233–36, with plate.

This is the definitive study for the painting, also at the Petit Palais, presented by David for the *Prix de Rome* in 1773. David, who had already lost the competition twice, lost again that year to Peyron (the painting by Peyron has vanished but the composition is known through the engraving and a preparatory drawing). Peyron's painting, as L. Hautecoeur humorously pointed out (1954, p. 28) is "more Davidian than David's". Peyron, indeed, turns himself toward Poussin's sobre expression while David remains attached to Boucher's effects. According to his habit, David separates the figure groups in his composition: the women with Pauline, Seneca's wife, are in the center to one side, and the men's group is profiled against "the usual curtain . . . blown by the tragical inspiration." The colors are vivid, almost crude: the whole is well executed but without profound originality. If one compares it to the *Mort de Socrate* (1787, New York, Metropolitan Museum) one sees the progress accomplished by the artist. In the Paris painting, there is nothing of the moving *exemplum virtutis* of the severe heroic lesson found in the New York picture, one of the artist's compositions which was to be widely imitated by the younger artists.

Paris, Musée du Petit Palais

JACQUES-FRANÇOIS DELYEN
Ghent 1684 (?)–Paris 1761

Pupil of Robert van Audenarde in Ghent and of Largillierre in Paris, Delyen exhibited portraits at the *Exposition de la Jeunesse* in 1722 and was received by the Académie in 1725 (no. 26). He exhibited at the Salon between 1737 and 1747. Delyen devoted himself primarily to portraits, with the exception of a few genre scenes such as the *Lanterne magique* and the *Marmotte* (1731; Puerto Rico, Ponce Art Museum). Only about twelve works have been attributed to Delyen thus far. A catalogue of the work of this fine portraitist was written by George Huard (1928).

26 *Portrait du sculpteur Guillaume Coustou,* 1725 PL. 29

Oil on canvas, 130 x 97 cm / 51¼ x 38¼ in.

PROVENANCE: Académie — Versailles during the Restoration — Ecole des Beaux-Arts, 1826 — Louvre, 1887; transferred to Versailles, 1921.

BIBLIOGRAPHY: Huard, 1928, p. 264, no. 1 — Frédéricq-Lilar in Ghent, Museum voor Schone Kunsten, 1975, no. 96.

Delyen has depicted the sculptor Guillaume Coustou pointing toward a bronze reduction of the Rhône river; this sculpture is one of his major works which adorned the pedestal of the equestrian statue of Louis XIV by Desjardins, in the place Bellecour at Lyons. It is with this portrait, engraved by N. de Larmessin in 1730 and the portrait of the painter Nicolas Bertin (no. 7), also at Versailles, that Delyen was received in 1725 by the Académie. The influence of Largillierre is, indeed, clear, but in the proud face of the model, carefully rendered and radiant with health, there is a life and a glow unknown to the magnificent portraits of Largillierre.

Versailles, Musée National du Château

JEAN-BAPTISTE DESHAYS
Rouen 1729–Paris 1765

Deshays was successively the pupil of Collin de Vermont, Restout and Boucher. He married the latter's older daughter in 1758. *Grand Prix* in 1751, he was received by the Académie in 1759 after a four-year stay in Italy. He exhibited at the Salon only four times, in 1759, 1761,

1763, and 1765 (posthumously, like Carle Van Loo, the same year), but each time with tremendous success. "The sunrise of French painting," Diderot considered Deshays, as early as 1761, "le premier peintre de la nation." There is in Deshays' work an easiness, a vivacity, a freedom of touch similar to Delacroix's (somewhat opposed to the most advanced trends of the art of his time) which allows us to compare his work, mostly religious and occasionally mythological compositions, to that of Fragonard. The study by Marc Sandoz (1959) is, with several other articles by the same author, the essential, modern basis to our knowledge of this artist who died at thirty-five and whose sketches are best indicative of his talent.

27 *L'Assomption de la Vierge* PL. 90

Oil on paper, 48.5 x 28.5 cm / 19 x 11¼ in.

PROVENANCE: H. L. Bishoffsheim, London, in 1907 — Knoedler and Co. — Charles E. Slatkin — acquired in 1961.

BIBLIOGRAPHY: Minneapolis, The Minneapolis Institute of Arts, 1971, no. 89; as Boucher.

Commonly attributed to Boucher, this sketch is definitely by Deshays: a comparison between the two kneeling figures in this picture and in the *Prédication de Saint Denis* (Nîmes) is sufficient proof of this. The Nîmes picture, until now catalogued as Sacchi (!), is in fact the painting of this subject catalogued in his sale after death (March 26, 1765, no. 110): it is a *modello* for a picture intended for the Church of Saint-Roch, Paris. Deshays was unable to finish it before his death, and the commission ultimately went to Vien.

Deshays received the commission of a large *Assomption* for the priory of Bellefonds, near Rouen. Seized during the Revolution, this painting has been lost since (see Beaurepaire, p. 421). More than the Edinburgh picture, still very close to Boucher (Edinburgh, National Gallery of Scotland, p. 96, no. 2719), the Minneapolis sketch — as well as the one in the Musée Magnin, Dijon (no. 275) — is probably the first *modello* for this commission. With its vigorous brushstrokes and the rigidity of line that differentiates it from Boucher's style, the Minneapolis sketch has this typically squarish aspect (slightly cubist) of Deshay's richly painted *bozzetti*.

The Minneapolis Institute of Arts, The Christina N. and Swan J. Turnblad Memorial Fund

FRANÇOIS DESPORTES
Champigneulles (Aube) 1661–Paris 1743

Pupil of the *animalier,* Flemish painter Nicasius Bernaert, Desportes sojourned in Poland in 1695 and first attempted a career as portraitist. It was, however, as *animalier* that he was received by the Académie in 1699, with his *Portrait en Chasseur* (Louvre). Thenceforth, he received many royal commissions (Ménagerie de Versailles, Marly, Meudon). Desportes went briefly to England in 1712. He worked untiringly for the Regent, the Savonnerie, Chantilly, Compiègne, Choisy, and so forth. Flower painter, painter of dead game, of royal dogs and of hunting scenes, Desportes remains an impassioned observer of the plants and animals he describes with clarity and respect. We await the forthcoming publication of the artist's *catalogue raisonné* by Georges de Lastic. This catalogue should include no less than two thousand entries!

28a *Etude de nuages éclairés par le soleil couchant* PL. 6

(P 2, 1814, no. 67)

Oil on paper laid on cardboard, 28 x 33 cm / 11 x 13 in.

28b *Etude de paysage: coin d'étang dans lequel se reflète le ciel et les coteaux* PL. 7

(P 2, 1814, no. 99)

Oil on paper laid on cardboard, 30 x 52 cm / 11¾ x 20½ in.

28c *Etude de deux plats, l'un d'argent, l'autre de vermeil (dont l'un aux armes royales)* PL. 8

(MP 5, 1814, no. 26)

Oil on canvas, oval, 82 x 96 cm / 32¼ x 37¾ in.

28d *Etude d'oiseaux: demoiselles de Numidie* PL. 9

Oil on paper laid on cardboard, 34.5 x 51 cm / 13½ x 20 in.

PROVENANCE: Belonged to the atelier of the artist; acquired from Desportes' nephew in 1784 and divided today for the most part between the Manufacture National de Sèvres, the Musée de Compiègne, the Musée de la Chasse et de la Nature, Paris and the Musée de la Chasse à Tir, Gien.

BIBLIOGRAPHY: Hourticq, 1920, pp. 117–36 — Compiègne, Musée National de Compiègne, 1961.

These studies are part of the contents of Desportes' studio, comprising some 600 works, the entirety of which was acquired in 1784 for the King. They are usually dated between 1690 and 1700. However, we do not see why Desportes should have ceased to do them after this date. Desportes painted a variety of subjects: some rare bird from the Jardin des Plantes du roi; a view of a pond; clouds in a sunset (one of the first renditions of this subject in Western art; see New York, Columbia University . . . , Knoedler, 1967, no. 59); or a piece of silver lent to him by his neighbor at the Louvre, Thomas Germain, and which he uses in several pictures. No matter what he paints, Desportes amazes one by the spontaneity of his vision, the correctness of his observation, and the cleverness and audacity of this composition. These studies give Desportes, who is too often considered an ordinary but good painter of still lifes and animals, his real dimension. His son described how his father worked, confirming that, indeed, these studies were done from nature: "He was going to the fields with his brushes and his loaded palette in tin cans; he had a cane with a long and sharp steel tip which held it tight into the ground. The steel head opened and a small steel stretcher could then be screwed on. He affixed to it the portfolio and the paper." (Dussieux, Soulié . . . , 1854–1856, II, p. 109).

28a–c: *Sèvres, Manufacture Nationale*
28d: *Paris, Musée de la Chasse et de la Nature (transferred from Sèvres in 1967)*

PIERRE DOMENCHIN DE CHAVANNES
Paris 1673–Paris 1744

Académicien in 1709 (his picture is at the Ecole des Beaux-Arts, Paris), Domenchin de Chavannes is one of the great landscape painters of his time: he executed more than twenty paintings for Versailles, Fontainebleau and the other royal residences. His life, as well as his production, are little known today. Whoever will try to reconstruct his *oeuvre* will have to look for his paintings among those attributed to later Venetian painters, such as Zaïs or Zuccarelli, or among the landscapes of Pianca, Tempesta or Locatelli.

Unlike those of Allegrain, his landscapes are lyrical and warm. His swaying figures and taste for somewhat unrealistic rocks make his works easily identifiable.

29 *Paysage au château,* 1737 PL. 53

Oil on canvas, 120 x 113 cm / 47¼ x 44½ in. (the painting was originally *chantournée*; its dimensions were then: 93 x 80 cm / 36½ x 31½ in.

PROVENANCE: One of two paintings executed in 1737 for the *petits appartements* at Fontainebleau; transferred from Versailles to Fontainebleau in 1965.

BIBLIOGRAPHY: Engerand, 1901, pp. 91–92.

It seems that Domenchin de Chavannes received a commission to do four paintings for Fontainebleau in 1737 and 1739. The first two, for which he was paid 600 livres for both and which were intended originally for the *petits appartements,* are now back in Fontainebleau; the other two for the *cabinet de la reine* were paired with two landscapes by Francisque Millet III (1697–1777) and seem to have been lost. Fontainebleau also owns two other landscapes by Chavannes, commissioned in 1709 and exhibited in Lille in 1968 (nos. 97 and 98). A comparison between these works and the 1737 pictures shows the artist's progress. He amplifies, with the years, the particularities of his style: free technique, heavy stroke, reddish and blue-green, occasionally chalky colors, and swaying figures in a rather hilly landscape. According to the 1737 payment, the picture we show here, considerably enlarged, represents a *Château dans le goux [sic] romain.*

Fontainebleau, Musée National du Château

GABRIEL-FRANÇOIS DOYEN
Paris 1726–Saint Petersburg 1806

Pupil of Carle Van Loo, *deuxième prix* in 1748, Doyen, after a short stay in the Ecole Royale des Elèves Protégés, left for Rome in 1750 where he lived until 1756. Like his comrades, he not only copied older masters, but also painted the *Junon et Eole* (Budapest museum; preparatory drawing at the Albertina) which shows his brilliant inclination toward painting. He stayed in Parma on his way back to France. *Agréé* in 1758, received by the Académie the next year, Doyen made himself known with his *Mort de Virginie* executed in 1760 for Parma. After the death of Carle Van Loo (1765), Doyen was selected to complete the decoration of the *chapelle Saint-Grégoire* in the Church of the Invalides. At the 1767 Salon, with his *Miracle des Ardents,* Doyen became famous, a hope of the new school. At the death of Louis XV, and with the appointments of Pierre and d'Angiviller to head the administration of the Fine Arts, Doyen no longer received first rate commissions and had a difficult time asserting himself. In 1791 he moved to Russia where he died.

A lyricism, a taste for movement, ample shapes, warm colors, and free handling of the brush (which he owes primarily to Rubens, and which differentiates him from his contemporaries) characterize Doyen. The studies of Marc Sandoz (1960) and the yet unpublished thesis of Martine Hérold enable us to know better the painter as well as the draftsman. Doyen had tried to guide French painting in a new direction, the same direction Gros, a half-century later, was to follow with great success.

30 *Le Miracle des Ardents,* 1767 PL. 108

Oil on arched canvas, 108 x 65 cm / 42½ x 25½ in.

PROVENANCE: Prosper de Baudicour; his sale, Paris, June 5, 1917, no. 21 — Baron Cassel; his sale, Paris, Hôtel Drouot, March 14, 1955, no. 73 — Marc Sandoz — acquired in 1966.

BIBLIOGRAPHY: Hérold, 1968, pp. 65–71.

Doyen exhibited, at the Salon of 1767, a very large painting (more than six meters high) which he had just completed for the Church of Saint-Roch in Paris (the painting is still there). At the same Salon, Vien exhibited another painting intended for the same church, *Saint Denis prêchant la foi en France* (cf. no. 27), also still in Saint-Roch. The critics did not miss the opportunity to compare these two paintings, so different in inspiration and intent. Doyen's picture represented the *Miracle des Ardents,* or, to quote the *livret* of the Salon, "In 1129, under the reign of Louis VI, a celestial fire fell over the city of Paris and, burning almost all the inhabitants, made them suffer a most cruel death; through the intercession of Saint Geneviève, this plague suddenly ceased." This work was preceded by several drawings (Bayonne, Moscow, Paris, Louvre and several private collections) and painted studies (Bayonne, Paris, Louvre and Musée Carnavalet; a copy by (?) Louis Boulanger is at Le Mans; another by A. Lenoir at Carnavalet). Some of these studies treat the subject formerly selected by the church's architect, Boullée: *Sainte Geneviève implorant le ciel contre les Huns.* The Douai grisaille sketch shows few differences with the finished picture, the most important being the gesture of the saint, who in the final version, opens her arms in a beautiful supplicating movement. Doyen's picture, "le plus beau du Salon," received enthusiastic success. Diderot praised "l'imagination et la verve" and added that "il produit un grand effet." Inspired above all by Rubens, Doyen tried, like many other artists of the time, to get French painting out of the impass into which Boucher and Carle Van Loo had brought it. With the near triumph of David, however, Doyen's attempts failed; only with Gros, Géricault and Delacroix was this attempt to find significance and to become understood.

Douai, Musée da la Chartreuse

FRANÇOIS-HUBERT DROUAIS
Paris 1727–Paris 1775

Son of Hubert Drouais (1699–1767), also a portraitist, father of Jean-Germain (1763–1788), who was the favorite pupil of David, François-Hubert was himself the pupil of Nonnotte, Carle Van Loo, Boucher and Natoire. Received by the Académie in 1758 with the portraits of Guillaume Coustou (Versailles) and of Edmé Bouchardon (Louvre), he exhibited regularly at the Salon. Mme de Pompadour, of whom he was the favorite painter, Mme du Barry, the royal family, and even an aging Louis XV (Versailles), who died a year before the painter, sat in his studio. Drouais likes to paint children and flatter his models. His cold approach is only pleasant, and his style, too sweet. Occasionally, as in the portrait of his wife, Françoise Doré (1758, Louvre), he shows his talent as an original colorist and a careful and vivacious observer. His work, admired during his lifetime and at the end of the nineteenth century, has not been much studied since C. Gabillot (1906).

31 *Le comte d'Artois et sa soeur, Madame Clotilde,* 1763 PL. 97

Oil on canvas, 129.5 x 97.5 cm / 51 x 38½ in.

Signed and dated lower right: *Drouais le fils 1763*

PROVENANCE: Salon of 1763, no. 113 — commissioned for the Royal collections in 1762 — Louvre since the Revolution.

BIBLIOGRAPHY: Seznec and Adhémar, 1957–1967, I, pp. 178–79, 232.

This often exhibited portrait, representing the future Charles X (1757–1836), younger brother of Louis XVI, and his sister (1759–1802), the future Queen of Sardinia, is one of the most popular pictures of the artist. It was engraved in 1767 by Beauvarlet. When it was first exhibited at the 1763 Salon, it was thought to be one of the best pictures there. Some reproached his use of colors which were "more brilliant than natural" (Diderot, who defended Drouais, essentially for his portraits of children, writes on his behalf that "by wanting to do white and milky flesh, he eventually makes them chalky"), but its "agreeable invention", "its brilliance and gracefulness" were usually admired. Today still, even if one regrets an undisputed insipidity, a somewhat superficial charm, it is impossible to resist the white goat decorated with ribbons, the basket of grapes and peaches, and this compassionate and amusing description of two children, who, according to the entire court, were "the two cutest one could see."

Paris, Musée du Louvre

FRANÇOISE DUPARC
Murcie 1726–Marseilles 1778

Two reasons explain the eclipse of the name and work of Françoise Duparc: the provincial origin of the artist and the fact that she was a woman. She was the daughter of the sculptor, Antoine Duparc, who had settled in Murcie, Spain. She received her first training in Marseilles and later from Jean-Baptiste Van Loo in Aix-en-Provence. She worked in Paris and London where we find her in 1763 and 1766 (she twice exhibited three portraits there). She also worked in Breslau and perhaps Russia. Around 1771, she went back to Marseilles where she was *agréé* by the local Académie in 1776. She bequeathed to the city of Marseilles at her death the only four works which are for certain by her hand; they are now in the Museum there. Like Greuze's canvases, these paintings are executed with a thick brushstroke. Their frankness, objective delicacy and realistic approach suggest the work of Chardin.

Joseph Billioud's article (1938) brings together most of the information we have on this artist.

32 *Femme assise les bras croisés* PL. 85

Oil on canvas, 72 x 58 cm / 28¼ x 22¾ in.

PROVENANCE: Bequeathed by the artist to the City of Marseilles; kept in the City Hall there until 1869 — Musée des Beaux-Arts after 1869; (see Marseilles, Musée des Beaux-Arts, 1908, no. 162.)

BIBLIOGRAPHY: Billioud, 1938, pp. 180, 184, fig. 4.

Sometimes called *La ravaudeuse,* or even *La blanchisseuse,* this portrait of an elderly woman, her arms folded and wearing a bonnet, is not only a superb painting, with its rich impasto, revealing a taste for Vermeer's opulent manner, but also a psychological document of great importance. Françoise Duparc gives to this common woman the same respect, without irony or caricature, which already differentiated the works of the Le Nain brothers from those of their northern contemporaries. In this reserved and simple portrait, executed in variations on white, one feels a dignity which anticipates the work of another great realist painter from Marseilles, who died a hundred and one years later than Duparc, Daumier.

Marseilles, Musée des Beaux-Arts

JOSEPH-SIFFRED (or SIFFREIN) DUPLESSIS
Carpentras 1725–Versailles 1802

Son of a surgeon, Duplessis went to Rome in 1745 and became friendly with Subleyras, whose work he copied. After returning to France in 1749, he arrived in Paris in 1752, but became famous only after 1769 when his pictures, exhibited at the Salon, were tremendously successful. *Agréé* the same year by the Académie, he was received as portraitist in 1774. Duplessis did the portraits of Louis XVI, Marie-Antoinette, the Comte de Provence, the Comte d'Angiviller, Necker, Franklin, and also of artists such as Gluck (1775), the sculptor Allegrain (1774) and Vien (1784).

He stopped producing during the Revolution and retired in Carpentras between 1792 and 1796. Director of the Versailles galleries under Louis XVI, a position he occupied again from 1796 on, he died forgotten and poor in 1802. Duplessis is, along with Roslin, the first portraitist of his generation. "If only Roslin painted carnations like Duplessis, and Duplessis, fabric like Roslin," wrote a critic in 1783. Duplessis excels in idealizing the faces, in making them relaxed and spiritual, while attending scrupulously to the likeness of his subjects. J. Belleudy (1913) wrote an excellent monograph on the artist.

33 *Portrait de Mme Freret-Déricour,* 1769 PL. 111

Oil on canvas, 82 x 63.5 cm / 32½ x 25 in.

PROVENANCE: Salon of 1769, no. 198 — Prince Paul Demidoff, San Donato; his sale, Paris, March 15, 1880 and following days, no. 1439 — Alfred de Rothschild, London, 1884 — Edouard de Rothschild, London — acquired in 1953.

BIBLIOGRAPHY: Belleudy, 1913, no. 67, pp. 322–23.

Considered until now as by Drouais, this magnificent portrait is in fact by Duplessis. Sufficient proof of this is the copy of the 1769 Salon *livret,* illustrated by Gabriel de Saint-Aubin (Dacier, 1909–1919, II, p. 83). This artist had drawn, alongside the entry of the *Portrait de Mme Freret-Déricour,* a quick sketch which identified, without doubt, both the sitter and the author of the Kansas portrait. If one knows nothing about the sitter, one should, however, mention that Duplessis exhibited, at the 1771 Salon, a *Portrait de M. de Héricourt.*

Duplessis showed, at the 1769 Salon, ten works which established his reputation, among which was the famous *Portrait de Mme Lenoir* (Louvre), less admired by the critics, headed by Diderot, than the *Portrait de l'abbé Arnaud* (Carpentras, museum). Duplessis had admirably rendered the rich dress of the model, her beautiful face, and her pet looking suspiciously at us as the mistress smiles with assurance.

Kansas City, Nelson Gallery–Atkins Museum, Nelson Fund

LOUIS-JACQUES DURAMEAU
Paris 1733–Versailles 1796

Pupil of the sculptor Defernex, Durameau received the *Grand Prix* in 1757. After three years spent, like most of his contemporaries, at the Ecole Royale des Elèves Protégés, directed by Carle Van Loo, he went to Rome where he stayed between 1761 and 1764. *Académicien* in 1774, he occupied in 1778 the position of *garde du cabinet du roi* and, in 1784, that of *garde des tableaux du roi* at Versailles; in 1794 he became curator of the galleries at Versailles. His major work is actually the ceiling of the opera there. It is the only one of his decorations, excepting a section for the *Galerie d'Apollon* (Louvre), still in location today. Durameau devoted himself mostly to history painting. "Witness of a transitory generation between Boucher and David," Durameau belongs to this stream of artists quite active under Louis XVI, who wanted to regenerate French art. Durameau strongly hoped for the advent of a more severe art form, intellectually more ambitious, without renouncing the elegance of his century. Anne Leclair has done fine studies on this artist; one can hope for the publication of her research in the near future.

34 *Achille pleurant Patrocle,* 1767 PL. 109

Oil on canvas, 53 x 72.5 cm / 20¾ x 28½ in.

PROVENANCE: Gift of the painter Louis Caradec around 1876.

BIBLIOGRAPHY: Paris, Musée du Louvre, 1974–1975, p. 59, with plate.

There is a signed and dated 1767 preparatory drawing for this painting in a private collection, Rennes. The subject, more rare than *Achille déposant le cadavre d'Hector aux pieds du corps de Patrocle* given at the 1769 Concours, reveals the new artistic ideal of the time: the cult of an exemplary and heroic death, of virile friendship. The composition is extremely simple, sculptural and monumental, but the free and heavy brushstroke remains that of an admirer of Boucher and of a rival of Carle Van Loo.

Brest, Musée des Beaux-Arts

HENRI DE FAVANNE
London 1668–Paris 1752

Raised in England, trained by Houasse, Favanne was in Rome between 1695 and 1700. In Spain at the beginning of the century, he became an *académicien* in 1704 (his reception piece is at Versailles) and exhibited, the same year, at the Salon. Along with Christophe, Charles Coypel, Cazes, Galloche, Lemoine, Oudry, Restout and Jean-François de Troy, he took part in 1724 in the decoration of the Hôtel du Grand Maître at Versailles, three years later in the 1727 Concours, and later in the 1737, 1746, 1747, 1748, 1750 and 1751 Salons. In 1748, he became *recteur* of the Académie. Nothing remains today, except the painted sketch at the Louvre, of his major enterprise, the decoration of the chapel, *salon* and *galerie* of the château at Chanteloup (1713–1716). Among the one hundred and fifty easel paintings attributed to him by his eighteenth-century biographer, Cousin de la Contamine, only about fifteen are known today, among which are the amazing *Autoportrait* (1745; Paris, Ecole des Beaux-Arts) and some mythological or historical scenes executed with strong and refined colors.

Antoine Schnapper's article (1972) summarizes what we know of this interesting painter who likes "simple costumes, solid volumes, figures with round and black eyes, twisted positions, often seen from the back and set in the foreground like screens." Favanne makes an unexpected link between Poussin and "Neoclassicism". Since Schnapper's article, several pictures (private collection, Upsala, signed and dated 1737; four in the church at Cuisery) have reappeared or have been reattributed to him (Louvre).

35 *Coriolan quittant sa famille pour combattre sa patrie*, 1725 — PL. 31

Oil on canvas, 97 x 129 cm / 38¼ x 50¾ in.

PROVENANCE: Acquired at public sale, Hôtel Drouot, Paris, 1971.

BIBLIOGRAPHY: Schnapper, 1972, pp. 362–63, fig. 2.

This picture and its pendant (also in Auxerre), *Coriolan supplié par sa femme et sa mère,* are dated around 1725 by Antoine Schnapper. It is, indeed, possible that the Auxerre pictures are the "two little subjects with Coriolan" exhibited at the *Exposition de la Jeunesse,* Place Dauphine, that year and mentioned by Cousin de la Contamine in his biography of the artist (1753). One finds in the Auxerre picture many characteristics of Favanne's style: small dark eyes, frieze-like composition, arrested gestures, a taste for "fuzzy" and dusty hues, affected and refined colors. What impresses one most, however, is the simplicity of the composition (one would like to say of the staging), "the clear definition of the space through architecture," in a word, the Classicism which owes much to the style of Poussin in the 1650's and which foreshadows the research of the French painters during the last twenty-five years of the eighteenth century.

Musée d'Auxerre

JEAN-HONORÉ FRAGONARD
Grasse 1732–Paris 1806

Grand Prix in 1752, Fragonard left for Rome at the end of 1755 after having completed three years at the Ecole Royale des Elèves Protégés, directed by Carle Van Loo. Fragonard stayed in Italy until 1761. There he became friendly with Hubert Robert. *Agréé* by the Académie with his immense *Corésus et Callirhoé* (Louvre) exhibited at the 1765 Salon, Fragonard never became an *académicien*, having failed to present his reception piece. He seldom exhibited at the Salon, preferring to work for a less official clientele. In 1769, he executed his *Figures de fantaisie* (eight at the Louvre) and in 1771–1773, his series of the *Progrès de l'Amour*, commissioned and eventually refused by Mme du Barry for Louveciennes (New York, Frick Collection).

In 1773–1774, Fragonard was again in Italy. To know many facts about his life during his last thirty years (for instance his appointment by David as curator of the Muséum des Arts in 1793) does not allow one to know the kind of work he then produced. Georges Wildenstein (1960), lists about 450 pictures executed before 1776 and little more than one hundred after that date.

Fragonard was most prolific, both in painting and drawing. Because he only occasionally signed his works, rarely exhibited them, and failed to have them engraved, it is hard, not only to distinguish his work from his imitators, or from his less gifted contemporaries, but also to date them correctly. Beyond a staggering virtuosity, delight in a brilliant execution, a freedom of the brush, and beyond the depiction of brisk and sensual scenes, yet never trivial or vulgar, Fragonard is an artist fully aware of the inventiveness of Rembrandt, Rubens, Frans Hals or Boucher. He is also a great poet, an artist who rejects formulas and who, varying his manner constantly, is able to adapt himself to the changes of taste and even to be, occasionally, an innovator.

36 *Le colin-maillard* — PL. 82

Oil on canvas, 117 x 91.5 cm / 46 x 36 in.

PROVENANCE: Baron de Saint-Julien sale, June 21, 1784, no. 75 with its pendant — M. [Orel] and others sale, May 3, 1786, no. 177 — Comte de Sinéty — Baron Nathaniel de Rothschild, Vienna — Baron Maurice de Rothschild, Prégny — acquired in 1954.

BIBLIOGRAPHY: G. Wildenstein, 1960, no. 47, fig. 31.

The pendant to this picture is the no less famous *Bascule* (collection Thyssen, Lugano; see Ebbinge-Wubben, Salm. . . , 1969, p. 113, no. 98). Both pictures were engraved in 1760 by Jacques-Firmin Beauvarlet (1731–1797) under both the names Boucher and Fragonard. In the catalogue of the sale held after the death of the Baron de Saint-Julien, one finds these two pictures (but with different dimensions). This would indicate that they were, in fact, large decorations which have been cut down at the top, probably in the nineteenth century.

One must concur with Charles Sterling's proposed date for these paintings: 1750–1752, the time at which Fragonard was probably in Boucher's studio. The painting still has the pinkish hues so characteristic of Boucher. The two children, as well as the luscious vegetation, are also borrowed from him. Already in *Le colin-maillard,* one senses, however, a freshness of expression, a taste for movement, and a verve which anticipate the mature Fragonard. The painter treated the same theme again: the first time in a clear, light green and gold, landscape (Washington); the second time, contrarily, in a Rembrandtesque twilight (before 1778, Louvre).

The Toledo Museum of Art, Gift of Edward Drummond Libbey

37 *Les cascatelles de Tivoli* PL. 93

Oil on canvas, 72.5 x 60.5 cm / 28½ x 24 in.

PROVENANCE: La Caze — bequeathed to the Louvre in 1869.

BIBLIOGRAPHY: G. Wildenstein, 1960, no. 108, fig. 72.

Entering the Louvre as a work by Hubert Robert, the attribution of this painting was rightly restored, by Charles Sterling in 1933, to Fragonard. There is, among the many drawings bequeathed to the city of Besançon by the architect Pierre-Adrien Pâris, a red chalk drawing signed *Frago* (Besançon, Musée des Beaux-Arts, 1957, no. 39 with plate) directly related to the Louvre picture. Pâris had this drawing which at one time belonged to the Abbé de Saint-Non, with whom Fragonard sojourned at the Villa d'Este and at Tivoli in the summer of 1760. Saint-Non also owned a painting of the same subject by Fragonard. The Louvre picture, with its warm green and gold harmonies, its washerwomen and the "tourists" who enliven this famous site near Rome (which was frequently painted by foreign artists), was painted in Italy, or shortly after his return to France in 1761. It is a vibrant hommage to Italy, more to its daily life, landscape and customs, than to antiquity and the masterpieces of the Renaissance to which Fragonard owed so much.

Paris, Musée du Louvre

38 *Portrait de Marie-Madeleine Guimard,* 1769 PL. 113

Oil on canvas, 81 x 65 cm / 32 x 25½ in.

PROVENANCE: Marcille sale, January 12–13, 1857, no. 64 — Hippolyte Walferdin sale, April 12–16, 1880, no. 35 — Mme Watel-Dehaynin — given to the Louvre as a tax credit in 1974.

BIBLIOGRAPHY: G. Wildenstein, 1960, no. 342, color reproduction facing p. 66 — Rosenberg and Compin, 1974, pp. 188–91, color reproduction p. 189.

Fourteen *Figures de fantaisie* by Fragonard are known today: eight are at the Louvre. One of the half-length costumed portraits bears the date 1769, usually assigned to the entire series. If these pictures represent, as one thinks, actual members of Fragonard's entourage (such as Diderot, or the Abbé de Saint-Non), then it is clear that the artist is less concerned with their likeness than with an image rendered with radiant vitality, and that the psychological analysis is less important than the virtuosity of the brush and plastic unity of the composition. It seems, despite its not having been established for more than a century, that this *Figure de fantaisie* represents Guimard (1743–1816), the famous opera dancer, known for her choreographic talents, her advanced taste in art (Ledoux, David) and her many and generous lovers. More than the slender figure of the dancer whose thinness was legendary, Fragonard has shown, in this surprising picture with its brown, red, green and gold chromaticism reminiscent of Rembrandt, the mobility of a lively face and its melancholy musing.

Paris, Musée du Louvre

LOUIS GALLOCHE
Paris 1670–Paris 1761

Pupil of Louis de Boullongne, (Galloche obtained the *Prix de Rome* in 1695 and stayed in Italy between 1699 and 1701. In 1711, he was received by the Académie where he led a brilliant career (after the death of Cazes, he replaced him as *chancelier* in 1754). He took part in the 1727 Concours (*Hippomène et Atalante*, lost but known through a photograph) and also in the 1747 Concours (*Coriolan*, Orléans). He exhibited at the various Salons which, from 1737 on, allowed the artists to show their work to the public. Today Galloche is only known to have been the teacher of Natoire and Lemoine. He outlived the latter by twenty-four years!

The four lectures he gave at the Académie between 1750 and 1753, known as his *Traité sur la peinture,* in which he said that "on the road the students must follow from the study of the antiques until they are able to operate by themselves," constitute an important documentation of a doctrine formulated by one who practiced it. To study this painter is a delicate task. His paintings are rare, his style difficult to define. His figures remain attached to the eighteenth-century tradition, but his taste for open air compositions and for clear and strong colors make him an excellent transitional artist.

After the Abbé Gougenot (1767), his eighteenth-century biographer, and Charles Saunier (1928), Galloche was studied by Marie-Catherine Sahut who wrote an important masters thesis, which will perhaps be published soon.

39 *Roland apprenant les amours d'Angélique et de Médor,* 1732 — PL. 42

Oil on canvas, 75.5 x 118 cm / 29¾ x 46½ in.

PROVENANCE: Commissioned in 1732 for the *cabinet de la reine* at Versailles; 750 livres paid, together with an *Allégorie de la reine sous la figure de l'Aurore* now in the Draguignan museum — sent in 1802 to Caen.

BIBLIOGRAPHY: Saunier, 1928, p. 225, no. 11.

More inspired by Quinault's opera (1685, music by Lulli), still very popular in the eighteenth century, than by Ariosto's *Orlando Furioso,* Galloche's picture shows an episode rarely represented by artists of the time: Roland hears from Coridon and Belise that Angélique has left with Médor. Furthermore, Belise's father, Tersandre, shows to the despairing Roland the bracelet Angélique offered him because he helped her to flee. In this mature work, Galloche is at his best: the sparkling colors, feeling of open air, contrast between Roland's despair, and the background with the frieze of dancers and musicians. It is fascinating to compare Galloche's picture with that of Cazes (no. 3). Both were commissioned, on the same date, for Versailles. Both artists, whose aesthetics remain attached to the principles in force at the end of Louis XIV's reign, tried to emulate the taste of the day.

Caen, Musée des Beaux-Arts

CLAUDE GILLOT
Langres 1673–Paris 1722

Pupil of Jean-Baptiste Corneille, *agréé* in 1710, *académicien* in 1715 (his reception piece, *Le Christ prêt à être attaché à la croix,* is in the church at Noailles), Gillot died unrecognized in 1722, a year after Watteau, his most famous pupil. His pictures, inspired by the theater, are rare; his engravings and drawings, executed in a nervous, mannered spirit, somewhat reminiscent of the sixteenth century, have always been in great demand. "His principal merit" wrote E. Dacier (1928), his best biographer, "is his ingenuity in opening new ways. He has been much more than an original artist, he has been an innovator." An avant-garde artist, "he mixes the picturesque and the religious, humanity and mythology, mythology and theater."

40 *La scène dite des deux carrosses* — PL. 20

Oil on canvas, 127 x 160 cm / 50 x 63 in.

PROVENANCE: Didot de Saint-Marc sale, Paris, November 30, 1835, no. 60; as Watteau — Alexandre-Ivanovitch Zimmermann, Saint Petersburg — Baron Rolf d'Ungern Sternberg — acquired by the Louvre in 1923.

BIBLIOGRAPHY: Dacier, 1928, pp. 181–82, 201–02, no. 2.

E. Dacier, François Boucher, who attributed this painting to its right author, and Paul Jamot have explained the subject of this picture for which we know several preparatory drawings (at the Louvre, and at the Lyons Library, for example) as well as a copy after it drawn by Lancret (G. Wildenstein, 1955, pp. 175–78): in 1695 the Italian comedians added a scene of their own invention to a play by Regnard and Dufresny, *La Foire Saint-Germain.* This scene, thereafter, continued to be performed: it is shown here, as performed in the theater, with its stage set. Two coaches, actually two *vinaigrettes* or small two-wheeled *chaises* drawn by footmen, meet in a narrow street in Paris, creating a "traffic jam". Neither of the ladies in the *vinaigrettes* will give up her right-of-way. A *commissaire* interferes to ask both *chaises* to go back. In the picture the two footmen, facing one another, rail at each other as the two actors, disguised as women, encourage them not to give up. The policeman's solution to the controversy is imminent.

One easily recognizes, to the right, and under the disguise of the woman with her huge *fontange,* Harlequin, who is wearing his mask; and on the left, one sees Scaramouche with his skull-cap and moustache. Painted renditions of theater scenes were tremendously successful in the eighteenth century. Gillot is seen here, not only as an innovator, but also as a forceful colorist using, in particular, the strongest scarlet reds. One should remember, about this street scene, the expressions on the faces, and the fast exchange of words, as well as the movements of the hands which are skillfully brought together in the center of the composition.

Paris, Musée du Louvre

JEAN-BAPTISTE GREUZE
Tournus 1725–Paris 1805

Greuze remains one of the most misunderstood artists of his time. During his lifetime, despite Diderot's enthusiastic defense, and despite the considerable sums he obtained for the sale of his paintings throughout Europe, and in Russia above all, Greuze was not received by the Académie as a history painter, as he had hoped to be, but as a genre painter (with his *Caracalla,* 1769, Louvre). The artist's disappointment was so great that he never exhibited at the Salon again. Trained in Lyons, *agréé* in 1755 (at which time he was noticed), Greuze went to Italy with the Abbé Gougenot (1756–1759). Upon his return, he quickly became known through his portraits which were remarkable for their Rembrandtesque realism (unknown until then in France); but he was more widely recognized because of genre scenes which, beyond their ambiguous sensuality and their sentiment content, and beyond the perfect knowledge of the painters of the past (Poussin notably), tended to "parler au coeur". Through the example they presented, they also tried to educate the viewer and to make him more "vertueux".

Since the eighteenth century, in spite of Diderot's lucid analysis, Greuze has been unlucky with the critics. The courageous studies of Louis Hautecoeur (1913), the excellent research of Edgar Munhall (1964, 1965, 1966), and the recent monograph of Anita Brookner (1972) have not helped him to regain, from the greater part of the public, the position that was rightly his during his lifetime. His birth, exactly two hundred and fifty years ago, has not been commemorated by one traditional exhibition!

41 *La paresseuse italienne,* 1756 PL. 87

Oil on canvas, 65 x 50 cm / 25½ x 19 11/16 in.

PROVENANCE: Salon of 1757, no. 114 — Boyer de Fonscolombe as early as 1757, Aix-en-Provence; his sale, Paris, January 18, 1790, no. 101 with its pendant — Prince Radziwill-Braniki — acquired from Wildenstein, 1934.

BIBLIOGRAPHY: Martin and Masson, 1908, p. 15, no. 187 — Brookner, 1972, pp. 59, 97, pl. 13.

This picture had for a pendant *L'Oiseleur qui au retour de la chasse accorde sa guitare* (Warsaw), also painted in 1756 in Rome and engraved by P. E. Moitte. The Wadsworth picture shows a slovenly woman, in a state of greatest disarray. Greuze wishes — an understandable concern from an artist who wants to make himself known — to show his ability to render the transparency of the glass bottles of Chianti, and of the water in the basin. The artist must have been aware, in Italy, of realistic genre scenes such as *La puce* by G. M. Crespi (Louvre), which seems to have had some influence on him. He also tries, beyond the sensual and erotic atmosphere indicated by the naked breast, and the disturbing contrast between the bare foot and the shod one, to paint a character, a symbol of indolence and laziness, to avert us from this deplorable example.

Hartford, Wadsworth Atheneum, The Ella Gallup Sumner and Mary Catlin Sumner Collection

42 *Le geste napolitain,* 1757 PL. 88

Oil on canvas, 73 x 94 cm / 28¾ x 37⅛ in.

Signed and dated lower right: *Greuze f. Roma 1757*

PROVENANCE: Salon of 1757, no. 113 — Abbé Gougenot — Princes N. N. and A. Demidoff, San Donato; sale, Paris, February 26, 1870, no. 108; 53,000 gold francs — acquired by Phillips probably for William I, Count of Dudley, died 1885 — Lord Masham — Viscountess Swinton — Koetser Gallery — Acquavella Galleries, New York — Alberto Reyna, Caracas — acquired in 1964 from French and Co., New York.

BIBLIOGRAPHY: Martin and Masson, 1908, p. 12, no. 152 — Brookner, 1972, pp. 59, 97, pl. 14 — Rich in Worcester, Mass., Worcester Art Museum, 1974, pp. 254–56.

The subject of this painting, for which we know a number of preparatory drawings and some painted studies, and which P. E. Moitte engraved as early as 1763, requires some explanation: a nobleman (he bears the *Ordre du Christ* and the Salon *livret* tells us he is Portuguese!) disguised as a peddler and offering a young maid "matches", tries to abuse her. His fraud is discovered by the maid-in-waiting. The young maid, putting her fingers under her chin, affects the *geste napolitain*. Painted in Rome with its pendant, *Les oeufs cassés* (Metropolitan Museum), this picture — in spite of his subject (the "Italian costumes" according to the *livret*, and fragments of antique capitals) owes little to Roman art of the time. Greuze wants to tell a story, condemn hypocrisy and lies, while perhaps trying to move us; each face must express a particular feeling. Greuze wanted also to prove his talent as a colorist (talent which assured him the admiration of the Abbé Barthélemy in Rome in 1757 and which can be witnessed here, for example, in the yellow-gold of the dress and the black coat of the peddler), using characteristic clear and light colors; he abandoned these colors after his return to France in order to adopt a Rembrandtesque chiaroscuro.

The group of the dog with the children was to be tremendously popular in his *oeuvre*.

Worcester Art Museum, Charlotte E. W. Buffington Fund

43 *Monseigneur de Valras* PL. 96

Oil on canvas, 145 x 115 cm / 57 x 45¼ in.

PROVENANCE: Seized during the Revolution in the residence of G.-F. Moreau, Bishop of Mâcon, between 1763 and 1790; the picture is listed among the inventory of his belongings, established in An II: "Tableau peint à l'huile portrait de l'évêque Valeras [*sic*], tête par Greuse [*sic*], 4 pieds 6 pouces de haut, 3 pieds 6 pouces de large, bordure dorée de 6 pouces, no. 95" (Lex, 1898, pp. 612, 632) — bequeathed to the museum in Mâcon in 1880 by Mlle Ronot, whose father, according to her, had acquired it for 2400 francs at the sale after the death of M. Pic, a lawyer in Mâcon, between 1823 and 1840 (Lex, 1898, p. 616 and note 2).

BIBLIOGRAPHY: Lex, 1898, pp. 606–39 — Martin and Masson, 1908, p. 78, no. 1267 — Brookner, 1972, pp. 104–05, pl. 32.

Henri-Constance de Lort de Sérignan de Valras (or Valreas) was Bishop of Mâcon between 1732 and 1763. One would think that Greuze executed this portrait shortly before his death. We do not know the origin of the portrait which belonged to his successor, who had it at the time of the Revolution (the dimensions given in the inventory correspond to 146 cm x 113 cm). The painting was, at that time, precisely described as being the portrait of Mgr. de Valras. Greuze had also been asked to portray G.-F. Moreau by the deputies of the Etats du Mâconnais in 1771, who wanted to show the Prelate their gratitude. The Prelate accepted the project (Lex, 1898, pp. 610, 622–23). There is no trace of this work which was intended for the *Salle des Etats*: one doesn't even know whether the project was actually executed. The same inventory established An II notes in Moreau's residence "dans la seconde pièce, salon: portrait du ci-devant évêque (Moreau), cadre doré, sans ver [*sic*], cinq pieds de haut (162 cm), no. 13 in." (Lex, 1898, p. 626 and note 2). Nothing indicates that it was also by Greuze. Mgr. de Valras' portrait, little known and poorly studied, shows a concern for reserve and austerity of composition, which does not prevent Greuze from showing his superb virtuosity in the rendering of the silks, the lace and the metal of the cross. The face is analyzed with objectivity, and Greuze tries to reveal his character. Occasional portraitist, Greuze makes an effort to restore the traditional conception of the genre and to place a new emphasis on the psychological aspect. He also anticipates the nineteenth century and shows himself to be an avant-garde artist.

Mâcon, Musée Municipal des Ursulines

ALEXIS GRIMOU
Argenteuil 1678–Paris 1733

Agréé by the Académie in 1705, Grimou, the "French Rembrandt", was dismissed four years later for having failed to submit his reception piece. Henceforth, he led his career at the Académie de Saint-Luc, rival of the

Académie Royale. Little is known of his life, and his reputation as a drunkard is ill-founded.

Grimou paints portraits, but familiar ones. He dresses his sitters in the costumes of pilgrims or the Spanish, and represents them (in half-length portraits) as drinkers or smokers. Grimou, like his idol, Rembrandt, whose warm and golden colors as well as taste for shadows he imitates, portrays himself constantly. If his "invention" is limited (to quote his obituary published in the *Mercure de France*), Grimou—like Raoux, who disappeared a year after him and who deserves to have been represented in our exhibition—knew how to create an original genre, that of the *portrait costumé* or of the *figure de fantaisie*, which became tremendously fashionable in the eighteenth century. Louis Réau's study (II, 1930), based upon the research of C. Gabillot (1911), must be completed with those of Claude-Gerard Marcus (1969) and G. Levitine (1969).

44 *L'Homme à la pipe*, 1726 PL. 35

Oil on canvas, 130 x 96.5 cm / 51¼ x 38 in.

Signed and dated lower right: *Grimou/f. 1726*

PROVENANCE: Cailleux, 1961.

BIBLIOGRAPHY: Marcus, 1969, p. 7, fig. 8.

This painting was engraved in the eighteenth century by Perret as a portrait of the famous corsair, Jean Bart. It is the portrait of a man dressed in a long red cloak, holding a long clay pipe and leaning against a table on which are a long-stemmed glass and a bottle (a pretext for the artist to show his ability to render the transparency and reflection of the glass), and it ranks among the best works of the painter. A year later than the famous *Jeune pélerin* and *Jeune pélerine* (Florence, Uffizi), it is in contrast to the works of the most laborious period of the artist (1720–1730) because of the assurance and the simplicity of the composition, the frankness of the execution and accuracy of the psychological aspect.

Paris, Collection Beytout

NOËL HALLÉ

Paris 1711–Paris 1781

Son and grandson of two renowned painters, Claude-Guy and Daniel, brother-in-law of Jean Restout, Noël Hallé obtained the *Grand Prix* in 1736. He was in Rome between 1737 and 1744. In 1748, he was received by the Académie where he pursued a successful career. A month before his death he became its *recteur*. *Surinspecteur* of the Manufacture des Gobelins in 1770, as a reward for his mission to Rome in 1775 to reorganize the Académie de France neglected by Natoire, he was made *Chevalier de Saint-Michel* in 1777. Hallé exhibited regularly at the Salon and received numerous commissions from the King and the Church. History painter above all, he is comfortable with large compositions; Hallé, however, had no contempt for genre pictures (*Education des riches*, *Education des pauvres*) or portraits. His style is easily recognized: he likes elongated figures, heads with long hair, faces topped by coiffures which stress their oval shape, and somewhat unbalanced silhouettes. His colors are pale, occasionally close to pastels; his brushstroke, wide and heavy in his beautiful sketches, becomes soft and porcelain-like in his large compositions. Since O. Estournet's monograph (1905), very little has been written about the artist.

45 *Joseph accusé par la femme de Putiphar*, 1744 PL. 67

Oil on canvas, 141.5 x 166.5 cm / 55¾ x 65 9/16 in.

PROVENANCE: Salon of 1748, no. 49 — sale after the death of Noël Hallé, July 2, 1781; because of family differences, this sale did not take place and the picture stayed in the Hallé family until recently — Pétin, Paris — sale, Paris, Hôtel Drouot, November 6, 1972, salle 14; not in catalogue; no attribution — Heim gallery, Paris and London — acquired in 1974.

BIBLIOGRAPHY: Estournet, 1905, p. 195, no. 3.

At the same 1748 Salon, Hallé exhibited his reception piece "*La dispute de Minerve et de Neptune pour donner un nom à la ville d'Athènes*" (Louvre) which he had just completed. This formal and elegant later work shows clearly the changes Hallé brought, in a few years, to his style. The Chicago picture (of which there is another, colder version), described by the September 1748 *Mercure de France* as "très beau d'effet et de composition" had been painted before the artist's return from Rome in 1744 and still has something of the Italian examples (Venetian and Roman) he was able to see. The richly ornamented bed, the vase, and the basin to the left, with their golden reflections, against the bodies of Potiphar's wife, of the servants and of Joseph, are the only light spots in the picture. The brushstroke does not yet have the metallic distinction of the later works; but already, Hallé tries to expose his subject with clarity, no matter the ambiguity or difficulty.

The David and Alfred Smart Gallery, The University of Chicago, Gift of the Mark Morton Memorial Fund and Mr. and Mrs. Eugene Davidson

46 *Le colin-maillard* PL. 94

Oil on canvas, 173 x 120 cm / 68 x 47¼ in.

PROVENANCE: Eugène Tondu sale, Paris, April 10–15, 1865, no. 209; as Hubert Robert — gift of the two brothers, Ernest and Olympe Lavalard, in 1894; again as Robert.

This picture, catalogued and exhibited several times as Hubert Robert (Nohlac, 1910, pl. 131), and sometimes compared to Fragonard, is actually by Noël Hallé, despite the fact that one does not find any mention of it in the literature on the painter (for that matter, the picture of the same subject, but different in composition, signed and dated 1773, sold in Paris, November 24, 1936 (no. 24), is not mentioned either). The broken folds of the dresses, painted like pieces put together, and the pale colors which resemble watercolor are trademarks of the artist. Even though this picture alludes to Italy, with its columns, its terrace, the umbrella pine, the portico transformed into a barn, we believe that it was executed in France when the artist had already reached his maturity. In any case, it shows that it is hasty to attribute only to Fragonard (cf. no. 36, the Amiens picture recalls the picture of the same subject by Fragonard in Washington) and Hubert Robert this kind of work which is both picturesque and amusing, and at the same time, rich in lively details (the parrot!) introduced to entertain the viewer.

Amiens, Musée de Picardie

MICHEL-ANGE HOUASSE
Paris 1680–Arpajon 1730

Son of Le Brun's collaborator, Réne-Antoine Houasse, Michel-Ange went to Rome with his father who had been appointed Director of the Académie de France (1699–1705). Michel-Ange was *agréé* in 1706 and received by the Académie the following year (*Hercule et Lycas,* Tours); he was in Madrid at the latest in 1715 where, during the next fifteen years, he devoted himself to the execution of official portraits, allegories, history paintings, genre scenes, bacchanals, landscapes, still lifes and representations of everyday life. An original artist in the choice of his subjects, Houasse remains unrecognized, in spite of the studies of Yves Bottineau (1960), Juan J. Luna (1974) and chiefly Jutta Held (1968). The dispersion among the collections of the Patrimonio Nacional of his astonishing topographical landscapes, in which accurate observation rivals the rendering of light, and of his scenes of popular life, is mostly responsible for this lack of recognition.

47 *Vue de l'Escurial* PL. 32

Oil on canvas, 50 x 82 cm / 19¾ x 32¼ in.

PROVENANCE: Inventoried as early as 1746 at La Granja.

BIBLIOGRAPHY: J. Held, 1968, p. 201, G. 45, fig. 20.

Houasse executed a series of topographical views of the Spanish official residences: this rapidly executed view of the Escurial (others are at La Moncloa), with a reading monk in the left foreground, is particularly interesting because of the way in which the harsh light of the sunset, which lengthens the shadows of the bushes in the foreground, is carefully observed. There are, in this work, which "expresses profound peace", a frankness, a simplicity, and a natural quality which have no equivalent at that time.

Madrid, Museo del Prado

JEAN-BAPTISTE HUET
Paris 1745–Paris 1811

Son of a *peintre artisan,* Huet was the pupil of the *animalier* Charles Dagomer and of Leprince. Received by the Académie in 1769, he regularly exhibited pastoral scenes and animal pictures at the Salon. Huet tried to be received a second time in 1779, as a history painter, but was unsuccessful. He was a prolific draftsman, fine engraver and receptive, during the Revolution, to the prevailing aesthetic. Huet exhibited until 1802 but ended his life almost entirely forgotten. If he often imitates Boucher or Leprince and extends their style until the Empire period, Huet, nevertheless, proves to be more inventive in his animal pictures, which owe much to Oudry, but are strongly colored and executed with remarkable boldness. Since C. Gabillot's study (1892) nothing essential has been written on Huet.

48 *Un renard dans le poulailler,* 1766 PL. 104

Oil on canvas, 98 x 131 cm / 38½ x 51½ in.

Signed and dated lower left: *J. B. Huet. 1766*

PROVENANCE: Salon of 1769, no. 138 — given to the museum in 1923.

At the Salon of 1769, the first one in which he participated, Huet exhibited more than twelve pictures: scenes with animals (among which were his reception piece, *Un dogue se jetant sur des oies,* Louvre, a *Laitière,* flower pieces, a moonlight landscape and drawings, one with a religious subject). The drawing executed by Gabriel de Saint-Aubin at the end of his own copy of the *livret* (Dacier, II, p. 89) confirms that the San Francisco picture is indeed the one exhibited at that Salon, and the one which was engraved by Jean-Baptiste Huets *fils.* The pictures Huet exhibited then had some success. Bachaumont, however, wrote of the San Francisco painting: "the fowl look like bats" and Diderot, for his part, reproached the artist because he did not have "enough drawing" and for the lack of "harmonies" in his pictures. Des Boulmiers, on the other hand, wrote in the *Mercure,* "His *Renard dans le poulailler* is the picture which does the most honor [to the artist] and which places him with the finest painters of this genre" (Gabillot, 1892, p. 50).

Huet is an exponent of the lesson of Oudry and wants to show his ability to render animals; he also succeeds in producing a colorful and lively composition full of picturesque details and movement.

The Fine Arts Museums of San Francisco, Gift of Mrs. Franck Wilkins in Memory of Charles Le Gay

JEAN JOUVENET
Rouen 1644–Paris 1717

Admirer of his Norman compatriot Poussin, Jouvenet, at the beginning of his career, participated with the pupils of Le Brun in the decoration of several rooms at the Tuileries and at Versailles. The first part of his life was devoted mostly to the decoration of royal residences and of Parisian hôtels. He seldom left Paris, excepting a few trips to Normandy and Rennes. The second part of his life (beginning in 1685) was devoted, in particular, to the execution of gigantic religious paintings; thus he became the most important religious painter of his generation. In spite of the paralysis of his right hand in 1713, he pursued his career as a painter. His *Magnificat,* completed shortly before his death, is one of the most grandiose and moving pages in French painting. One should not forget the artist's portraits: dignified and reserved, the finest psychological analysis is combined with a sobriety of means.

Prolific but not inventive (he draws from a repertoire of forms, using them from one painting to the next), Jouvenet created a personal style which was rigorous and lucid, inspired by Poussin, Le Brun, Rubens or the Carracci, but never confused with those of his contemporaries. His lesson remained valid through the eighteenth century and his work returned to the topical with the rise in popularity of David. Like his paintings, Jouvenet's drawings (mostly black chalk studies for single figures later used in his canvases) are firm, neat, refined and distinct.

Antoine Schnapper's monograph on the artist (1974) is perfect. One can only wish that it would serve as an example for those who would like to devote a comparable study to one of the artists represented in this exhibition, few of which have received such magistral attention.

49 *La déposition de croix,* 1709 PL. 4

Oil on canvas, 179 x 137 / 70½ x 54 in.

Signed and dated lower center: *Jouvenet 1709*

PROVENANCE: Private collection, Montpellier — Heim gallery, London — acquired in 1974.

BIBLIOGRAPHY: Schnapper, 1974, pp. 26, 143–144, 214, 216, cat. no. 126, fig. 141.

This recently rediscovered painting is, according to Antoine Schnapper's careful analysis, an autograph version showing considerable changes (namely the addition of figures on both sides of the composition): first, from the painting of the same subject exhibited at the Salon of 1704 (lost, but known through the engraving by Alexis Loir; Schnapper, fig. 134); and second, from the painting, today in the church of Saint-Maclou in Pontoise (Schnapper, fig. 135), signed and dated 1708, repeated and copied several times by the artist and his studio throughout the eighteenth century. Schnapper catalogues only one copy of the Toledo picture, recently published with an attribution to Piazzetta's pupil,

Giulia Lama! In this picture, which was executed eight years before his death, Jouvenet aims chiefly toward a clear and perfectly readable composition. The pure, strong colors call to mind those of Carlo Dolci and of Philippe de Champaigne who, like Jouvenet, never went to Italy. We are attracted by the arch formed by the body of the dead Christ; the main figures, like the *pleurants* of a Medieval entombment group, are plunged into deep meditation. Serious and reserved, this painting, by no means declamatory, indicates the nobleness of French painting during the last years of Louis XIV's reign.

The Toledo Museum of Art, Gift of Edward Drummond Libbey

SIMON JULIEN
Toulon 1735–Paris 1800

Simon Julien is confused even today with Jean-Antoine Julien, called Julien de Parme (1736–1799). It is not our purpose to attempt here the separation of the lives of these two artists whose works are equally confused. A pupil of Dandré-Bardon in Marseilles and of Carle Van Loo in Paris, Simon Julien obtained the *Grand Prix* in 1760 (no. 50), left in 1763 for Rome where he stayed until 1771, but was *agréé* only in 1783. However, he never submitted his reception piece (*Tithon et l'Aurore*; picture, sketch, 1783, and drawing, 1782, in Caen). During his stay in Italy he apparently lived by producing copies or fakes. He exhibited at the *Salon de la Correspondance* in 1782 and 1785 and at the Salons of 1783, 1785, 1787 and 1800 (posthumously). Julien left some very beautiful engravings, remarkable drawings (which he fortunately signed) and some pictures, such as the *Martyre de saint Hippolyte* (Lyons, Cathedral of Saint Jean), which reveal a great artist.

Since Prosper de Baudicour (1859) and Bronze (1862), without forgetting Bellier and Auvray's dictionary (1882–1885) as well as his autobiography (see Bronze, 1862), no significant study of this artist has been made to distinguish him from his namesake.

50 *Le sacrifice de Manué, père de Samson*, 1760 PL. 95

Oil on canvas, 146 x 115 cm / 57½ x 45¼ in.

PROVENANCE: Seized at the Académie during the Revolution; sent to the Musée de Tessé, An VII; catalogued the following year (see Mauclay, An VIII, p. 10, no. 95).

Still catalogued in 1932 as *Le Barbier*, this picture was recognized in 1910 (Fontaine, p. 225) as being a work by Simon Julien. It is with this work that the artist won in 1760, before Lagrenée *le jeune*, the *Prix de Rome* which opened to him the doors of the Académie de France. He left for Rome only after completing three years at the Ecole Royale des Elèves Protégés.

The subject is rather common in French painting: Lesueur (Toulouse and Montauban) and his great rival Le Brun treated the subject in works Julien certainly remembered (he even imitated Lesueur's clear and suave colors). It was by a return to the purism and "neo-Raphaelism", characteristic of French painting in the preceding century, that Julien endeavored to exploit his talents among the young painters of his generation.

Le Mans, Musée de Tessé

CHARLES-FRANÇOIS GRENIER DE LA CROIX, *dit* LACROIX DE MARSEILLE
Marseilles ca. 1700 (?)–Paris or Berlin 1782

Little is known about Lacroix, who was called della Croce by the Italians, and who never was the subject of an important study. His first paintings date from 1743. He was certainly in Rome in 1750 where he met Vandières. It is only after Vernet's departure from Rome, in 1753, that his signatures appeared regularly on his paintings. In 1757 he was in Naples. He exhibited at the *Colisée* in 1776, and at the *Salon de la Correspondance* in 1780 and 1782. In May of 1780, the *Annonces, Affiches et Avis divers* mentioned that "M. Delacroix, painter of architecture, of seascapes and landscapes, who has lived for a long time in Italy, wishes to take students at his place, rue de Vaugirard, facing the Luxembourg." One can conclude from this that he was certainly in France by then. A contemporary of the artist, Pahin de la Blancherie, said that he died in Berlin in November 1782.

Lacroix must have known Manglard, and like Vernet, occasionally copied and often imitated him. He worked mostly for Italian, but also for French, customers; this is proven by the sale in Paris, December 19, 1866, "of eighteen pictures . . . by La Croix, all signed and dated, intended for the city hall of one of the southern French departments" (see Lugt, 1964, p. 76, no. 29403). In his best works, Lacroix differentiates himself from Vernet by his taste for fantastic architectural settings, *capriccios*, and for more ambitious and descriptive compositions, which link him sometimes to Dughet and sometimes to Rosa.

51 *Vue d'un port méditerranéen*, 1750 PL. 77

Oil on canvas, 94.5 x 167 cm / 37¼ x 65¾ in.

Signed and dated lower left: *Grenier de La/ Croix fecit Rom./ 1750.*

PROVENANCE: Mrs. F. R. Wynne, Tempsford Hall — sale, Sotheby's, London, November 19, 1952, no. 68 — Agnew, London — Cailleux, Paris — acquired in 1956.

This picture, often compared to the one in the National Gallery in London, and cautiously attributed to Vernet (Davies, p. 218, no. 1393), is without doubt the masterpiece of this mysterious artist. Like Henry d'Arles and Volaire, Lacroix imitates Vernet but introduces into his strongly colored pictures his own architectural inventions. The charming group of figures, descending the stairs on the right, and the three orientals in the center enliven this austere composition where one finds both imagination and precise topographical elements.

The Toledo Museum of Art, Gift of Edward Drummond Libbey

CHARLES DE LA FOSSE
Paris 1636–Paris 1716

La Fosse, the oldest painter represented in our exhibition, is also the one who learned the most from the examples of Le Brun and Poussin. In fact, he collaborated extensively with Le Brun at Versailles. La Fosse was in Italy between 1658 and 1663 (in Venice more than Rome). Upon his return, he worked on the decorations of the *Salon de Diane* and *Salon d'Apollon* at Versailles, the Trianon, and the Church of the Assumption in Paris. In 1690, he went to London where he decorated Montagu House. Thanks to the patronage of the *Surintendant*, Hardouin-Mansart, he obtained a large part of the commission for the Church of the Invalides. In 1709, he decorated the *cul-de-four* in the apse of the chapel at Versailles. Acquainted with the financier and collector, Crozat, he met at his residence the young Watteau, on whom he had significant influence. From his early years on, La Fosse displayed his predilection for colors, turning himself toward Veronese, the Venetians in general, and Rubens. His art, which does not tend toward rigorous academism, is sumptuous, noble, warm and sometimes moving. His partiality is to warm hues, saffron and autumnal reds. By finding his inspiration in those sources generally neglected by most of the artists of his generation, La Fosse gave French painting a new orientation. In a more modest sense, his attempt is comparable to that of Watteau.

The essential study on La Fosse, which was limited to his paintings, was published by Margaret Stuffmann (1964). Since then many paintings have appeared; this allows a better understanding of the painter's style and of the chronology of his *oeuvre*. La Fosse the draftsman, neglected until now, tended to combine red, black and white chalks.

52 *Le Christ au désert servi par les anges* PL. 5

Oil on canvas, 91.5 x 167 cm / 37¼ x 65¾ in.

PROVENANCE: Cardinal Fesch; his sale, Rome, March 17–18, 1845, no. 361–2954, acquired by "Williams" — Thomas J. Bryan — offered by him to the New York Historical Society — sale, New York, Parke-Bernet, December 2, 1971, no. 117.

BIBLIOGRAPHY: Stuffmann, 1964, p. 112, no. 70, with figure.

La Fosse has treated this subject several times: among the various known versions of it (Grenoble, engraving by Mariette after a lost painting), that which is most like the New York painting in composition is the Leningrad version (Stuffmann, no. 44, with figure). The workmanship of these pictures, however, is extremely different. The Russian picture, hardly larger than the New York one, is smoother and more carefully executed: the well-balanced composition the artist seeks owes much to Le Brun. The New York picture is freely handled and audacious in its chromatics. M. Stuffmann rightly mentions, in regard to this picture, the names Watteau (who knew La Fosse) and Rembrandt. A late picture — or at least, so it seems, considering what little information we have of the artist's chronology — it is characteristic of the originality of La Fosse's talent. A taste for color and movement is emphasized to the prejudice of correct drawing. The crepuscular light gives this work a curiously pre-romantic atmosphere.

New York, Private collection

LOUIS-JEAN-FRANÇOIS LAGRENÉE, *dit* LAGRENÉE L'AÎNE
Paris 1724–Paris 1805

Pupil of Carle Van Loo, like most history painters of his generation, Lagrenée obtained the *Grand Prix* at the Académie in 1749 and stayed briefly in Rome in 1751. *Académicien* in 1755, Lagrenée occupied the position of *Premier Peintre de l'Impératrice* in Saint Petersburg from 1760 to 1762 and succeeded Vien as Director of the Académie de France at the Palazzo Mancini from 1781 to 1787. In 1785 he was made *recteur* of the Académie.

A prolific painter (his *livre de raison* was published by the Goncourts in 1877), Lagrenée worked for the Church, for the King and for a large clientele of financiers and noblemen. Diderot, who defended him, rightly wrote: "the more his canvas expands, the more his talent diminishes." He likes the finish, the *"belles draperies"*, and uses strong and fresh colors. A French interpreter of Pompeo Batoni's style (see Sandoz 1962 and 1963), Lagrenée reacted against the careless and unfinished manner of Boucher and his peers. His works, elegant and seductive, are not, however, rich in drama or psychological insight; they are neither moral lessons nor *exempla virtutis*.

53 *Allégorie à la mort du Dauphin*, 1767 PL. 105

Oil on canvas, 128 x 96 cm / 50 x 37¾ in.

PROVENANCE: Salon of 1767, no. 19 — commissioned by the Duc de la Vauguyon (1706–1772) — Charles Vail, about 1870 — Mme Gravelin-Braquenié — acquired by Versailles in 1953, transferred to Fontainebleau in 1956.

BIBLIOGRAPHY: Lossky, 1967, pp. 184–86, with plate.

Louis XV's older son, the Dauphin, Louis de Bourgogne, died at Fontainebleau in 1765 shortly before his wife, Marie-Josèphe de Saxe. The preceptor of their children, the Duc de la Vauguyon, first commissioned Greuze, then Lagrenée (who received 4000 livres), to execute a commemorative picture while the Dauphin's wife was still alive. The future Louis XVI, Louis XVIII and Charles X are at their father's bedside while in the sky their older brother, deceased a few years earlier, only girdled with the blue sash of the *Ordre du Saint-Esprit,* puts a star crown over the head of the Dauphin.

The picture was well received by the critics at the Salon; they found it "touching", "pathetic and affecting" and compared its author to Guido Reni. Only Bachaumont ("Le Dauphin grimace") and Diderot, who was usually laudatory, expressed their reservations.

The best aspect of this work, above the "émotions du coeur", is its masterful accomplishment, the taste for a "smooth and creamy" surface, the fresh, precise and skillfully selected colors and the perfect execution of the painting.

Fontainebleau, Musée National du Château

54 *"Une femme endormie sur un lit parsemé de roses"*, 1773 PL. 122

Oil on copper, 34 x 42 cm / 13¾ x 16½ in.

PROVENANCE: Salon of 1773, no. 10 — (?) Duc de Chartres — Cailleux, Paris — acquired in 1975.

BIBLIOGRAPHY: *Catalogue de l'oeuvre peint de Lagrenée* (ms.), p. 264, no. 208 (?).

The Bibliothèque Doucet (Paris) keeps a *Catalogue de l'oeuvre peint de Lagrenée* written by the artist and published in part by the Goncourts (1878, p. 331 ff.). It is possible to associate the Clermont-Ferrand picture with several paintings mentioned in the original manuscript: for instance, there is mention of a *Volupté,* sold for the considerable amount of 1200 livres to the Duc de Chartres, which is certainly the picture exhibited at the Salon of 1773 under the title we have given to the Clermont-Ferrand copper; there is also mention of a *Jeune berger trouvant sa maîtresse endormie,* also painted in 1773 (without price). The opinion of one critic of the Salon of 1773 confirms the fact that the Clermont-Ferrand picture is, indeed, the one exhibited then. He mentions (Paris, Bibliothèque Nationale, fonds Deloyne, *"Entretiens de M. l'Abbé A*** avec Mylord B***,"* X, p. 248; p. 16) the "accentuated hip" of the sleeping woman and criticizes the "silly look" on the "man's" face.

Clermont-Ferrand, Musée des Beaux-Arts

JACQUES DE LAJOUE
Paris 1686–Paris 1761

Lajoue exhibited several architectural landscapes in 1721, the year he was received by the Académie, and in 1725, at the *Exposition de la Jeunesse,* Place Dauphine. He received in 1731 his first official commissions. Between 1737 and 1753 he exhibited at every Salon. Lajoue executed stage designs, added a painted perspective to the Bibliothèque Sainte-Geneviève, worked for the *cabinets* of the Duc de Picquigny, Bonnier de la Mosson, and received the commission of an important *Allégorie à la gloire du Roi* for Mme de Pompadour (Salon of 1753).

Lajoue is not only chiefly a painter of architectural ruins and of ornaments (the purest representative of the "rococo trend" in French art under Louis XV; "tout était livré à l'esprit de vertige," wrote Cochin subtly), but he also left seascapes, allegories, portraits (his own portrait with his family is at Versailles) and even some religious compositions. The figures in his decorative paintings are often inspired by engravings after Lancret, Boucher, and above all, Watteau. His own productions were known throughout Europe through the many engravings done after them.

Lajoue's works are numerous, uneven, and seldom dated: thus the establishment of their chronology is a rather delicate problem. We hope that the research of Marianne Roland-Michel will clarify the points still obscure in the studies of Mlle Bataille (1930, in Dimier) and of J. Cailleux (1957) on the relationship between Watteau and Lajoue.

55 *Paysage composé, au Neptune mutilé,* 1746(?) PL. 72

Oil on canvas, 81.5 x 101.5 cm / 32 x 40 in.

Signed in the center, on the arch: *La/ Joue*

PROVENANCE: Cailleux before World War II — Humbert de Wendel, 1930 — Baronne de Becker Rothschild — exhibited in 1953 at Frank T. Sabin, London, no. 13 in catalogue — sale, Paris, June 7, 1955, no. 67, with its pendant, today in a private collection, Paris — acquired from Cailleux in 1965.

This picture and its pendant could be assimilated to two works by Lajoue exhibited at the Salon of 1746 (nos. 90 and 91). Lajoue, however, plays untiringly with a limited number of motifs, and the description given by the *livret* is not sufficient to firmly establish that these are indeed the paintings of 1746.

Lajoue delights in painting staircases whose curves repeat those of the trees, as well as the fountains and pyramids of an imaginary architecture. Like Watteau, Lajoue prefers sculptures which take life; in this picture the river gods mingle with the couples seated on the steps. From this world of dreams, a stage setting where water and stone, trees and ruins blend, a nostalgic and dreamy feeling emanates, reinforced by the moving image of Neptune and his mutilated sea horses carried away by the waves.

Paris, Musée du Louvre

JEAN-BAPTISTE LALLEMAND
Dijon 1716–Paris 1803

Lallemand, the son of a tailor, went to Italy in 1744. He married there, was quite successful and returned ultimately to Paris only in 1764. The same year, he exhibited at the Académie de Saint-Luc, Paris. In 1770, Lallemand went to Dijon and three years later to London. He exhibited at the *Exposition du Colisée* in 1776, at the *Exposition de la Jeunesse* in 1783 and at the *Salon de la Correspondance* in 1786.

His production is consequential: it consists primarily of imaginary landscapes, or cityscapes, ruins in the style of Panini, seascapes in the style of Vernet, oils, gouaches and drawings which imitate, down to the ink color, those of Piranesi. Perhaps a minor artist, Lallemand is, nevertheless, the perfect example of a pleasant *petit maître* who is not particularly inventive but who spreads a style which is proof of itself and which pleases a large clientele.

P. Quarré and Mlle Geiger devoted an exhibition to this painter (1954); its catalogue is the basis of our knowledge on the artist.

56 *Vue du château Saint-Ange à Rome* PL. 78

Oil on canvas, 48 x 74 cm / 19 x 29¼ in.

Signed lower right: *Lallemand*

PROVENANCE: Bequeathed by Gaston Joliet in 1925.

BIBLIOGRAPHY: Quarré, 1954, no. 10, pl. IV.

Painted without doubt in Rome, with its pendant, the *Ponte Rotto sur le Tibre,* during the artist's long stay there: these pictures recall the two compositions of the same subject by Joseph Vernet (1745, Louvre).

Lallemand carefully describes the site, the Ponte della Consolazione with the Castel Sant'Angelo and San Pietro in the background. He chose also a late hour of the day, when the sun casts a golden light on the stones of these famous monuments. This type of picture (the Dijon museum owns another version with changes, painted in gouache) was likely to find easily a clientele among the tourists who wished to take home with them a souvenir of their trip abroad. Lallemand, however, distinguished himself from his numerous rivals through such details as the lacy vegetation, the group of fishermen, looking unbalanced on the ground, and his somewhat dull colors.

Dijon, Musée des Beaux-Arts

NICOLAS LANCRET
Paris 1690–Paris 1743

Pupil of Pierre Dullin and of Gillot, Lancret was for a short time in contact with Watteau; the two soon quarreled. Lancret was received by the Académie in 1719, before Watteau died. As early as 1723, the *Mercure* wrote of Lancret that he was "the pupil of the late M. Gillot and rival of the late M. Watteau." Henceforth he worked for the Duc d'Antin, Crozat, Tessin, the Prince de Carignan, and Frederic II, among others.

His production, mostly pastorals, *fêtes galantes,* scenes of comedy where music and dance play an important part, is considerable (over seven hundred pictures according to G. Wildenstein's monograph and *catalogue raisonné* of the artist, 1924). A stronger artist than Pater, more varied in his subjects and in the search for new settings for his figures, Lancret works with a limited repertoire of physiognomic types and psychological situations.

"His work, charming and accurate, reflecting the spirit and manners of our eighteenth century" has often been considered the symbol "of one of the most seductive expressions of French art" (G. Wildenstein, 1924, p. 37).

57 *La danse devant la tente* PL. 55

Oil on canvas, 60 x 50.5 cm / 23½ x 20 in.

PROVENANCE: Sale after the death of Mme Lancret, April 3–5, 1782; 250 livres, 19 sols — Galerie Cailleux, Paris — acquired in 1972.

BIBLIOGRAPHY: G. Wildenstein, 1924, no. 169.

This picture, kept by Lancret's widow until her death shortly before the Revolution, is one of the most accomplished works by the artist. Watteau's entire repertory can be found in it: the hurdy-gurdy player, the boy getting the wine bottles from the basket, the dancing couple with its swaying attitude, the table placed in the open air under a tent. Lancret gives this enchanting scene an atmosphere of festivity, made even more attractive by his glistening palette. Lancret has kept Watteau's inventions without either attempting to understand their true lesson or to renew their significance.

The William Hayes Ackland Memorial Art Center, University of North Carolina, Chapel Hill, Ackland Fund

NICOLAS DE LARGILLIERRE
Paris 1656–Paris 1746

Trained in Anvers with Antoine Goubaud, Largillierre went to England where he worked with Peter Lely between 1674 and 1680. Upon his return to France, he was received by the Académie in 1686. Henceforth, he devoted himself principally to portraits but did not neglect landscapes. Unlike the court painter, Rigaud, Largillierre worked mostly for a wealthy, bourgeois clientele. His rivalry with Rigaud was also aesthetic. Rigaud preferred cold hues, straight lines, and a rigorous composition. Thanks to his Flemish training, Largillierre used warm hues, a broad and thick brushstroke, and curves which give his paintings a deliberate dynamism.

Largillierre's production was immense (Mariette thought that, at that time, there were between twelve and fifteen hundred portraits by him in Paris), and the chronology of his work is not well established. We hope that the research of Georges de Lastic will reveal the generous personality of this great painter, who was studied only superficially by Georges Pascal (1928).

58 *Nature morte au tapis* PL. 11

Oil on canvas, 86 x 131 cm / 33¾ x 51½ in.

PROVENANCE: Acquired with its pendant, *Nature morte sur une table de pierre avec un bas-relief,* on the Italian art market in 1967.

BIBLIOGRAPHY: Lastic, 1968, pp. 233–40, fig. 3.

"Never has a painter been as universal as M. de Largillière" wrote Mariette (III (1854–1856), p. 61), referring to the religious pictures, the landscapes, and the still life pictures of the artist. This picture, dated by Georges de Lastic between 1700 and 1720, ranks among the most sumptuously executed ones by Largillierre. The rug, which recalls those in the works of Francesco Fieravino, Il Maltese, and the fruit basket, profiled against a yellowish drapery, show the progress accomplished by the artist since his first attempt in 1677; at that time the virtuosity and the search for *trompe-l'oeil* effects were still prevalent. Here, the warmth of the colors and the freedom and spontaneity of execution triumph.

Musée de Dunkerque

59 *Portrait de François-Jules du Vaucel,* 1724 PL. 28

Oil on canvas, 138 x 105 cm / 54¼ x 41¼ in.

Signed and dated lower left: *Peint. par. / N. de Largillierre./ 1724*

PROVENANCE: La Caze — bequeathed to the Louvre in 1869.

BIBLIOGRAPHY: Brière, 1919, pp. 144–45.

The identification of the sitter, François-Jules du Vaucel (1672–1739) — *fermier général* in 1721, *payeur des rentes de l'Hôtel-de-Ville,* Paris, in 1728 — is confirmed by the inscription on the letter which rests on the piece of furniture to the right; *A Monsieur / Du Vaucel con*[er] */ Roy maison couronne.* A marble bust (a terracotta version is also known) of the same man by Coysevox was part of the Jacques Doucet sale in 1912 (Paris, Galerie George Petit, Part II, p. 13, no. 107; later in New York, collection of Jules Bache). This little known picture, which does not figure in the recent catalogues of the Louvre because of its location since 1952 at the *Présidence du Conseil,* Hôtel Matignon, is a magnificent portrait executed in the artist's mature style.

The attitude is noble; the sumptuous outfit and the fat and pudgy hands, all curved, and the arabesques of the apparel make this picture something other than the truthful portrait of a rich *fermier général.* It is an authentic creation where the artist's methods are as important as his model.

Paris, Musée du Louvre

60 *Paysage silvestre avec deux personnages* PL. 14

Oil on cardboard, 36 x 64 cm / 14¼ x 25¼ in.

PROVENANCE: Acquired by the Louvre in Switzerland, 1971.

BIBLIOGRAPHY: Rosenberg, 1973, pp. 89–90, fig. 1.

Largillierre was not only a portraitist. He executed some religious paintings (Louvre, Arras), and we show here (no. 58) one of his most beautiful still lifes. Furthermore, Largillierre did some pure landscapes, a field in which he might have been trained by his father-in-law, the landscape painter, Jean Forest (ca. 1635–1712). The Louvre picture is the first one to reappear. The attribution of the work is certain. In addition to an inscription on the back, which perhaps copies the signature of the artist, the comparison with the backgrounds in some of his portraits is evidence of the accuracy of the attribution: one sees the same golden, warm colors, violent strokes of light, the gnarled and twisted trunks of half-dead trees, and reddish autumnal foliage.

We are less certain about the date of the painting; it is probably from his late career if we judge by the extraordinary audacity of execution and modernity of inspiration.

The history of landscape painting in France during the first half of the eighteenth century remains to be studied: the Louvre picture proves that a portraitist as famous as Largillierre was not contemptuous of this often disregarded genre. Largillierre chooses a lyrical formula, free and direct, a warm rather than formal composition; in one word, he chooses the "Flemish cause" — that of color.

Paris, Musée du Louvre

SÉBASTIEN II LE CLERC
Paris 1676–Paris 1763

Son of the draftsman and engraver Sébastien I (1637–1714), father of Jacques-Sébastien Le Clerc, called des Gobelins (1733–1785), Sébastien II only recently was recalled from obscurity. He seldom exhibited at the Salon, but his reputation was sufficient that he was selected to participate, in 1747, in the Concours intended to put in opposition the twelve best history painters of the time. Le Clerc was a pupil, like Tournières, Cazes and Bertin, of Bon Boullongne. He was received by the Académie as early as 1704 with his *Déification d'Enée* (Tours); his works, mostly allegorical compositions, were popularized through the engravings by Edmé Jeaurat (an unpublished series is at the main office of the Banque de Paris et des Pays-Bas). Le Clerc tries, in a style which makes him easily recognizable (shape of the heads and of the eyesockets, pointed noses, full draperies which seem to impede the movements of the figures), along with Vleughels, Bertin, Favanne and Houasse, to modernize history painting.

The artist's biographer, Antoine Schnapper (1973, p.

246), has recently written: "There is . . . in Leclerc's art, a somewhat naïve vivacity which is not without charm [and which is] increased by very light colors, sharp draftsmanship and [a] kind of exoticism which appears here and there."

61 *La mort de Saphire,* 1718 PL. 18

Oil on canvas, 90.5 x 72 cm / 35½ x 28¼ in.

Signed lower right: *Le Clerc*

PROVENANCE: Formerly in the sacristy of the Church of Saint-Germain-des-Prés, Paris; seized during the Revolution.

BIBLIOGRAPHY: Schnapper, 1973, pp. 245–46, fig. 8.

This picture is the reduction, without significant changes, of the 1718 *May* of Saint-Germain-des-Prés, today again in that church (another version, belonging to M. Cornillon, was exhibited in 1783 at the *Salon de la Correspondance,* no. 32; see Pahin de la Blancherie, 1783).

The subject, popularized by Raphael and Poussin, shows Saint Peter striking Sapphira and her husband, Ananias, to sudden death for having lied to him about the price of a field. Mariette quotes an amusing comment by Watteau about Le Clerc's large picture (III (1854–1856), pp. 113–14): "The older men in the picture look like big children with beards." The boy with the turban to the right, and the mother and the young girl with the sprightly face, who more astonished than uneasy, look at the scene, are charming passages. What surprises one most about this curious artist are the acid colors, deliberately unrealistic, the unquestionable originality of inspiration and an obvious attempt to diverge from the fashionable style.

Paris, Musée du Louvre

FRANÇOIS LEMOINE
Paris 1688–Paris 1737

Stepson of Tournières and pupil of Galloche, Lemoine won the *Grand Prix* in 1711; *agréé* in 1716, he was received two years later with his *Hercule et Cacus* (Paris, Ecole des Beaux-Arts). Lemoine wanted to devote himself to important decorations: he executed a sketch for the ceiling of the Banque de France (Hôtel de Law) with the intention of competing with Pellegrini's composition (unfortunately destroyed). He painted the *Transfiguration* for the ceiling of the Church of Saint-Thomas-d'Aquin and left for Italy with his patron, M. Berger (1723–1724), where he completed his *Hercule et Omphale* (Louvre). Upon returning, he produced a painting for the Hôtel du Grand Maître in Versailles; he participated in the 1727 Concours and shared the prize with Jean-François de Troy (both contestants' paintings are in Nancy). He also decorated the cupola of the *chapelle de la Vierge* in Saint-Sulpice, Paris. His major accomplishment is the ceiling of the *Salon d'Hercule* at Versailles, one of the rare ceilings in French painting executed *à ciel ouvert* and conserved until now. Unveiled for the King on September 26, 1736, this very fine realization procured the artist the title of *Premier Peintre du Roi.*

Anxious, never happy with himself, Lemoine took his life the next year, during a crisis of persecution. An ambitious artist, Lemoine wanted to follow the example of the great Italian masters of the seventeenth century and become, in the first place, the painter of major ceiling decorations. His easel paintings—praised by his eighteenth-century biographers such as Caylus, Nonnotte, Dézallier d'Argenville, for their "freshness"—are elegant and are both more finished in their execution and more intellectual in their sensuality than those of his rival, Jean-François de Troy. His drawings, usually black chalk on blue paper, are of the utmost elegance. Charles Saunier (in Dimier, 1928) has devoted a chapter to Lemoine. We hope the monograph presently prepared by Jean-Luc Bordeaux will replace it soon.

62 *Pygmalion voyant sa statue animée,* 1729 PL. 39

Oil on canvas, 212 x 168 cm / 83½ x 66¼ in.

PROVENANCE: (?) *Fermier général* Etienne-Michel Bouvet — Jean-Joseph de Laborde, Méréville, after 1762 — Grimod de la Reynière; his sale, August 21, 1797, no. 2 — Radix de Sainte-Foy; his sale, January 16, 1811, no. 44 — M. S. sale, June 14, 1900, no. 6 — Villeroy sequestered sale, April 28, 1922, no. 44 — anonymous sale, May 6, 1931, no. 14 — George Jay-Gould, Château du Sentier in Mosnes, near Amboise — given to the Musée des Beaux-Arts, Tours, in 1951.

BIBLIOGRAPHY: Lossky, 1962, no. 68 with figure.

Pygmalion's sculpture, with which he fell in love, is already very much alive: Lemoine has given the sculpture the appearance of some beautiful woman of the time, but certainly not that of Mme de Pompadour (as stated in the catalogue of the Radix de Sainte-Foy sale) who, in 1729, was only eight years old! It is with his usual elegance that Lemoine treats this difficult subject. He gracefully renders the folds of the draperies, the movement of the figures, and the expression on the faces. The curly hair pulled back on both heroes is the trademark of the artist.

Tours, Musée des Beaux-Arts

63 *Narcisse contemplant son reflet dans l'eau* PL. 41

Oil on canvas, 56.5 x 105.5 cm / 22¼ x 41½ in.

PROVENANCE: Thiébault-Sisson before 1932 — private collection — Heim-Gairac Gallery, Paris, 1972.

Lemoine treated the same subject in a vertical composition, signed and dated 1728, and engraved by Jean Pelletier (Hamburg, Kunsthalle). Several replicas of variable quality are in Munich, Dôle, Autun and a French private collection. The Strasbourg picture (see London, Royal Academy of Arts) uses, without major changes, the figure in Narcissus but changes considerably the landscape in the background. Furthermore, the dog one sees in the Hamburg version does not appear here. Its fresh colors, the elegant simplicity of the composition, and the melancholy and musing attitude of the smiling Narcissus make this painting one of the most exquisite accomplishments of French painting around 1730.

Strasbourg, Private collection

NICOLAS-BERNARD LÉPICIÉ
Paris 1735–Paris 1784

Son of François-Bernard Lépicié, *graveur du roi* and *secrétaire de l'Académie*, Nicolas-Bernard, pupil of Carle Van Loo, obtained the second *Grand Prix* in 1759. He was *agréé* in 1764 and received as a history painter in 1769. From 1765 on, he exhibited regularly at the Salon, sending numerous pictures each time. Until 1773, he devoted himself to history painting as well as to large and somewhat conventional religious compositions, and spent the last ten years of his short life executing genre paintings. One must admit that it is in these carefully rendered little pictures that he shows best his talent for observation, so much in favor then among the French public (which was also fond of the Dutch seventeenth-century *petits maîtres*).

Paradoxically, Lépicié shows in this genre, more than in his large paintings, his awareness of a new style. He likes simple compositions: a flat surface, without effects, and a dark and sober color scale with "gingerbread" hues. His less ambitious works, which occasionally call to mind those of Chardin or Greuze, release a simple charm and poetic discretion which make his description of familiar scenes of his time particularly attractive.

Florence Ingersoll-Smouse's articles (1923, 1924, 1926, 1927) and the remarkable *catalogue raisonné* of P. Gaston-Dreyfus (1922), if not adequately illustrated, have not yet been replaced.

64 *Portrait d'Emilie Vernet, future Madame Chalgrin, 1769* PL. 112

Oil on canvas, 42 x 32.5 cm / 16½ x 12¾ in.

Signed and dated lower right: *Lépicié 1769*

PROVENANCE: Carle Vernet and his descendants, Hippolyte Lecomte and Général Cabrié — Mesdemoiselles Cabrié — Cailleux — acquired by the Musée du Petit Palais in 1967.

BIBLIOGRAPHY: Ingersoll-Smouse, 1921, pp. 323–29 — Gaston-Dreyfus, 1922, no. 67.

Lépicié enjoyed painting the children of his friend, Joseph Vernet. There are several portraits of Carle (1758–1836), the most famous of his pupils (two at the Louvre, one of which was done in 1772, and a 1769 portrait at the Petit Palais), Livio and Emilie. These portraits have generally remained, until recently, in the families of the descendants of the sitters. This is the case with the portrait of Emilie Vernet (1760–1794). The future wife of the famous architect Chalgrin, Emilie was decapitated in 1794. There is nothing tragic in this portrait; it is just the charming representation of a nine-year-old child, already coquettish; note the affected movement of her right hand, her necklace and her grown-up's hat.

Thanks to the sobriety of his colors, the silvery whites in contrast to the background simply covered with a thin wash, Lépicié asserts himself as a portraitist, fully aware of the evolution of this genre, losing in sumptuousness what he gains in frank and natural effects.

Paris, Musée du Petit Palais

65 *Le lever de Fanchon, 1773* PL. 123

Oil on canvas, 74 x 93 cm / 29 x 36½ in.

Signed and dated lower right: *Lépicié 1773*

PROVENANCE: Salon of 1773; among the several pictures listed under no. 35 — Briant, his sale, March 27–28, 1851, no. 117 — Baronne du Teil Chaix d'Est-Ange — given to the museum in 1921.

BIBLIOGRAPHY: Gaston-Dreyfus, 1922, no. 169 — Ingersoll-Smouse, 1924, pp. 127–30.

There is another, larger version of this picture published by G. Wildenstein (1928, pp. 199–200) and two studies for the bust of Fanchon (Gaston-Dreyfus, no. 67; Paris, Gallerie Heim, 1974, no. 38). The title of the work, which in fact represents a maid getting out of bed, putting on her stockings while a cat rubs against her leg, must be recent: Fanchon is the nickname for Françoise, the maid's name, and is not found in the *livret* of the Salon.

Lépicié draws his inspiration from Greuze (see no. 41) but lacks his sensual ambiguity and lacks, of Chardin, the descriptive meticulosity of the maid's modest room. Boldly turning his back on the naughtiness of Boucher, Lépicié accurately describes the domestic implements, the candle, and the boards of the bed, as well as the maid's clothes. If the charm of the picture belongs to the past, its fresh, simple colors, classical composition, "familiar realism", and lack of gesture make it exemplary of the new aesthetic.

Saint-Omer, Musée de l'Hôtel Sandelin

JEAN-BAPTISTE LEPRINCE

Metz 1734–Saint-Denis-du-Port, near Lagny, 1781

Pupil of Boucher, Leprince went in (?) 1758 to Russia for five years and worked at the Imperial Palace in Saint Petersburg. He also travelled extensively in the country. *Agréé* in 1764, he was received the next year with his *Baptême russe* (Louvre). He exhibited regularly at the Salon, specializing thereafter in popular scenes and representations of daily life in Russia. He also painted many pastoral scenes in the style of Boucher and so contributed to the vogue of the genre established by his master. A prolific and pleasant draftsman, able but uneven painter, typical *petit maître*, Leprince owes his reputation to the painters he untiringly imitated. One seldom finds works, such as the Toledo picture, where he shows real personal invention and inspiration. Since Jules Hédou's monograph (1879), no one has cared to study Leprince, whose name, however, occurs frequently in sales catalogues.

66 *La crainte,* 1769 PL. 115

Oil on canvas, 50 x 64 cm / 19¾ x 25¼ in.
Signed and dated lower left: *J. B. Leprince 1769*

PROVENANCE: Salon of 1777, no. 55 — Duc de Liancourt, eighteenth century — Sénateur Boittelle, Paris; his sale, April 24–25, 1866, no. 89 — Baronne d'Erlanger, London, 1932 — Dr. Ernest L. Tross — sale, Sotheby's, London, May 14, 1958, no. 144 and sale, Christie's, June 29, 1962, no. 48 — Comte Guillaume de Belleroche, 1968; sale, February 22, 1970, no. 37, Versailles — acquired in 1970.

BIBLIOGRAPHY: Chiego, 1974, no. 1, pp. 11–14 — Cailleux, 1975, p. 300.

Engraved by Noël Lemire, this picture (a copy of which is at the Louvre; RF. 1970–46), although signed and dated 1769, was exhibited only at the Salon of 1777. It was well received, because of its subject (understood by a contemporary, Mathieu-François Pidanzat de Mairobert, as follows: "everything characterizes a daring lover who did not have the strength to be guilty and went elsewhere to hide his shame and his despair;" see "Lettres sur l'Académie . . . ," p. 230) and for its innovation of execution.

It is not surprising that Lemire's engraving — or at least its second and more frequent state (1784), in which the engraver had added the figure of a young man lifting the curtain to the left — has "been paired with the engraving of *Le verrou*" after Fragonard (*Journal Général de France,* January 11, 1785, quoted in D. Wildenstein, 1975, p. 24, n. 20). Both works, in effect, share not only the spirit of their subjects, but also a new way of treating this almost licentious genre, considering, of course, the difference between a *petit maître* with exceptional inspiration and a first rate artist able to create one of the most popular images in the entirety of French painting, reminiscent of Rembrandt.

The Toledo Museum of Art, Gift of Edward Drummond Libbey

JEAN-ETIÉNNE LIOTARD

Geneva 1702–Geneva 1789

It may seem paradoxical to include Liotard in an exhibition of French painting. Isn't he above all a pastellist; and doesn't his birth in Geneva make him a Swiss painter? We must remember that his family, like Rousseau's, came from France, and that he studied in Paris. His style, however, is less "French" than Roslin's.

Liotard arrived in Paris in 1723. He studied there with Massé and stayed in France until 1736. He then went on a *grand tour* to Naples, Rome, Florence, Malta, the Greek Islands, Constantinople, Vienna, Venice, and Germany. In 1748, he was briefly in Lyons before settling in Paris for five years. He then went to London, Amsterdam, returned to Paris in 1757 and 1758, and left once again for Geneva and Vienna before returning to Paris in 1770 and 1771. He then went to London, Geneva, Vienna and again Geneva and Lyons. In 1781, he finally settled in Geneva where he remained until the end of his life.

In pastel or oil, Liotard is above all a portraitist. His compositions, with their figures clearly set against the ground, the clear and cold light he uses, his taste for strong, even rough, colors announces Ingres as well as Degas. He also painted the Orient (its costumes more than its customs) which, still generally unknown, fascinated everyone. François Fosca has written two monographs on his compatriot (1928 and 1956).

67 *Dame franque et sa servante* PL. 62

Oil on canvas, 72.5 x 57 cm / 28½ x 22½ in.

PROVENANCE: Colnaghi's, London, in 1953 — acquired in 1956.

BIBLIOGRAPHY: Kansas City, William Rockhill Nelson Gallery . . . , 1956, p. 29, no. 67 and pp. 86–87, fig. 57.

It was in Constantinople, where he stayed between 1738 and 1743 with Sir William Ponsonby, the future Lord Bessborough, that Liotard was able to see this *Dame franque et sa servante* for which a study with some changes was in the Heseltine collection (Geneva, Musée d'Art et d'Histoire; Fosca, 1956, plate III; two other pastel versions are in the Oskar Reinhart collection, Winterthur and in the Bernard Naef Collection, Geneva).

As we know, the Koran forbids the representation of human figures, and Moslems strictly respected this law. In addition, Turkish women were veiled; it is therefore likely, as Fosca thinks, that Liotard represented here a Frankish woman (a European woman from the Levant, usually from the Greek neighborhood of Galata) in the hamman, dressed as a Turk. One should notice the magnificence of the costumes, the Oriental pattens with double heels and the long *chibouk*, the red spot made by the tips of the henna-dyed fingers against the olive green background, the Gerôme-like detail of the tub, the coffeepot, and the comb on the tray held by the young servant. A precise and falsely naïve observer, Liotard, even more than his successor in Constantinople, Favray, knows how to create a melancholy and poetic world, simultaneously refined and silent.

Kansas City, Nelson Gallery-Atkins Museum, Nelson Fund

PHILIPPE-JACQUES DE LOUTHERBOURG
Strasbourg 1740–London 1812

In Paris as early as 1755, Loutherbourg was, like so many other artists of his time, the pupil of Carle Van Loo and also of the battle painter (and brother of the author of the *Memoirs*), François-Joseph Casanova. After being *agréé* in 1763, Loutherbourg exhibited successfully at the Salon. Four years later, he was received by the Académie; in 1768, he was recorded as being in Marseilles, perhaps in Italy the same year, as well as in Germany and Switzerland. In 1771 he definitely left Paris for London where he started a new career, devoting himself in turn to stage settings, genre scenes, landscapes, seascapes, battle paintings, and religious paintings, not to mention his extraordinary *Eidophersikon*. During the years he exhibited at the Paris Salons, Loutherbourg affirmed his talent through his virtuosity, his ardor, his brilliant transcription, into a modern language, of the work of the northern landscape painters, such as Berchem, and showed himself to be one of the most gifted seascape and battle painters of his generation.

Rüdiger Joppien, author of the exhibition catalogue *Loutherbourg* (1973) has completed the monograph of this painter (to be published). Although this artist is chiefly of interest in regard to the history of English painting, he, nevertheless, has his place in every study devoted to French painting during the last years of Louis XV's reign.

68 *Combat sur mer, 1767* PL. 110

Oil on canvas, 58 x 82 cm / 22¾ x 32¼ in.

Signed and dated lower right: *P.J. de Loutherbourg 1767*

PROVENANCE: Salon of 1767, no. 124, with five other pictures — Gustaf Philip Creutz, Swedish Ambassador in Paris, in 1767 — Gustaf III — Drottningholm Palace — transferred to the Nationalmuseum, 1865.

BIBLIOGRAPHY: Joppien, 1973, no. 53.

At the Salon of 1767, the young Loutherbourg exhibited no less than fifteen pictures, not to mention drawings. They were mostly landscapes with animals, battle scenes, *tempêtes* and seascapes which were greatly admired. Diderot, for instance, although he preferred Vernet to Loutherbourg and reproached the artist for his routine, admired the "intelligence" of his works. The figures of this confused naval battle still owe much to Carle Van Loo. Loutherbourg skillfully uses the contrasts between the very simple pyramidal composition, the multiplicity of the motions, and of the details which attract one "in the middle of the agitated and foamy waves" of this "battle without heroes", reminiscent of Falcone.

Stockholm, Nationalmuseum

PHILIPPE MERCIER
Berlin 1689–London 1760

It may seem paradoxical to include Mercier in an exhibition devoted to French art. Born in Berlin of Huguenot parents, Mercier was possibly in London as early as 1711 (Eidelberg, 1969, p. 275). In any case, he got married there in 1719 after a short trip to Italy and France. Thereafter, his career took place exclusively in England, except for a brief stay in Portugal in 1752. Painter to the Prince of Wales from 1729 to 1736, he worked in London, then in York from 1739 to 1751, before returning to London. Mercier has certainly contributed to French painting being known in England. He had possibly met Watteau during his trip to London (1719–1720) and was continuously inspired by French engravings.

Painter of portraits, genre scenes and conversation pieces, Mercier is at his best when he paints joyful and playful children. The good catalogue of the Mercier exhibition (York, City Art Museum, 1969) states the true position of this artist, famous because expatriated.

69 *L'éducation du chien,* 1744 PL. 65

Oil on canvas, 127 x 100 cm / 50 x 39½ in.

Signed upper left, vertically on the tree trunk: *Ph. Mercier f.*

PROVENANCE: Miss Mary Mackensie — Koetser, London — Aram Gallery, New York, 1949 — given to the Detroit Institute of Arts in 1950.

BIBLIOGRAPHY: Wescher, 1951, pp. 188–89, fig. 1, p. 178.

This painting was engraved by J. Faber in 1744, the approximate date of the picture. The engraving bears a long inscription in verse which explains the subject: a young boy prepares himself for his future career as an officer by training a begging dog. The boy has leaned a staff against the sitting dog's chest; a young girl and another young boy look amusedly toward the viewer.

Here the influence of Watteau is eclipsed by that of Chardin; this is clearly evidenced in the general theme as well as in details such as the headdress of the boy who trains the dog.

This picture confirms the fact that Chardin, whose work was occasionally engraved by Faber, was, during his lifetime, already well known in England (Carritt, pp. 502–09).

The Detroit Institute of Arts, Gift of Mr. and Mrs. Edgar B. Whitcomp

LOUIS-GABRIEL MOREAU, *dit* MOREAU L'AÎNÉ
Paris 1739–Paris 1805

Brother of the draftsman and engraver Jean-Michel Moreau *le jeune* (born in 1741), Louis-Gabriel was the pupil of Demachy. He exhibited at the *Salon de la Jeunesse* in 1760 and 1761. In 1764, he was received by the Académie de Saint-Luc. He exhibited there in 1764 and 1774 and participated in the *Salon de la Correspondance* in 1778 before becoming painter to the Comte d'Artois. He tried unsuccessfully to be *agréé* by the Académie Royale and exhibited at the Salon only after it was open to all painters (between 1791 and 1804).

Engraver, watercolorist, painter of gouaches, Louis-Gabriel Moreau seldom used oil and even then preferred to apply it on paper rather than on canvas.

Misunderstood during his lifetime, unknown until the middle of the nineteenth century, Moreau owes his fame to George Wildenstein's book (1923) and to the collecting of David David-Weill and Arthur Veil-Picard. Some wanted to make him, perhaps by comparison with Hubert Robert alone (1733–1808), an isolated figure and a precursor. Indeed, very few artists have carried so far the study of nature and have neglected so much the human figure. We should, however, remember the studies by Desportes (no. 28), and one should not forget that Valenciennes, of whom the Louvre owns an incomparable series of studies of the sky, clouds and trees, was born only eleven years after Moreau. Because of his natural elegance and the refinement of his compositions, Moreau belongs entirely to his time, a period during which all of Europe discovered, with Rousseau, the beauties of nature.

70 *Vue des coteaux de Bellevue, prise du parc de Saint-Cloud* PL. 126

Oil on paper, 56 x 82.5 cm / 22 x 32½ in.

PROVENANCE: Humbert de Wendel.

BIBLIOGRAPHY: Cailleux and Roland-Michel, 1958, no. 61, pl. XVI.

This picture is very close to the one of the same subject at the Louvre. Both works share the same format and the same composition. In the Louvre picture, however, Moreau gives more importance to the numerous figures; it differs also from this picture by its light and bright colors, so different from the dark greens which create the particular charm of the painting shown here.

It is rather difficult to ascertain the precise date for this work: the chronology of the gouaches and oils of the artist is not certain. If one accepts a date around 1770 for the Louvre picture (the same as for the dated picture of the *Vue prise aux environs de Corbeil,* see G. Wildenstein, 1923, no. 40, pl. XX), it is impossible to date this work much later.

Nevertheless, this study, painted from nature, has a spontaneity, a freshness, a feeling for open air and vast spaces which foreshadow the landscape painters of the first half of the nineteenth century in France as well as in England.

France, Private collection

CHARLES NATOIRE
Nîmes 1700–Castelgandolfo 1777

The prolific artist, Natoire, has dealt with all genres: history, mythology, sacred history (the destruction in 1750 of the decorations of the *Chapelle des Enfants Trouvés* is an irredeemable loss to the knowledge of this part of his work), French history (his series of the *Histoire de Clovis,* Musée de Troyes, foreshadows the comparable series commissioned by d'Angiviller for Louis XVI), and allegories, as well as portraits and subjects inspired by literature. He was also an elegant and productive draftsman. His *Paysages,* watercolors representing views of Rome and her surroundings, the only part of his work not completely neglected, are in favor again today. Securing the *Grand Prix de Rome* in 1721, Natoire stayed in Italy between 1723 and 1729. *Académicien* in 1734, the same year as Boucher (Natoire's reception piece is now in the Louvre), he is often associated with this artist in numerous decorative ensembles (Hôtel de Soubise, Versailles, Marly, Fontainebleau, Bibliothèque Royale, today Nationale). Natoire also worked for the Manufacture de Beauvais *(Histoire de Don Quichotte* and for the Manufacture des Gobelins *(Histoire de Marc-Antoine).* He exhibited regularly at the Salon.

In 1751, he was appointed Director of the Académie de France à Rome, replacing J.-F. de Troy. Five years later, to thank him for painting the ceiling of the Church of San Luigi dei Francesi in Rome, the King ennobled him. Because management of the Académie was not entirely satisfactory, he had to resign, but he never left Italy. The *catalogue raisonné* of his *oeuvre* was compiled by Ferdinand Boyer (1949). One hopes that the bicentennial of his death will be commemorated by an exhibition which should give him the place he deserves in the history of eighteenth-century French painting.

71 *L'entrée solennelle de Monseigneur de Paris à Orléans en 1733* PL. 69

Oil on canvas, 55.5 x 77 cm / 22 x 30¼ in.

PROVENANCE: At the museum since 1834 (?).

BIBLIOGRAPHY: Boyer, 1949, no. 143.

This is a sketch for the picture (375 x 490 cm !) exhibited at the Salon of 1745. The picture, intended for the Château of Meung-sur-Loire, the country residence of the Evêques d'Orléans, is today at the Bibliothèque d'Orléans, the former Bishop's palace. The composition shows the Dean of the chapter giving the new Bishop (whose portrait, also by Natoire, dated 1746, is at the Musée des Beaux-Arts, Orléans) the book of the Gospel in front of the old Porte Bourgogne in Orléans. Royal judges attend the ceremony, Daniel Jousse (see no. 80) and Robert-Joseph Potier (whose beautiful portrait by S. B. Lenoir is also in Orléans) are among them.

If there is something theatrical in this sketch which recalls the tapestry cartoons for the series of *Don Quichotte* (Compiègne), there is also, in the contrast between the black costumes with broken folds of the judges and the glittering of the ecclesiastical vestments, as well as in the design of this immense composition, as much ability as knowledge. Some faces, such as that of the kneeling woman to the left, and the harmony of the whole painting with its gray-green and yellow-gold, are typical of Natoire's style.

Orléans, Musée des Beaux-Arts

72 *La toilette de Psyché*, 1745 PL. 68

Oil on canvas, 198 x 169 cm / 78 x 66½ in.

PROVENANCE: Joseph Bonaparte (1768–1844), older brother of Napoleon — sale in Bordentown, N. J., September 17–18, 1845, no. 17 — James Robb, New Orleans, between 1845 and 1897 — Randolph Newman, New Orleans, between 1897 and 1940.

BIBLIOGRAPHY: Boyer, 1949, no. 115; as *Vénus à sa toilette* — Benisovich, 1956, p. 298, fig. 5.

The story of Psyché has inspired Natoire several times: his most famous work, based on this legend, is an ensemble of eight decorative panels, executed between 1737 and 1739 for the *grand salon* of the Hôtel de Soubise (Paris; today Archives Nationales). The New Orleans picture is, without doubt, later. All the "mannerisms" of Natoire can be found here: a predilection for gracious and youthful bodies: zigzagging and somewhat "broken", crumpled draperies: heads with elaborate hairdos and affected expressions.

If one compares this picture to Boucher's masterpieces, Natoire's *toilette* is, indeed, less refined and naughty, but well composed. Its colors are sparkling, dominated by the artist's own yellows; and its obviously decorative effect is intended to please.

Lise Duclaux called our attention to a beautiful preparatory study (British Museum: 1850–3–9.2), for the central figure of the New Orleans picture.

New Orleans Museum of Art, Purchased through the Bequest of Judge Charles F. Claiborne

JEAN-MARC NATTIER
Paris 1685–Paris 1766

The son of a completely forgotten portraitist, Jean-Marc Nattier began his career under his godfather, Jouvenet, and Rigaud. Jean-Marc did a drawn copy of Rigaud's *Portrait de Louis XIV*. His oldest daughter, who eventually married the painter Tocqué, was the first to write her father's biography. She reports that, after seeing this work, the King said: "Monsieur, you must go ahead and work. You will become a great man." Nattier was also influenced by Le Brun and Rubens; he copied Rubens' *Battles* and, specifically for the engraving, the *Vie de Marie de Médicis*.

In 1717, he left for Holland where he worked for Peter the Great (*Bataille de Poltava*, Moscow); the following year, he was received by the Académie (no. 73). Henceforth, he executed oil or pastel portraits, most of which were mythological. In a certain way, he re-established this genre, in favor during the sixteenth century, but treated it in a completely different spirit. Nattier represents his sitters, usually the King's favorites or daughters, with the attributes of the Olympian goddesses. The end of his life was saddened by the death of his son who drowned in Rome in 1754, a few months after arriving at the Académie de France. Financial problems and illness made Nattier stop painting in 1762. His daughter wrote: "He accomodated so well these two important parts of art in his works that the enlightened public often did not know what to admire most in him, the history painter or the portraitist. Moreover, one will wonder less about the successful way M. Nattier combined the two genres if one realizes that his first and major studies had all been done with the intention of following the compositional genre, and that only later circumstances made him change his object" (Dussieux, Soulié, . . . eds., II, p. 354).

Since those studies done by P. de Nolhac (1925) and G. Huard (1930), nothing essential has been published on this painter who is so well represented in American museums.

73 *Persée, assisté par Minerve, pétrifie Phinée et ses compagnons en leur présentant la tête de Méduse*, 1718 PL. 19

Oil on canvas, 113.5 x 146 cm / 44¾ x 57½ in.

PROVENANCE: Académie Royale — seized during the Revolution — transferred to Tours in 1803.

BIBLIOGRAPHY: Nolhac, 1925, pp. 48–50 — Huard, 1930, no. 143 — Lossky, 1962, no. 78, with figure.

This is the painting Nattier presented to the Académie in 1718 for his reception as history painter. His daughter, later the wife of the painter Tocqué, wrote that it was various "circumstances", primarily financial, which influenced the artist to paint portraits. Even then, he tried to make this genre more "noble" by identifying his models with mythological figures, muses or goddesses.

The Tours picture is flagrant evidence of Nattier's gifts as a painter: he places his composition in an imposing architectural frame; the colors, deliberately wrong, are original; his figures, which show his admiration for Le Brun and Jouvenet, are noble and grandiloquent like those of a theatrical production. The subject allows Nattier the opportunity to depict the figures suddenly arrested and petrified at the horrible vision of Medusa's head, while the victorious hero turns himself gratefully toward the helpful Minerva.

Tours, Musée des Beaux-Arts

74 *Mme Crozat de Thiers et sa fille (?)*, 1733 PL. 48

Oil on canvas, 138 x 105.5 cm / 54¼ x 41½ in.

Signed and dated lower right: *Nattier pinx.* 1733

PROVENANCE: Michel Ephrussi, 1905 — Princesse de Faucigny-Lucinge, 1934 — sale, June 12, 1953, Paris, Hôtel Charpentier, no. 1 — given to the Museum in 1972.

BIBLIOGRAPHY: Nolhac, 1925, pp. 180–81, 225, 251 — Huard, 1930, no. 74.

According to Nolhac, this portrait represents the Marquise de Chatel (née Gouffier, daughter-in-law of the financier Crozat le cadet and wife of Louis-François Crozat) with her daughter Antoinette-Eustachie (born in 1728, later the wife of the future Duc de Gontau and mother of the Duc de Lauzun). However, according to the entries in the catalogues of the *Siècle de Louis XV* (Paris, Gazette des Beaux-Arts, 1934, no. 125) and of the *Chefs d'oeuvre de l'art français* (Paris, Palais National des Arts, 1937, no. 189) it represents Marie-Louise-Augustine de Montmorency-Laval, wife of Louis-Antoine Crozat, Baron de Thiers (1699–1770); this opinion is shared by Miss Stuffmann in her study of the pictures of the Pierre Crozat collection (1968, p. 34).

In any case, this picture is especially noteworthy for the charm of some of its details, such as the ribbon around the neck of the sitter, the flowers the mother puts in the hair of her mischievous-looking daughter, and the flowers the daughter holds. Thus, this portrait, which lies between reality and artificiality, likeness and invention, becomes a true creation, full of rich innovations.

Indianapolis Museum of Art, Gift of Mrs. Herman C. Krannert

DONAT NONNOTTE
Besançon 1708–Lyons 1785

A pupil of his uncle, Jean Nonnotte, Donat came to Paris in 1728, and from 1731 on he collaborated with Lemoine on the frescoes for the Church of Saint-Sulpice in Paris, as well as on the ceiling of the *Salon d'Hercule* at Versailles. The suicide of the *Premier Peintre du Roi* in 1737 created financial difficulties for Nonnotte who overcame them by marrying a rich widow. He was received by the Académie in 1741 as a portraitist and exhibited regularly at the Salon until 1755 (and a last time in 1765). In 1754, he settled in Lyons where he directed the free school of drawing. In his new town, Nonnotte gave, between 1754 and 1772, a whole series of *Discours sur la peinture* and wrote an important *Vie de Lemoine*.

Nonnotte was a good portraitist, without too much imagination perhaps, but honest and precise. He would have occupied an entirely different position in the history of eighteenth-century painting if he had been employed by a foreign court.

Basic study on the painter has been done by Jules Gauthier (two articles, 1902).

75 *Portrait du graveur Jean Moyreau*, 1742 PL. 60

Oil on canvas, 91 x 73 cm / 35¾ x 28¾ in.

Signed and dated upper right: *Nonnotte / Pinx.* 1742

PROVENANCE: Salon of 1745, no. 85 — probably acquired in 1842 at a Geffrier-Delisle sale; Geffrier-Delisle may have been a relative of Jean Moyreau.

BIBLIOGRAPHY: Gauthier, "Donat Nonnotte de Besançon. . . ," 1902, p. 53, no. 13.

"Nonnotte lacks genius, but not sedulousness and scrupulousness. His *Portrait du graveur Jean Moyreau* (Orléans), dated 1742, is actually a sort of official report" wrote Paul Fierens (1933, p. 55) in a comment on the exhibition of the masterpieces from provincial French museums (Paris, Musée Carnavalet, 1933) where this portrait was shown.

Moyreau (1690–1762), from Orléans, engraved this portrait in 1742 and used it in 1749 as the frontispiece for a work by Wouwermans, a very popular artist in France during the eighteenth century. Moyreau specialized in reproducing his pictures.

The engraver, himself an *académicien* since 1736, is elegantly dressed: a velvet frock coat, a shirt with a lace frill, a powdered wig. Nonnotte describes him with perfect objectivity without trying to penetrate the personality of his sitter.

Orléans, Musée des Beaux-Arts

JEAN-BAPTISTE OUDRY
Paris 1686–Beauvais 1755

A pupil at the Académie de Saint-Luc, Oudry began his career under its protection. He later studied with Largillierre, commencing as a portraitist. *Agréé* by the Académie in 1717, he was received two years later as a history painter, and became a professor in 1743. Protected by the Duc d'Antin, he not only obtained the directorship of the Manufacture de Beauvais in 1734, but also worked for the Manufacture des Gobelins (cartoons for the series of the *Chasses de Louis XV*). Burdened with commissions (*Portrait du tsar;* paintings for Tessin, the King of Denmark, and the Prince of Mecklemburg who assembled the most beautiful ensemble of works by Oudry, today in the museum in Schwerin), Oudry executed portraits, some history and allegorical pictures, occasionally genre pictures, but devoted himself mainly to still lifes, landscapes, hunting scenes of all animals, especially the King's dogs of which he was, so to speak, the official painter. Less moving than that of Chardin, Oudry's work aims toward virtuosity, illusion and stunning effects. His son, Jacques-Charles (1720–1778), imitated his father's style.

Oudry's work is enormous. Opperman (1972) has catalogued over six hundred paintings and one thousand drawings by the artist. We hope that his research, which received in 1974 the *Prix Cailleux*, will be published soon, thus replacing the monographs by Locquin and Vergnet-Ruiz.

76 *"Teste bizarre d'un Cerf pris par le Roy le 3 juillet 1741"*, 1741 — PL. 59

Oil on canvas, 114 x 67 cm / 45 x 26¼ in. (11 cm added to the top and 4 cm at the bottom).

Signed and dated lower left: *Peint par J. B. Oudry 1741*

PROVENANCE: Salon of 1741, no. 36 — Louis XV — Musée du Louvre; transferred to Fontainebleau, November 7, 1845, to decorate the *passage* of the *appartement des chasses* of the Ducs d'Aumale and de Montpensier, where it remains today, encased between the wainscotting.

BIBLIOGRAPHY: Opperman, 1972, II, 1, pp. 520–21, no. P. 507, fig. 283.

Exhibited at the Salon of 1741 and widely admired by the critics, this painting of antlers is the first of a series commissioned by the King (the series is, for the most part, kept today in Fontainebleau). After Oudry's death in 1755, Bachelier (no. 3) took over the task of representing the trophies that the King, a dedicated hunter, wanted to keep as souvenirs.

In this *trompe-l'oeil,* Oudry wanted, before all, to show his technical virtuosity. He has forced illusionism to the point of nailing a piece of paper onto the boards which frame his composition, which renews — in the middle of the eighteenth century! — the tradition of the *cartellino,* on which the subject of his canvas is explained: the "curiosité" he was charged to immortalize — this head called *bizarre* or *bizarde* — because of the abnormal formation of the antlers.

Fontainebleau, Musée National du Château

77 *Un vase de fleurs avec un parterre de tulipes, un perroquet et des papillons de nuit,* 1744 — PL. 63

Oil on canvas, 146 x 181 cm / 57½ x 71¼ in. Signed and dated lower left on the marble slab beneath the vase: *J. B. Oudry / 1744*

PROVENANCE: M. de la Bruyère at the time of the Salon of 1745 where it was shown, no. 33 — Marquis de Breteuil — Galerie Heim, Paris — acquired by the Detroit Institute of Arts in 1967.

BIBLIOGRAPHY: Opperman, 1972, II, 1, pp. 501–02, no. P. 457.

On January 10, 1761, the Abbé Gougenot read, at the Académie, a *Vie de M. Oudry* (Dussieux, 1854–1856, II, pp. 365–403) which he followed by a catalogue, the first of the four catalogues of his work to be compiled (the others are by Locquin, Vergnet-Ruiz and Opperman). The Detroit picture is described similarly to the way it was described in the *livret* of the Salon of 1745: "A painting . . . representing a vase of flowers, jacinths among others, ordered in Holland by the King. Next to the vase, a corner of tulip-beds, painted after those in the garden of M. de la Bruyère," the first owner of the picture (Dussieux, 1854–1856, II, p. 398).

One doesn't know what is most admirable in the Detroit picture: the imagination of the artist, who, to enliven this botanical plate, adds a parrot and two large moths, the originality of the design with its subtle play of straight lines on the ground, or the sumptuous colors. To break the monotony of the architectural background, Oudry curves the right wall and opens his composition on one corner to the sky and trees.

The Detroit Institute of Arts, Founders Society Purchase, The John N. and Rhoda Lord Family Fund and General Endowment Fund

PIERRE PARROCEL
Avignon 1670–Paris 1739

"How is one to know where one is among all these painters who are of the same name, sometimes the same first name, lived at the same time and are all relegated to the darkest provinces?" wrote J. J. Guiffrey as early as 1881 (p. 156).

If the personalities of Joseph Parrocel (1646–1704) and of his son Charles (1688–1752) (unfortunately, not included in this exhibition) are today relatively well-known, it is not the same, by far, for Jacques-Ignace (1667–1722), his son Etienne Parrocel called le Romain (1696–1776), Pierre and his two sons, Pierre-Ignace (1702–1775?) and Joseph-Ignace-François (1704–1781). All of them worked in southern France, Paris and Rome, specializing in battle scenes and large religious compositions. Pierre, pupil of his uncle Joseph and, in Rome, of Carlo Maratta, worked first in southern France and later executed sixteen large paintings for the Hôtel de Noailles in Saint-Germain-en-Laye (now in Marseilles). He was *agréé* in 1730.

No recent study has been devoted to him; the nineteenth-century publications concerning this painter should be used prudently.

78 *Jeune femme lisant devant une cheminée*, 173(5?) PL. 51

Oil on canvas, 36 x 47 cm / 14¼ x 18½ in.

Monogrammed and dated lower right, at the base of the mantel: *.P.P.I.F./173(5?)*

PROVENANCE: Bought for the collection of Queen Louise-Ulrique of Sweden by C. G. Tessin, delegate to Paris in 1741; Drottningholm Palace — Nationalmuseum since 1865.

BIBLIOGRAPHY: Stockholm, Nationalmuseum, p. 218.

When the *Surintendant de Fredenheim* wrote the catalogue (1760) of the paintings belonging to the Queen Louise-Ulrique (Lespinasse, 1912, p. 233), he described this one as "a child playing with soap bubbles." This subject (Chardin had just painted his version of it), set in a delicate interior where the artist plays cleverly with the contrast of the reading woman's blue dress and the fire in the fireplace, is quite different from the large religious compositions Parrocel usually painted.

One could criticize us for having represented the dynasty of these painters with one atypical work. In any case, it shows that these artists could execute delightful works, especially because of their daily realism.

Stockholm, Nationalmuseum

JEAN-BAPTISTE PATER
Valenciennes 1695–Paris 1736

Born in Valenciennes like Watteau, Pater was his pupil in 1713 and worked again with him shortly before his death in 1721. He was received by the Académie only in 1728 as a "peintre de sujets modernes" with a *Fête champêtre* (Louvre; the same year, another pupil of Watteau, Bonaventure de Bar, was received with a picture of the same subject, also at the Louvre). In the eighteenth century, Pater's fame approached that of Watteau, and Frederic II owned more than forty pictures by him.

Not particularly inventive, Pater not only gets his inspiration from Watteau, but copies himself constantly. His light touch, sharp blues and pearly pinks make his many works easily recognizable. He is the *petit maître par excellence* who benefited (excessively, if one thinks of the way so many great artists of the time have been forgotten) from Watteau's immense glory.

Florence Ingersoll-Smouse compiled an exemplary and well illustrated catalogue of his work (1928).

79 *La foire à Bezons*, 1733 PL. 49

Oil on canvas, 106.5 x 142 cm / 42 x 56 in.

PROVENANCE: Espagnac or Tricot; sale, Paris, May 22, 1793, no. 101 — Alfred-Charles de Rothschild, Paris — Almina, Lady Carnavon, London — sold by Duveen to Jules S. Bache — bequeathed with the Bache collection to the Metropolitan Museum in 1949.

BIBLIOGRAPHY: Ingersoll-Smouse, 1928, pp. 11, 17, no. 55, pl. 45 — Sterling, 1955, pp. 112–14, with figure.

French artists at the beginning of the eighteenth century often painted the fair at Bezons (near Versailles), one of the most popular ones around Paris. It opened the first Sunday in September. Among the painters who have treated the subject, we can mention J. Parrocel (Tours), Lancret (G. Wildenstein, 1924, no. 40), and Octavien, another pupil of Watteau, who presented this subject as his reception piece to the Académie in 1725.

Pater's picture — perhaps his largest work and his masterpiece — can be dated around 1733, the year the artist painted a slightly smaller picture (Sanssouci, Potsdam), similar in composition but different in the organization of the figures.

Pater draws his inspiration for his figures from Watteau; he uses the same costumes and the same attitudes. Figures are placed under the same large trees. If he transforms and idealizes the reality of the scene, surprisingly, he lacks poetry and remains an outsider to the world he describes.

New York, The Metropolitan Museum of Art, The Jules S. Bache collection

JEAN-BAPTISTE PERRONNEAU
Paris 1715 (?)–Amsterdam 1783

Trained as an engraver, Perronneau is above all a pastellist (his first pastels were done in 1743); he is, however, less exclusive than his great rival Maurice Quentin de La Tour (1704–1788), for he also executed oils. He was received by the Académie in 1753 with two portraits, those of the sculptor L. S. Adam and of Oudry (Louvre). Perronneau had difficulty finding a clientele in Paris; therefore, he led a wandering life, from Spain to Hamburg, from Russia to Italy and England, and from Poland to Amsterdam where he died.

Little known during his lifetime, Perronneau was rediscovered in the nineteenth century. Primarily a portraitist, he gave more attention to his model than did his rival, Quentin de La Tour; he was more vigorous, virtuosic, capricious, "spiritual" and perhaps more irritating. One finds in Perronneau a need for realism, a growing anxiety, and a careful attention to serve and understand the model (La Tour, on the other hand, uses the model to his own advantage). Perronneau's sincere qualities have been clearly emphasized in the excellent monograph of L. Vaillat and P. Ratouis de Limay (1923).

80 *Portrait de Daniel Jousse* PL. 98

Oil on canvas, 80 x 64 cm / 31½ x 25¼ in.

PROVENANCE: Given in July 1860 by Mlle Regnard, grand-niece of the sitter.

BIBLIOGRAPHY: Vaillat and Ratouis de Limay, 1923, pp. 162–63, 239, 244.

Daniel Jousse (1704–1781), *Conseiller au présidial d'Orléans,* was one of the most famous jurisconsults of his century: he is shown in Natoire's picture *L'entrée de Monseigneur de Paris à Orléans* (the sketch for this is no. 71).

The *Portrait de Daniel Jousse* was formerly attributed to S. B. Le Noir whose masterpiece, the *Portrait de Pothier,* is also owned by the Musée des Beaux-Arts, Orléans; Pothier is also represented in Natoire's picture. The *Portrait de Daniel Jousse* was painted between 1755, date of the publication of the *Traité de la Sphère* (the globe to the right refers to this publication) and 1775, the date at which the engraving of the portrait by Lucas was featured as frontispiece of the new edition of the *Traité.* It is likely that the portrait was executed around 1765–1767, the years during which Perronneau lived in Orléans. Natoire, incidentally, is said to have been Perronneau's first teacher.

The proud attitude of the sitter who places his hand on his chest, an attitude one might see in a portrait by El Greco or Van Dyck, gives him a dignity proper to his function. His face, upon which a smile may or may not appear, is beautiful, and his glance seems to look through the viewer. The portrait is painted with the artist's typical bursts of cold, shiny light and a strange impassibility.

Orléans, Musée des Beaux-Arts

ANTOINE PESNE
Paris 1683–Berlin 1757

The son of a painter, nephew of La Fosse, *Grand Prix* in 1703, Pesne was in Italy between 1704 and 1710. He stayed in Rome, where he married the daughter of a still life painter, Dubuisson, and also in Venice where he became acquainted with Andrea Celesti. In 1710, he settled in Berlin. He worked almost exclusively for the German courts of Berlin and Dresden, and served successively Frederic, the first King of Prussia, Frederic-Wilhelm I, the Sergeant-King, and Frederic the Great. He stayed in London and Paris in 1723–1724. In 1720, he was received by the Académie. Primarily a portraitist, Pesne also painted a few mythological and religious pictures as well as some large decorations.

> "Quel spectacle étonnant vient de frapper mes yeux
> Oui, Pesne, ton pinceau te place au rang des dieux."

If these verses prove that their author, Frederic II, could express himself perfectly well in French, one should find them, however, excessively flattering.

A good portraitist (like so many other artists in the eighteenth century), Pesne owes his fame and the immense literature devoted to him (particularly the monograph by Berckenhagen, Colombier, Kühn and Poensgen) to the fact that he pursued his career outside France and in a country where good painters were, at that time, extremely rare.

81 *Portrait du graveur Jean Mariette,* 1723 — PL. 27

Oil on canvas, 113 x 93 cm / 44½ x 36½ in.

PROVENANCE: Acquired in 1889 from M. Dangibaud.

BIBLIOGRAPHY: Berckenhagen, Colombier, Kühn, Poensgen, 1958, p. 160, no. 226, pl. 49 — Paris, Musée du Louvre, Galerie Mollien, 1967, no. 282.

This portrait was painted during Mariette's first stay in France, in 1723, at the same time as the portrait of Vleughels (Louvre), whom he had probably known in Venice. It was engraved by Jean Daulle in 1747, and shows the features of one of the most famous members of this dynasty of print dealers, Jean Mariette (1660–1742), son of Pierre II and father of the great drawing collector and scholar, Pierre-Jean.

Pesne has represented the engraver and publisher, then over sixty years old, his left hand resting on a portfolio of prints, and his right one holding a pencil. The elegance of the attitude and the precise psychological analysis make this portrait Pesne's masterpiece.

Paris, Musée Carnavalet

JEAN-BAPTISTE-MARIE PIERRE
Paris 1714–Paris 1789

Pupil of Natoire, Pierre obtained the *Grand Prix* in 1734 and left for Rome the following year, where he stayed five years. Received by the Académie in 1742 (his reception piece, *Diomède tué par Hercule* is in Montpellier), Pierre rapidly ascended through the various echelons of the academic career.

After Boucher's death in 1770, he became *Premier Peintre du Roi* and Director of the Académie. After his ennoblement, he practically ceased to paint.

It is no exaggeration to say that, next to D'Angiviller, Pierre played the principal rôle in the administration of the French artistic life under Louis XVI. A history painter, he has also tried to execute large decorations. His rare genre scenes are full of fantasy and are as brilliantly painted as his sketches. He was also a remarkable draftsman and engraved. Pierre wanted a return to a flatter and more linear, sober, classical style. His works are evidence of a concern for sobriety and self-control, and effectually, a reaction against the works of those predecessors who had held the position of *Premier Peintre du Roi,* Carle Van Loo and Boucher.

Monique Halbout has studied this painter; we hope that her work will eventually become a publication devoted to the artist who was not only misunderstood during his lifetime and is forgotten today, but also was the "master of the arts" in France when a new aesthetic was being elaborated.

82 *Bacchanale,* 1747 — PL. 70

Oil on canvas, 115 x 147 cm / 45¼ x 57¾ in.

Signed and dated left of center: *Pierre/1747*

PROVENANCE: Salon of 1747, no. 55 — seized during the Revolution — transferred from the Louvre to Le Puy in 1872.

Pierre exhibited several pictures at the Salon of 1747: a *Saint François méditant dans sa solitude* (Paris, Church of Saint-Pierre-du-Gros-Caillou), a *Saint Nicolas, évêque de Myre* (Paris, Church of Saint Nicolas-des-Champs), a *Sculpteur dans son atelier* (probably the picture sold in Paris, March 26, 1953, no. 111, with plate) and a *Bacchanale* the dimensions of which were given in the *livret* (probably erroneously) and which correspond only vaguely to the ones of the Puy picture. Aside from two religious pictures and a genre scene, all quickly executed, Pierre exhibited a painting, in the genre of Boucher, but which is more flat and cold, with raw and enamel-like colors. Pierre expresses in it his principal concern for rhythm and line. This elegant canvas shows how wide Pierre's repertoire can be: within a few years he painted works as different as the *Mort d'Harmonia* (New York, Metropolitan Museum), the *Adoration des Bergers* (which we regret we are unable to show and which is in the Church of Saint-Sulpice, Paris), the *Mauvaise nouvelle* (Paris, Musée Nissim de Camondo) or the *Maîtresse d'école* (Auxerre, Musée des Beaux-Arts).

Le Puy, Musée Crozatier

JEAN RANC
Montpellier 1674–Madrid 1735

Jean Ranc was Rigaud's pupil and the son of Antoine Ranc. Rigaud himself had been a disciple of Antoine and married in 1715 a niece of his. Ranc became an *académicien* in the category of portraiture in 1703, and tried unsuccessfully to become a history painter. He went to Spain in 1723 on the recommendation of Rigaud and became *Premier Peintre* to the court of Philippe V.

His work, principally portraiture, has been studied successively by C. Ponsonailhe (1887) and Bottineau (1960, see particularly pp. 443–50). Ranc introduced to Spain the style established by Rigaud. His preference for glossy silks and light reflections makes him close to Michel-Ange Houasse, who had preceded him in Spain almost ten years earlier.

83 *Vertumne et Pomone* PL. 25

Oil on canvas, 170 x 120 cm / 67 x 47¼ in.

PROVENANCE: Sale, Paris, Hôtel Drouot, January 30, 1933, salle 6, no. 18 — acquired from Marcus in Paris, 1964.

If the composition of this painting does not fail to recall Goya's *Las Niñas* (Lille), nothing is more remote, both in its spirit as well as in its technique, from Goya's painting than this work by Ranc. Was it even painted in Spain where Ranc settled in 1723? In any case, it was engraved, at an unknown date, by Nicolas-Etienne Edelinck (1681–1767; the engraving, mentioned by Baré, 1884–1885, p. 39, does not figure in the collection of the Bibliothèque Nationale; see Roux, VIII, 1955, p. 453, no. 31). According to the popular mythological legend (Ovid, Metamorphoses, XIV, 609–97), Vertumnus, god of the gardens, disguised himself as an old woman in order to seduce Pomona, goddess of the fruits. Ranc's main concerns, however, are to render the rays of the autumnal sun through the parasol, to play with the changing lusters of the bright, silky dress and to render also the particular features of an older woman looking with admiration at a young and elegant woman, thus showing his ability as a portraitist.

Montpellier, Musée Fabre

JEAN RESTOUT
Rouen 1692–Paris 1768

Nephew of Jouvenet, Restout was in Paris as early as 1707. He was *agréé* by the Académie in 1717 and received three years later. Like all the best painters of his generation, he painted in 1724 a composition for the Hôtel du Grand Maître in Versailles; he took part in the 1727 Concours and ten years later in the decoration of the Hôtel de Rohan in Paris. In 1729, he married Claude-Guy Hallé's daughter, thus becoming part of another great dynasty of artists. He exhibited regularly at the Salon and took an active part in the reunions of the Académie, of which he became *chancelier* in 1761. Restout painted mostly for the Church, taking over, to a certain extent, Jouvenet's position: he painted also for Frederic II and the courts of Denmark and Sweden. He painted about one hundred and fifty pictures, a relatively small amount, but one should not forget that some of them are extremely large. His colors are often dark and his compositions zigzagging. As his style developed, the elongated figures, with their small heads, became more dance-like, and their gestures more irregular.

Restout seems a singular figure in his time. In reality, he is clearly part of a period much more varied than is usually thought. He is also important because of the sobriety of his colors, the discretion of his approach (see his portraits for instance) and the sincerity of his analysis.

The catalogue of the *Restout* exhibition (Rosenberg and Schnapper, 1970) was designed to establish a complete list of his works (paintings and drawings) and to return the artist to the position which was his during his lifetime.

84 *Portrait de l'architecte Pierre de Vigny* PL. 34

Oil on canvas, 81.5 x 64.5 cm / 32 x 25½ in.

PROVENANCE: Comte de Beaumont in Saumur, about 1890; the Comte was a descendant of the sitter.

BIBLIOGRAPHY: Gallet, 1973, pp. 263–86, fig. 1.

Restout's portraits are rare. This one was unknown to us at the time of the *Restout* exhibition (Rosenberg and Schnapper, 1970). It is dated around 1727 by M. Gallet who was the first to call attention to it. The architect Pierre Vigné de Vigny (1690–1772) got married in 1727. Shortly before 1722, his master, Robert de Cotte, had sent him to Constantinople to study a project for the French embassy. This portrait can be compared stylistically to the more formal *Portrait dit de Boffrand* (1734, Nancy) or to the *Portrait de François Pourfour du Petit* (1737, Paris, Faculté de Médecine).

The sitter's attitude — his pensive and intense face, the head looking back, the long and nervous fingers — is typical of Restout, as are the colors. The artist uses knowingly — and very differently than the "professional" portraitists, Largillierre and Rigaud — the white harmonies of the sleeve and of the shirt against the blue-green and purple ones of the sitter's jacket. Restout knows primarily how to give the sharp-looking architect, who holds steel compasses, a simple and strong rendition, without complacency, but not without charm.

Private collection

85 *La mort de sainte Scholastique,* 1730 PL. 40

Oil on canvas, arched with shoulders, 338 x 190 cm / 133 x 78¾ in.

Signed and dated lower left: *JRestout 1730* (J and R are interwoven)

PROVENANCE: Painted for the Convent of Bourgueil — seized during the Revolution and transferred to the museum in Tours since its establishment.

BIBLIOGRAPHY: Rosenberg and Schnapper, *Jean Restout,* 1970, no. 7, pl. IX.

This picture, engraved by Jean Audran, is the artist's most famous work. The picture, with its pendant, *L'extase de saint Benoit* (1730, Tours, Musée des Beaux-Arts), is regularly exhibited and reproduced. The colors still recall those of Jouvenet, with their gold and dark-blue, almost black, harmonies and their predilection for "wrong" and glaucous hues. The large Z described by the composition and its utmost simplicity emphasize the impression of "joyful annihilation", wrote Restout's first biographer, Jean Messelet (1938, p. 117). The surprising effect of the painted wooden floor, the crucifix held in its fall by the two attendants of the expiring saint, the skull, and the hourglass give evidence of this "predilection for reality" that Restout never quite abandoned.

Tours, Musée des Beaux-Arts

HYACINTHE RIGAUD
Perpignan 1659–Paris 1743

Rigaud outlived Louis XIV by twenty-eight years. His greatest rival, Largillierre, three years older than he, outlived him by three years. Thus it is excessive, or at least too restrictive, to see nothing in these two painters but the official portraitists of Louis XIV's reign. It is equally exaggerated to limit their production to portraits. Rigaud, for instance, was received by the Académie in 1700 as a history painter; the same year he produced his two most famous works, the portraits of Louis XIV and of Philippe V. The artist successfully allied a realism, which he owed to his formative years in the south of France where he was born, to more formal and solemn aspects. Rigaud was able to give his sitters a natural superiority which made his old biographers compare him to Van Dyck. He describes their costumes with utmost care; his ability to render particular qualities and his concern for details are almost surrealistic. Since J. Roman's publication of Rigaud's *Livre de raison* (1919), nothing essential has been published on him. After Claude Colomer's study (1973), we impatiently await the monograph of G. Van Derveen Gallenkamp, devoted to both the painter and the draftsman.

86 *Portrait du cardinal Dubois,* 1723 PL. 26

Oil on canvas, 146.5 x 113.5 cm / 57¾ x 44¾ in.

Signed and dated on the base of the clock, in the middle toward the right: *Fait par Hyacinthe Rigaud 1723*

PROVENANCE: Château d'Eu in 1723 (?) — Mlle Violet, heiress of Cardinal Dubois, Château de Villemenon, near Brie-Comte-Robert— Georges, last Comte d'Egremont, sale, Christie's, May 21, 1892 — Rodolphe and Edouard Kann — acquired in 1967.

BIBLIOGRAPHY: Roman, 1919, pp. 195, note 1, 233 and 284— Tzeutschler-Lurie, 1967, pp. 230–38, color pl. p. 229 — Tzeutschler-Lurie, 1974, pp. 667–68, pl. p. 669.

Engraved in 1724, a year after its execution, this portrait (for which was paid 3000 livres — 300 for the two commissioned copies; this is recorded in the artist's *Livre de raison*) shows the cardinal (1656–1723) the year of his death. Born in 1656 at Brive-la-Gaillarde, he became in 1687 preceptor of the Duc de Chartres, the future Philippe d'Orléans. When the later became Regent, before Louis XV became of age, the cardinal, who was then only the Abbé Dubois, played a most important political part. His aim was to maintain the *paix d'Utrecht*: in trying to accomplish this, he allied France to England and Holland, as well as to Austria, and defeated Spain. If the man's morality is doubtful (Saint-Simon describes him in a less than flattering light) his political sense is outstanding. Rigaud describes him at the height of his power: cardinal in 1721, *premier ministre* the next year, he became a member of the Académie Française in 1723. That same year he announced Louis XV's majority and lost all political importance. Rigaud has shown him smiling. The harmony of the reds, the whites, and the golds of the arm chair is particularly successful.

The Cleveland Museum of Art, John L. Severance Collection

87 *La présentation au temple,* 1741–1743 PL. 61

Oil on canvas, 83 x 68 cm / 32½ x 26¾ in.

PROVENANCE: Bequeathed by the artist to Louis XV in 1743 — at the Louvre since the Revolution.

BIBLIOGRAPHY: Roman, 1919, pp. VIII and 221.

"His propensity to execute history paintings occasionally burst. He has done . . . . a presentation in the temple in the manner of Rembrandt which he bequeathed to the King at his death." (Dézallier d'Argenville, 1762, IV, p. 318).

We know, through his will written April 9, 1741, that he had, at that time, almost completed this painting to which, according to his *Livre de Raison,* he added the last touch the year of his death.

Inspired by Rembrandt's followers, such as Dou, as well as by the master himself (whose works Rigaud collected; he owned, over the years, seven paintings by him), this glistening picture shows the diversity of the artist's talent. As in his portraits, he enjoys rendering the changing lustre of the silk and the bright colors, which demonstrates a refined predilection for the mysteries of chiaroscuro.

Paris, Musée du Louvre

ANTOINE RIVALZ
Toulouse 1667–Toulouse 1735

Son of Jean-Pierre Rivalz, himself an artist of outstanding rank in Toulouse, Antoine is one of the rare great painters of the century whose career took place exclusively in the provinces. He went to Paris, was trained at the Académie there, and spent the last twelve years of the eighteenth century in Rome where he won, in 1694, a first prize at the Accademia di San Luca for a large drawing, the *Chute des Géants,* (still at the Accademia). However, upon his return, he devoted himself mostly to decorating the various churches of Toulouse and of the surrounding area with large, animated and lyrical compositions whose dark and vigorous colors owe little to Parisian examples of the time.

Robert Mesuret has devoted many articles to the paintings and drawings of Antoine Rivalz, many of which are still in the Toulouse area. A list of them can be found in his excellent work, *Les expositions de l'Académie royale de Toulouse de 1751 à 1791* (posthumously published in 1972). We can only hope that a monograph will soon be written on the whole Rivalz dynasty, and that a *catalogue raisonné* of their works will give these painters the importance they deserve.

88 *Autoportrait,* 1726–1728 (?) PL. 33

Oil on canvas, 83 x 64 cm / 32½ x 25¼ in.

PROVENANCE: Belonged in 1751 to the artist's son, Pierre Rivalz — Académie des Arts de Toulouse — Ecole des Beaux-Arts — at the museum since its establishment during the Revolution.

BIBLIOGRAPHY: Mesuret, 1972, p. 19, no. 109.

This picture, of which a replica has been known since 1783 (Toulouse, Moulas collection), was engraved by Barthélémy Rivalz, the artist's cousin. Rivalz showed himself completing a large drawing of *Saint Michel terrassant les anges rebelles*; we have recently identified this drawing and have been able to persuade the Toulouse museum to purchase it (see P. Rosenberg, 1975). This drawing is actually a study for the huge picture, today in the Cathedral at Narbonne. This picture was intended to replace the *Résurrection de Lazare* by Sebastiano del

Piombo (London, National Gallery) which was bought by the Regent shortly before his death in 1723 for his collection at the Palais-Royal.

This portrait, executed between 1723 and 1728, is extremely different from the solemn and sumptuous images of themselves which his contemporaries usually executed. If his is shown — not without pride — in front of one of his major realizations, he has, nevertheless, given to his face an anxious and severe expression, moving in its profound sincerity.

Toulouse, Musée des Augustins

HUBERT ROBERT
Paris 1733–Paris 1808

Pupil of the sculptor M. A. Slodtz, Robert accompanied the ambassador of France, the Comte de Stainville, later Duc de Choiseul, to Rome in 1754. This trip gave him the opportunity to meet Panini, his ideal. Like him, he rapidly specialized in renderings of somewhat imaginary or fantastic ruins and architecture. Robert came back to France in 1765; a year later, he was *agréé* and received by the Académie with his *Port de Ripetta* (Paris, Ecole des Beaux-Arts). In 1767, he exhibited for the first time at the Salon. Protected by the Comte d'Angiviller, he obtained living quarters at the Louvre and was made designer of the King's gardens. Robert represented successively Versailles, Ermenonville, Méréville, and Marly, as well as Paris and its modern buildings, the *Grande Galerie* at the Louvre under various (occasionally the most fantastic) aspects, and the Roman monuments of the south of France.

During the Revolution, Hubert Robert was incarcerated at Sainte-Pélagie first and later at Saint-Lazare, before becoming, like his friend Fragonard, curator at the Muséum des Arts. Robert has imitated mostly Panini, but he has not been insensitive to Piranesi's engravings: his immense production (uneven especially in his later years) makes him the propagator in France of an antique and modern Rome, interpreted in more or less fantastic terms; it also makes him the principal witness of a Paris in complete urban renewal.

After C. Gabillot's (1895) and P. Nolhac's studies (1910), and the catalogue of the Robert exhibition (Paris, Musée de l'Orangerie, 1933), Robert has been somewhat neglected. He would of course deserve a study in depth and a *catalogue raisonné*.

89 *L'escalier tournant du Palais Farnèse à Caprarola* PL. 102

Oil on canvas, 24.5 x 33.5 cm / 9¾ x 13¼ in.

PROVENANCE: Dr. La Caze — given to the Louvre in 1869.

There is a preparatory drawing for this picture (Valence, Musée des Beaux-Arts; Beau, 1968, no. 47) probably executed during Robert's stay in Caprarola in 1764 (one should note that the eighteenth-century sales catalogues often mention this subject, usually painted on a vertical panel). The Valence drawing and the Louvre picture are much alike with some exceptions: in the painting, Robert has pierced the bay windows, compartmentalized the coffered vault, and added the amusing feminine figures which go up or down the famous staircase of the Palace built by Vignola.

If, as it is generally thought, this painting was executed in 1765, it then shows the high degree of perfection the artist had attained before his return to France. Robert uses with virtuosity the curve of the turning staircase and gives the architecture an animated depth which the viewer follows without being able to focus on any particular spot.

Paris, Musée du Louvre

90 *La découverte du Laocoön, 1773* PL. 124

Oil on canvas, 119.5 x 162.5 cm / 47 x 64 in.

Signed and dated lower right: *H. Robert 1773*

PROVENANCE: Maurice de Rothschild, Château de Prégny — acquired in 1962.

BIBLIOGRAPHY: New York, Wildenstein and Company, Inc., 1968, no. 36, with plate.

Painted eight years after the return of the artist to France, this painting is the imaginary representation of the discovery of the *Laocoön* in a fantastic Roman basilica (the discovery was in fact made in 1506 on the Esquiline, in the ruins of Nero's *Domus aurea*). In 1766, the publication of Lessing's *Laocoön* increased the popularity of this Hellenistic group.

The painting, for Robert, is a pretext to represent a sculpture, the memory of which could move all those who had been able to admire it in Rome, and to represent a sculpture for those who wished actually to see it. The artist surrounds it with many figures — the first visitors, the workers entrusted with moving it, in short, so many scenes of daily life which give the composition its life and give the gigantic basilica its scale. At the end of the gallery, slightly off center toward the left, an opening into light emphasizes the depth of the canvas and shows the artist's ability to render perspective.

Richmond, Virginia Museum of Fine Arts

PAUL PONCE ANTOINE ROBERT, *dit* DE SÉRY
Séry-en-Porcien 1686–Paris 1733

Pupil of Tisserand in Reims and of Jouvenet in Paris, Robert was in Italy as early as 1706 where he stayed in Venice, Parma and Rome. Art dealing seems to have assured his living in Rome: he probably met Vleughels there, as well as Caylus and Mariette, his best, but not indulgent, biographer. His meeting with the Cardinal de Rohan in Rome in 1724 prompted his return to Paris and gave his career a new direction. In spite of Crozat's protection, he failed at the Académie and, unknown, died of consumption.

Only some very beautiful engravings and a handful of paintings by Robert de Séry are known today (museums in Vienna, Charleville, Lille (1722), Versailles (1729) and in the churches of Yville (1727) and Saint-Merry, Paris (1730), for instance). They show his admiration for Correggio and Barocci.

A curious and marginal personality, mostly attached to the Flemish milieu and to the Parmesan painters, Robert surprises us less when one thinks of the variety of research undertaken by many French painters between 1715 and 1730.

The study on this painter by H. Bourin (1907) is essential. We are now preparing an article on this too little-known painter.

91 *Portrait de femme,* 1722 — PL. 23

Oil on canvas, 71 x 57 cm / 28 x 22½ in.

Signed and dated lower left: *P. P. Robert 1722*

PROVENANCE: Gift of Paul Leroi, alias Leon Gauchez, the dealer, in 1883.

BIBLIOGRAPHY: Paris, Orangerie . . . , 1957, no. 75, pl. v — Cailleux and Roland-Michel, 1968, no. 84 — Châtelet, 1970.

Engraved by the artist himself in 1723, this painting, executed in Rome, is the only work by Robert still famous today. If its subject is more pleasant than those of the large religious compositions of Saint-Merry or Yville, it is, however, not of higher quality. The influence of Rubens is clear; this is a surprising aspect for a painting done in Rome, one year after Watteau's death and by an artist in residence there for sixteen years. The fresh colors (in particular the salmon pinks and reds), the modernity of the psychological analysis, and the realism of the approach have all brought to mind the names Courbet, Manet and Renoir.

Lille, Musée des Beaux-Arts

HENRI-HORACE ROLAND DE LA PORTE
Paris 1724 (?)–Paris 1793

Pupil of Oudry, *agréé* in 1761, received in 1763 as "peintre dans le genre des animaux et des fruits" with his *Vase de lapis, sphère et musette* (Louvre), Roland de La Porte exhibited regularly at the Salon until 1771 and again from 1787 on. Between these two dates he was away from Paris, perhaps at the court of the Margrave of Baden-Dürlach, as advanced by M. Faré. He worked for the Marquis de Beringhen, Marigny, La Live de Jully and seems to have enjoyed a certain renown which Diderot, eager to defend Chardin, tried to obstruct.

His reserved colors and design and his predilection for extremely simple compositions actually owe more to Oudry than to Chardin. Roland de La Porte is not only a virtuoso of imitation and *trompe-l'oeil,* he also foreshadows some "Neoclassical" painters such as Boilly.

In addition to the study by Gerda Kircher (1928), one should read the pages devoted to him by M. Faré (1962).

92 "*Les apprêts d'un déjeuner rustique*", 1763 — PL. 101

Oil on canvas, 92 x 73 cm / 36¼ x 28¾ in.

PROVENANCE: Salon of 1763, no. 143 — Marquis de Ménars, sale, end of February 1782, no. 95; the sale actually took place March 18–April 6; bought by M. de La Live de la Briche — Comte Molé — given by the Comte Molé to M. Saint; his sale, Paris, May 4, 1846, no. 49; bought by Dr. La Caze for 301 francs — La Caze — given to the Louvre in 1869.

BIBLIOGRAPHY: Faré, 1962, pp. 168, 229.

It is not surprising that this painting bore in the nineteenth century, even for a while in the collection of its famous owner, Louis La Caze, the name Chardin. Did Diderot not write, unjustly, in his account of the Salon of 1763 where this painting was most certainly shown, that "As for Roland de La Porte, he is another victim of Chardin?" At the same Salon, Roland de La Porte exhibited seven other pictures, among which was the famous *Oranger* (Karlsruhe), an imitation bas-relief with its frame, which represented the head of an emperor and which an enthusiastic critic considered a "triomphe d'illusion". Diderot, while admiring its "effet surprenant", added: "the common people are made to be stunned; they ignore how easy this sort of illusion is."

The simple colors and classical composition are in contrast to the brio with which the crust of the bread, the curve of the pitcher and the transparence of the glass are painted. There is nothing spectacular in this still life which tries to be "true" and aims toward formal perfection, perhaps to the prejudice of "emotion".

Paris, Musée du Louvre

ALEXANDRE ROSLIN
Malmö 1718–Paris 1793

Born and trained in Sweden, Roslin stayed in Bayreuth and spent four years in Italy: Venice, Bologna, Florence (where he became a member of the local Academy), Naples, Parma, and so forth. He arrived in Paris in 1752 and made the acquaintance of Pierre and Boucher, whose portrait he executed (1760, Versailles). He was received by the Académie in 1753 with the portraits of two other artists: *Collin de Vermont* (Versailles) and *Jeaurat* (Louvre). Roslin often painted artists, architects, painters or sculptors *(Vernet, Pajou),* scholars and writers (for example, *Marmontel, Linné, Daubenton*). He married in 1759 the pastellist M. S. Giroust (1734–1772) and took, between 1774 and 1778, a triumphant trip to Sweden, Saint Petersburg, Poland and Vienna.

An outstanding portraitist, Roslin considered himself Swedish, but the largest part of his career took place in Paris and his work, close to that of Duplessis and superior to that of F. H. Drouais, belongs to the French tradition of the portrait, so brilliant during the eighteenth century.

His catalogue, established by his remarkable biographer G. W. Lundberg, lists about 625 entries, most of which are portraits.

93 *Portrait de l'abbé Terray, 1774* PL. 120

Oil on canvas, 129 x 97 cm / 50¾ x 38¼ in.

Signed and dated upper right: *Roslin. Chev. de l'ordre de Vasa / 1774.*

PROVENANCE: Commissioned September 25, 1773, by the Académie Royale de Peinture; payment of 2000 livres on April 6, 1774 — National collections since the Revolution.

BIBLIOGRAPHY: Lundberg, 1957: I, p. 308, pl. p. 151; II, pl. 114; III, p. 66, no. 349

In 1773 the Académie decided to own a portrait of the Abbé Terray (1715–1778), the most powerful and less-than-popular *Contrôleur général des Finances* since 1769. Terray, who prided himself as an art connoisseur and who collected modern paintings (Vernet, Lépicié, to name just two), accepted this honor and allowed the Académie to choose the painter. Roslin obtained the commission. He delivered his picture (engraved the same year by Cathelin) on April 30, 1774, the very day he was leaving his colleagues of the Académie for a trip that took him to Russia and his own homeland.

Terray is depicted in his full power, before being replaced in his briefly occupied function of *Surintendant des Beaux-Arts* by d'Angiviller, shortly after Louis XVI's succession to the throne. He was also replaced by Turgot as *Ministre des Finances.*

Roslin is without peer at that time in France in the rendering of shimmering fabrics and in the expression of a severe face which attempts to look pleasant and well-intentioned. He does not disappear behind his sitter, however, and tries to please him without altering his features.

Versailles, Musée National du Château

GABRIEL-JACQUES DE SAINT-AUBIN
Paris 1724–Paris 1780

Saint-Aubin, like Watteau, is rightly considered one of the greatest draftsmen of the eighteenth century. His projects for illustrations, his drawings in the margins of many Salon *livrets* and also in those of the guides of Paris or sales catalogues are not only accurate witnesses of eighteenth-century Paris but also masterpieces in their own right. Very seldom has any artist, in so few strokes and on so small a surface, proved his sense of observation with such precision and detail, and very few have been able to retain the essentials without ever lacking humor.

Both a very rare engraver and painter, Saint-Aubin is not inferior as a draftsman. A pupil of Jeaurat and Boucher, Saint-Aubin failed three times to win the *Prix de Rome* and modestly exhibited at the Académie de Saint-Luc where he also taught, and at the *Colisée* in 1776. Little known during his lifetime, Saint-Aubin sacrificed his attire as well as his household to his curiosity for Paris and his passion for drawing and painting. He almost died of want.

Emile Dacier's two volumes (1929–1931), and his facsimile publication of some sales *livrets* give us a better idea of this great master. Many drawings remain to be reproduced, and many discoveries can still be made in this fascinating work which is inexhaustible in its information of all kinds and a most lively chronicle about the time.

94 *La promenade,* 1760 PL. 92

Oil on canvas, 80 x 63 cm / 31½ x 24¾ in.

PROVENANCE: Came to the museum with the Palégry collection, 1840, attributed to Lancret.

BIBLIOGRAPHY: Dacier, 1929–1931: I, pl. v; II, pp. 91–92, no. 529.

This picture was reattributed to Saint-Aubin in 1925. It can be both dated around 1760 and considered the pendant for the *Parade du boulevard* (London, National Gallery); a preparatory drawing (Leningrad, Hermitage) was discovered in 1954 and shows the same scene viewed from a slightly different angle. In the drawing, the group of drinkers with the beggar to the left is more in the foreground; and the couple in the foreground of the picture is, in the drawing, in the back. This drawing, engraved by the artist, and two other drawings (one of which is at the Institut Néerlandais, Paris) make the attribution of the Perpignan painting certain. On each side of the elegant main group, two lines in perspective, which recede into the picture, give depth to this probably Parisian *promenade.* Saint-Aubin not only uses perspective skillfully, but his natural, pensive elegance also creates, through refined colors, a poetic mood of which the sober charm is quite unique in the whole century.

Perpignan, Musée Rigaud

PIERRE-HUBERT SUBLEYRAS
Saint-Gilles-du-Gard 1699–Rome 1749

Subleyras' career was straightforward: the son of a modest painter from Uzès, Pierre Subleyras was trained in Toulouse, in the studio of Rivalz. In 1726, he went to Paris and won the *Grand Prix* the next year. On July 20, 1728, he left for Rome and lived until 1735 in the Palazzo Mancini, then directed by Vleughels. In 1739, he married the miniaturist, Felice Maria, the daughter of the musician Tibaldi (two Subleyras portraits of her are in Baltimore and Worcester). In 1747, already ill, he went to Naples. He died after returning to Rome in 1749, leaving the first place in the Roman art world to Pompeo Batoni.

Subleyras painted for the Duc de Saint-Aignan (*Remise du Saint Esprit,* Paris, Musée de la Légion d'Honneur), the order of Saint-Jean de Latran (*Repas chez Simon,* Paris, Louvre), the Olivetans in Perugia and the Camillians among other orders. His patrons often became his sitters. His most famous work, for San Pietro, is the large *Saint Basile* (Rome, Santa Maria degli Angeli). In addition to portraits (*Benedict XIV,* 1741) and history paintings, Subleyras executed genre paintings (the delightful *Atelier,* Vienna, Akademie, for example) or sometimes nimble-witted illustrations for La Fontaine's *Contes.* Odette Arnaud's excellent study on Subleyras dates from 1930. We have been preparing, for several years, a study and *catalogue raisonné* on this painter who, like Poussin, is as Roman as he is French. He is soon to occupy, once again, the position that was his both during his life and until the second half of the eighteenth century.

95 *Nu de femme* PL. 64

Oil on canvas, 74 x 136 cm / 29 x 53½ in.

PROVENANCE: Given in 1945 by the Marchesa Mariarosa Gabrielli Gagliardi — Galleria Nazionale d'Arte Antica, Palazzo Barberini; transferred to Palazzo Corsini.

BIBLIOGRAPHY: Rosenberg, 1970, pp. 641–42, fig. 122.

Formerly attributed to Piazzetta and to one of the Gandolfis, this astonishing female nude ranks among the most perfect realizations of Subleyras. The flat technique, so particular to the artist, is rather clear, as well as the fine strokes vigorously and regularly applied like hatchings. The simple audacity of the composition, the beauty of this curved feminine body and the harmony of blacks, whites and pinks give this painting (unusual in Subleyras' *oeuvre*) a position, in the history of the Nude, among the *"Rokeby" Venus* by Velazquez, and those of Courbet and Manet.

Rome, Galleria Nazionale d'Arte Antica, Palazzo Corsini

96 *Le bienheureux Jean d'Avila* PL. 66

Oil on canvas, 136 x 98 cm / 53½ x 38½ in.

Inscribed lower foreground, on the pulpit:
VENER . . . MAG • IOANNES DE AVILA/ VANDA . . .
LICIE • APOST OBIIT MON/TILLIE . . .
DIE X MAIIAN • MDLXIX

PROVENANCE: Cardinal Albani at Soriano del Cimino — Prince Lodovico Chigi until 1959 — acquired in 1959 from Colnaghi.

BIBLIOGRAPHY: Arnaud, 1930, II, pp. 63, 84, no. 146 — London, Royal Academy of Arts, 1968, no. 653.

The subject of this painting is identified by the long inscription in the lower foreground. A replica of it (formerly in the Comte de Saint-Bon collection, Rome and in 1914 in the Cremer collection, Dortmund) was last sold under a Spanish attribution in Berlin (May 29, 1929). H. Voss reattributed it to Subleyras.

The Blessed John of Avila (1500–1569), sometimes called the Apostle of Andalusia, the confessor of Saint Teresa, is represented in this posthumous portrait "preaching from the pulpit, holding the crucifix, an unforgettable figure with his glance engaged in a prophetic vision. His left hand, so admirably real, punctuates the sentences of his speech" (Arnaud, p. 63).

The large white expanse, against which John of Avila's biretta contrasts, the blue touch of the fabric resting on the pulpit to the left, and the *trompe-l'oeil* of the crucifix show the painter's abilities as a colorist. A striking impression of monumentality emanates from this large and classical composition which the artist deliberately wanted static.

Birmingham, City Museum and Art Gallery

97 *Saint Camille de Lellis sauvant des malades d'une inondation,* 1746 PL. 73

Oil on canvas, 205 x 280 cm / 81 x 110 in.

Signed and dated on the stretcher, lower right:
P. Subleyras Pinx. 1746

PROVENANCE: Commissioned by the Camillians on the occasion of their founder's canonization and offered to Pope Benedict XIV — Colonna — Barberini — acquired by the Museo di Roma in 1960.

BIBLIOGRAPHY: Arnaud, 1930, II, p. 77, no. 55 — Pericoli, 1961, pp. 37–43, with plate.

This picture shows Saint Camille of Lellis (1550–1614), founder of the order of the Camillians (Fathers of the good death), saving the sick people in the Ospedale di San Spirito, Rome, from drowning during the terrible flood on the night of December 24, 1598. The Pushkin Museum, Moscow, owns a painted study for the group of the Saint holding the sick man.

Never during his career has Subleyras asserted, to this extent, the refinement of the juxtaposition of pure colors, the ability to articulate different groups, and the emotion in so dignified and solemn a scene. This, however, does not prevent his making the basket of dishes in the center of the picture one of the most beautiful still lifes of the entire century.

Rome, Museo di Roma, Palazzo Braschi

LOUIS TOCQUÉ
Paris 1696–Paris 1772

Pupil of Nicolas Bertin and Nattier, Tocqué was *agréé* by the Académie in 1731 and was received, three years later, as a portraitist (no. 98). He travelled to Russia (1756–1758) and Denmark. In 1747 he married Nattier's older daughter. Exclusively a portraitist and a specialist in royal effigies, Tocqué also executed more informal figures of artists or members of the "bourgeoisie". Tocqué "preferring the sincere and true expression . . . to the affected, the formal and the conventional . . . is clearly reacting to his predecessors; he accomplishes a step forward toward the simplicity and the realism which became tomorrow's taste" (Doria, 1929, p. 47; this monograph remains exemplary).

98 *Portrait du sculpteur Jean-Louis Lemoyne,* 1734 PL. 50

Oil on canvas, 130 x 98 cm / 51¼ x 38½ in.

PROVENANCE: Académie Royale, seized during the Revolution — at Versailles since 1820 — Ecole des Beaux-Arts, 1826 — at the Louvre since 1887.

BIBLIOGRAPHY: Doria, 1929, p. 117, no. 169, fig. 33.

This portrait and the *Portrait de Galloche* (no. 39; Louvre) were Tocqué's reception pieces to the Académie in 1734. He painted Lemoyne (1665–1755), one of his intimate friends, several times

(Doria: no. 170, fig. 35, Doria collection; no. 171, fig. 120. This picture, shown at the Salon of 1743, no. 66, is today on the Paris art market).

According to Jean-René Gaborit, one can see the feet of Innocence from Lemoyne's group, the *Crainte des traits de l'Amour* in the background of the painting (rather than the group called *La Compagne de Diane*).

Lemoyne is represented smiling and seated on a golden, cane-bottomed chair. He holds a chisel and wears a blue scarf around his neck. The proud and radiant face of the sumptuously dressed sculptor is analyzed with realistic care; one also feels the warm friendship between the painter and his model.

Paris, Musée du Louvre

ROBERT LEVRAC, *dit* TOURNIÈRES
Caen 1668–Caen 1752

A pupil in Paris of Bon Boullongne (whom he met when the latter had been asked to work on the decoration of the Château de Balleroy, near Caen), Levrac married in 1693 the widow of one of the King's postillions, Françoise Lemoine, mother of the famous painter. He was *agréé* in 1701 and received by the Académie, first as a portraitist in 1702, and later as a history painter in 1716. He was, nevertheless, primarily a portraitist.

"Encouraged by the auspicious success of his small pictures, Tournières abandoned larger compositions and devoted his career to painting small *portraits historiés* or *sujets de caprice* in the manner of Schalken or Gerard Dou. His aim was to imitate their beautiful colors, their seductive reflections and this precious *fini* which must be appreciated" (Dézallier d'Argenville, 1762, IV, p. 363).

Marie-Louise Bataille's study (1928) on Tournières has not been replaced.

99 *Allégorie de l'été*, 1717 PL. 16

Oil on canvas, 128 x 95 cm / 50½ x 37½ in.

Signed and dated lower left: *RL* (interwoven) *Tournières 1717*

PROVENANCE: Bequeathed by Jules Audéoud to the Rouen Museum, 1885.

BIBLIOGRAPHY: Bataille, 1928, I, p. 237, no. 4 — Rosenberg, 1966, no. 126, with plate.

Far less popular than its pendant *L'Automne*, which was executed a year later (also in the Rouen museum) and of which many copies are known, the *Allégorie de l'été* explains why Dézallier d'Argenville called Tournières the "French Schalken". If the composition is inspired by Bon Boullongne, the artist's teacher, the smooth finish recalls, indeed, the style of the Dutch master: on the other hand, nothing is more "French" than the graceful attitude, the somewhat affected expression and the movement of the model who is surrounded by a garland of honeysuckles and roses.

Rouen, Musée des Beaux-Arts

PIERRE-CHARLES TRÉMOLIÈRES
Cholet 1703–Paris 1739

Pupil of Jean-Baptiste Van Loo in Paris, second *Grand Prix* in 1726—the year he engraved a few plates of the *Figures de différents caractères* after Watteau—Trémolières stayed in Italy between 1728 and 1734 at the Académie de France, then directed by Vleughels. He went to Rome in the company of Subleyras, Blanchet, the sculptor M. A. Slodtz, the architect Le Bon and there met Dandré-Bardon, Carle Van Loo and his nephews Louis-Michel and François, as well as Boucher. Before leaving Rome, Trémolières married Isabella Tibaldi whose sister married Subleyras. On his way back, he stopped in Lyons where some of his best pictures are today. *Agréé* in 1736, he was received the next year. He exhibited at the Salon and participated, with equal success, in the decoration of the Hôtel de Soubise (today the Archives Nationales) with Boucher, Restout, Carle Van Loo and Pierre. He died at age thirty-five, when he seemed ready to occupy the position left vacant by Lemoine's suicide.

An elegant artist and refined draftsman, he knew how to drape his figures admirably. According to his patron and biographer, the Comte de Caylus, he died when "il entrait dans l'âge où l'on bâtit."

The catalogue of the Trémolières exhibition (Rosenberg, Méjanès and Vilain, 1973) is in some ways a monograph of this artist.

100 *Ulysse, sauvé du naufrage par Minerve, aborde à l'île de Calypso*, 1737 PL. 54

Oil on canvas, 168 x 198 cm / 66¼ x 78 in.

PROVENANCE: Académie Royale — seized during the Revolution in 1794 — sent to Montpellier in 1803.

BIBLIOGRAPHY: Rosenberg, Méjanès, Vilain, 1973, no. 15, pl. XXXVII.

This is the reception piece to the Académie, painted by Trémolières in 1737, two years before his death. Its very rare subject was inspired by Homer's *Odysseus*. Ulysses, exhausted, fell asleep on his ship as he was trying to sail across the Straits of Messina between Charybde and Scylla. His companions then killed the oxen of the Sun. Zeus, to satisfy Helios' revenge, struck Ulysses' boat with his lightning. Only Ulysses was saved from drowning. Thanks to Minerva, he reached the island of Ogypia where, seduced by Queen Calypso, he stayed for seven years.

If Trémolières fills his canvas and has some difficulty placing his figures in the space, he is, however, a master in the art of rendering the bodies, which are linked to each other with skill and elegance. The rhythm and the smoothness of the composition, and the light colors make Trémolières' reception piece a sort of manifesto of the new aesthetic inaugurated by the generation of 1700.

Montpellier, Musée Fabre

FRANÇOIS DE TROY
Toulouse 1645–Paris 1730

François de Troy went early to Paris. He became the pupil of Nicolas Loir and of the portraitist Claude Lefèvre. François de Troy was received by the Académie as a history painter in 1674. In 1708, he became its director. Portraitist above all, he exhibited many works at the only two Salons in which he was able to participate (1699 and 1704). "He knew well what was proper, and omitted the fuss of draperies which, attracting the viewer too much, distracts him from the principal object," wrote Dézallier d'Argenville (1762, IV, p. 220) who added: "He was particularly good at painting women . . . they knew he had the ability to make them look beautiful." The style of François de Troy, the father of Jean-François, cannot be confused with those of his contemporaries, Largillierre or Rigaud. More direct and realistic, also more severe, less grandiose and formal, this artist (studied about twenty years ago by Paul Detroy, 1955–1956) ranks among the good portraitists of his generation.

101 *La duchesse de La Force (?)* 1714 PL. 12

Oil on canvas, 144 x 111 cm / 56¾ x 43¾ in.

Signed and dated to the left on the sculpture's pedestal: *PEINT A PARIS PAR FRANCOIS / DE TROY EN 1714*

PROVENANCE: (?) Château de Bosmelet, near Aullay — possibly sent to Paris when the museum was founded in 1803.

BIBLIOGRAPHY: Detroy, 1955–1956, pp. 230–38 — Rosenberg, 1966, no. 130, with plate.

This portrait is presumably of Anne-Marie de Beuzelin de Bosmelet who married, in 1698, Henri-Jacques de Caumont (1675–1726), later, in 1699, the Duc de La Force. It is, without doubt, the artist's masterpiece. De Troy renders with equal success the peaches and the silk of the dress, as well as the regular features of the somewhat heavy, dark-haired model. The Duchess is painted outside, in front of a sphinx which bears, on its base, the proud signature of the artist who also specified that the picture had been executed in Paris. A young servant, richly dressed with a tufted toque, looks at his noble mistress, probably flattered by the artist who did not completely sacrifice the likeness.

Rouen, Musée des Beaux-Arts

JEAN-FRANÇOIS DE TROY
Paris 1679–Rome 1752

Son of François de Troy, Jean-François went to Rome without having obtained the traditional *Grand Prix*. In 1699, he joined the Académie de France, then directed by the pupil of Le Brun, René-Antoine Houasse. He quickly left the Palazzo Capranica, where the Académie was installed, to wander through Italy (one of his many love affairs made him stay for rather a long while in Pisa). Upon his return to France, he was received and *agréé* (1708) by the Académie with his *Apollon et Diane perçant de leurs flèches les enfants de Niobé* (Montpellier). He participated in the decoration of the Hôtel du Grand Maître in Versailles, in the 1727 Concours (picture in Nancy) against Lemoine, his main rival in the decoration of the *chambre de la reine* at Versailles and in the King's *petits cabinets*. He also produced cartoons for the Manufacture des Gobelins *(Histoire d'Esther, Histoire de Jason et de Médée)*. In 1738, he was made *chevalier* and replaced Vleughels, dead the year before, at the head of the Académie de France à Rome. Rich through his marriage, de Troy was able to lead a luxurious life while taking care of his new position. "Prince" of the Accademia di San Luca in 1744, he took an essential part with the *pensionnaires* (nos. 4 and 142) in the Carnival of 1748 (*La Caravane du Sultan à La Mecque*). In 1750, he received in Rome the future Marquis de Marigny, brother of Mme de Pompadour, who was there with Cochin, Soufflot and the Abbé Le Blanc; Marigny eventually decided to replace de Troy with Natoire.

His eighteenth-century biographers have given him an attractive image. Prolific artist, Jean-François de Troy treated all genres: not only history, mythological or religious subjects, but also portraits, landscapes and genre paintings (he did a beautiful series of *Tableaux de mode*). Extremely gifted, sensual, sometimes slightly superficial, a sumptuous and warm colorist, this "French Jordaens" deserves to recover the rank that was his in the eighteenth century.

Since Gaston Brière's important study (1930), a few pictures of his have been separately published (Talbot, 1974, for instance). We hope that the important monograph Jacques Vilain is writing will soon be completed.

102 *L'éducation de Bacchus*, 1717 PL. 15

Oil on canvas, 140 x 165 cm / 55 x 65 in.

Signed and dated lower right: *de Troy 1717*

PROVENANCE: C. Soulzener, Paris; bought in 1875 from X. Pittet — Marquise d'Escayrac-Lauture, daughter of C. Soulzener, Paris — acquired with its pendant, *Bacchus et Ariane*, also signed and dated 1717, in 1961.

BIBLIOGRAPHY: Brière, 1930, II, p. 36, no. 36.

As early as 1717 de Troy reached a mature style which did not have at that time the loose qualities for which he was later reproached. He likes smiling and opulent models with fine hands, turned-up noses, slightly open mouths, deep green and orange harmonies, and elegant and lithe compositions. He wants above all to make mythology pleasant, without vulgarity, but also without severity. What impresses one most about the Berlin picture is the *joie de peindre* shown by the artist and, in addition to its zest and generosity, its chromatic richness.

Staatliche Museen, Preussischer Kulturbesitz, Gemäldegalerie Berlin (West), Property of the Kaiser-Friedrich-Museums-Verein

103 *La moissonneuse endormie* PL. 52

Oil on canvas, 105 x 139 cm / 41¼ x 54¾ in.

PROVENANCE: At the museum since 1844.

BIBLIOGRAPHY: Nîmes, Musée de Nîmes, p. 252, no. 98; as "Detroy (Ecole de Rubens)" — San Diego, 1967–1968, n.n.

G. Brière did not accept this picture (1930, p. 46), which owes its title to the sheaf under the resting young woman, as being a work by Jean-François de Troy. Today it is unanimously attributed to him. In this magnificent and freely executed picture (above all the study of a female body), de Troy shows his usual sensuality which foreshadows Courbet's *Les Demoiselles des bords de la Seine*. The harmony of the pink cheeks and lips and the saffron and browns of the dress are typical of de Troy's work.

Nîmes, Musée des Beaux-Arts

104 *Le marquis de Vandières*, 1751 PL. 81

Oil on canvas, 132 x 96 cm / 52 x 37¾ in.

Signed and dated lower left on the entablature: *de Troy 175 (1?)*

PROVENANCE: Cailleux, 1931 — Versailles since 1953.

BIBLIOGRAPHY: Rosenberg, Compin and Guilmard, 1974–1975, no. 123, pl. p. 103.

"M. le Marquis de Marigny [1727–1781] . . . was travelling in Italy in 1750 and, during his stay in Rome, sojourned in the palazzo of the Académie de France; the joy of all *pensionnaires* could not be expressed . . . To show our appreciation of the honor done to us," wrote the sculptor, Caffieri in 1762 (Dussieux, II, pp. 283–84), "we decided to ask him to celebrate all together this happy event and, to leave a souvenir to posterity, to give us his portrait . . . After seeing him, we went to M. de Troy . . . and asked him to please execute the portrait of M. le Marquis de Marigny. He favored our request with his usual benevolence. . . ." In 1750 the future Marquis de Marigny and Marquis de Ménars was only Abel Poisson, Marquis de Vandières. He had been sent to Rome by his sister, the Marquise de Pompadour, to polish his artistic education. Upon his return from Italy, he occupied, for the rest of Louis XV's reign, the position of *Surintendant des Bâtiments* and thus played an essential part in the French artistic life of the second part of the King's reign.

The sumptuous Versailles portrait is very characteristic of de Troy's style, especially the rendering of the hands. Not only does this portrait represent a man (also portrayed by Tocqué, Roslin and L.-M. Van Loo) whose importance has not been fully studied yet (see, however, Ericksen, 1962), it also enables us to confirm two things: the attribution to de Troy of the *Portrait d'homme,* so-called Marquis de Marigny (Pittsburgh, Frick Art Museum), executed during his Roman period; and the reattribution to de Troy of the beautiful *Portrait d'homme* until now given to Tocqué (Paris, Musée Jacquemart-André; see Doria, 1929, p. 133, no. 276, fig. 10).

Versailles, Musée National du Château

ANNE VALLAYER-COSTER
Paris 1744–Paris 1818

Anne Vallayer-Coster was, along with Mme Vigée-Lebrun (born in 1755) and Mme Labille-Guiard (born in 1749), the most famous woman painter of the eighteenth century in France. As early as 1770, she was received by the Académie (see no. 105). One does not know precisely where she was trained. A prolific artist (between 400 and 500 pictures), she obtained living quarters at the Louvre in 1780. She married the next year an *Avocat au Parlement,* Jean-Pierre-Silvestre Coster. She painted still lifes, flowers, portraits, and miniatures. Little by little, during the Revolution, she survived in spite of her royalist convictions; under the Empire, she lost the prominent position that had been hers until 1785. She tried only occasionally, one should add, to adapt herself to the new aesthetic.

Anne Vallayer-Coster is without any doubt one of the best, but not one of the most original, still life painters of the second half of the eighteenth century. Marianne Roland-Michel's perfect monograph (1970) has done justice to her underestimated merits.

105 *Instruments de musique,* 1770 PL. 116

Oil on canvas, 88 x 116 cm / 34¾ x 45¾ in.

Signed and dated to the right, halfway up: *Me Vallayer 1770*

PROVENANCE: Salon of 1771, no. 149 with its pendant, also the Louvre — Académie — Louvre since the Revolution.

BIBLIOGRAPHY: Roland-Michel, 1970, no. 258.

Anne Vallayer-Coster presented two pictures for her reception at the Académie in 1770. Both are at the Louvre, the *Attributs de la peinture, de la sculpture et de l'architecture* and the picture shown here: it represents a still life of musical instruments, a horn, a bagpipe, a lute resting on a music sheet, a flute, an oboe, and a violin on a green rug with gold fringe. The success of this painting and of Anne Vallayer-Coster's other works presented at the Salon of 1771 was tremendous: "so much art, for a young lady!" wrote the critic of *La Muse*; Diderot remarked that "It is not Chardin, but below this master it is, however, far above [the art of] a woman." In fact, this work is very different from Chardin's mysterious compositions: Vallayer-Coster is more descriptive, more detailed; she pays less attention than Chardin to the composition, the planes and masses, and the harmony of the colors put together. Because of her accomplished *métier* and her inspiration, perhaps more traditional than innovative, she creates works such as this in which the "poetic realism is reassuring" and which are extremely seductive.

Paris, Musée du Louvre

CARLE VAN LOO
Nice 1705–Paris 1765

Charles-André, called Carle Van Loo, is the most famous member of this family of artists, Dutch in origin. He was the grandson of Jacob, the son of Louis, the brother of Jean-Baptiste, the uncle of Louis-Michel and Charles-Amédée and the father of Jules-César-Denis, all of whom were painters. Very early Carle followed his brother, Jean-Baptiste, to Rome, where he became the pupil of B. Luti and of the sculptor Le Gros. In Paris again in 1719, he won the *Grand Prix* in 1724 and went again to Italy in 1727. He stayed there until 1734. He painted a ceiling for San Isidoro in Rome and worked in Turin for the Palazzo Reale and Stupinigi. After his return, he was received by the Académie—there he occupied all possible functions. Director of the Ecole Royale des Elèves Protégés in 1749 and in 1762, *Premier Peintre du Roi,* Van Loo was ennobled in 1751.

Carle Van Loo treated all genres: religious subjects (Church of Saint-Sulpice and Notre-Dame-des-Victoires in Paris), history paintings, mythological compositions, portraits, genre scenes and allegories (Fontainebleau, Bibliothèque Nationale). He had immense success: Grimm called him "le plus grand peintre de l'Europe," and Voltaire compared him to Raphael. Shortly before his death, he began the decoration of one of the chapels of the Church of the Invalides (*Vie de saint Grégoire*).

Carle Van Loo is today one of the least known and most misunderstood painters of the eighteenth century. To compare him to Boucher, whose spirit he does not have, is rather uncalled for. There is, however, in his work, a security, a consciousness, a power, and a sense for composition which is nothing but admirable. He does not stir emotions but forces respect.

To study Van Loo today, one must consult either the eulogy written by Dandré-Bardon (1765) with its *catalogue raisonné*, or the already old and poorly illustrated study by Louis Réau (1938). Therefore, it is hard to pretend that what is written on the painter today is done knowingly! An exhibition, accompanied by a large, fully-illustrated catalogue of his work, is being prepared.

106 *Le voeu de Louis XIII au siège de La Rochelle*, 1746 — PL. 71

Oil on canvas, arched with shoulders, 77 x 62 cm / 30¼ x 24½ in.

Signed below center: *Carle Van Loo*

PROVENANCE: Sale after death of Louis-Michel Van Loo, November 1772, no. 69; 300 livres; acquired by Donjeu — acquired in Tours in 1953.

BIBLIOGRAPHY: Montgolfier, 1956, pp. 10–11, with illustration.

The fact that this is the painting sold after Louis-Michel Van Loo's death is confirmed by the drawing, in the margin of the sale catalogue, done by Saint-Aubin on his own copy (Paris, Bibliothèque Nationale, Cabinet des Estampes; see E. Dacier, 1909–1919, VI (1911), p. 33). It is the sketch for the large painting by Carle Van Loo exhibited at the Salon of 1746 (no. 30); today it is above the main altar of the Church of Notre-Dame-des-Victoires in Paris. The painting is now surrounded by six large compositions, by the same artist, with subjects from the life of Saint Augustine. A few changes occur between the sketch and the finished painting: the position of the Virgin and the angels; the position of Richelieu, to the left of the King in the finished painting instead of behind him. Furthermore, the background of the altarpiece represents the City of La Rochelle rather than an equestrian battle near the sea. Louis XIII, after the defeat of the Protestants at La Rochelle in 1625, had made the vow to build a convent for the order of the Reformed Augustinians, whose church would be dedicated to Notre-Dame-des-Victoires: it is this event Van Loo's picture commemorates. The sketch, freely executed, surprises by its colors: the cold and glaucous shades are dominated by greens and blues, creating a beautiful pearly harmony.

Paris, Musée Carnavalet

107 *Allégorie de la peinture*, 1753 — PL. 83

Oil on canvas (formerly a shaped canvas), 84 x 86.5 cm / 33 x 34 in.

Signed lower left: *Carle Van Loo*

PROVENANCE: Salon of 1753, no. 180, with the three other overdoor paintings, executed for the Marquise de Pompadour, Château de Bellevue — Marquis de Ménars sale, end of February, actually March 18 — April 6, 1782, no. 124; bought by Basan for 3500 livres — Louis-Philippe; sale, London, Christie's, May 28, 1853, no. 190(?) — several English nineteenth-century auctions — Baron Nathaniel de Rothschild, Vienna, 1903 — acquired from Rosenberg and Stiebel, 1953.

BIBLIOGRAPHY: Réau, 1938, p. 60, no. 73.

This painting, which brought 800 livres, belongs to a series of four, formerly shaped, overdoor paintings, which were intended for the Marquise de Pompadour's residence at Bellevue. There are many copies of this series, some from the artist's studio, and some by Carle Van Loo himself; but the San Francisco pictures, engraved by Etienne Fessard in 1756, in spite of their unclear provenance, are the only ones which used to be shaped and are signed, as was customary for overdoor paintings. The Art Institute of Chicago owns a preparatory drawing for the head of the young girl (see Rosenberg, 1972–1973, no. 142). In this important commission, Carle Van Loo proves to be a painter aware of the particular qualities of childhood. The idea of the picture within the picture, perhaps common in the eighteenth century, is used with refinement in this allegory, which has no other pretension than to please.

The Fine Arts Museums of San Francisco, The Mildred Anna Williams Collection

JEAN-BAPTISTE VAN LOO
Aix-en-Provence 1684–Aix-en-Provence 1745

Grandson of the Dutch painter, Jacob Van Loo, who settled in France and became an *académicien* in 1669, Jean-Baptiste, father of Louis-Michel, worked in the south of France: Toulon (1706), Aix (1707–1712), Nice, Monaco, Turin ((1712–1715) where he became affiliated with his patrons, the Princes de Carignan) and Rome (1715–1718, with the painter B. Luti). He settled in Paris between 1720 and 1739, was *agréé* in 1722 and was commissioned to execute portraits (in 1724 and 1727) either full-length or equestrian, of the King. In 1731 he became an *académicien.* Thenceforth, he spent his time in Aix, where he painted portraits, in Paris, where he worked for the Church, and in London where he lived between 1738 and 1742 and met with tremendous success (Portraits of Horace Walpole and Alexander Pope).

Prolific artist, Jean-Baptiste Van Loo is difficult to judge: many of his works have disappeared; many attributions to him are not satisfactory. Colette Mouton-Gilles' thesis (1970; unfortunately unpublished; see, however, Mouton-Gilles, 1972, pp. 187–91) puts in his real place an uneven artist, whose portraits, as well as his history paintings, show inspiration.

108 *Renaud dans les bras d'Armide* PL. 45

Oil on canvas, 130 x 200 cm / 51¼ x 78¾ in.

Signed and dated lower right: *J B Van Loo*

PROVENANCE: Beringhen, *premier écuyer du roi*; sale, July 2, 1770, no. 46 — according to the cataloguer, the painting is "d'après Lemoine"! — Blondel de Gagny; sale, December 10–24, 1776, no. 237 — Marquis de Livois — seized during the Revolution and given to the museum at the time of its foundation in 1799.

BIBLIOGRAPHY: Planchenault, 1933, pp. 223–25.

This picture is dated by Mme Mouton-Gilles, in her unpublished thesis, during the artist's Parisian stay between 1730 and 1735. Mme Mouton-Gilles compares it to the *Diane et Endymion* (Louvre) which opened to the artist the doors of the Académie in 1731 as a history painter. The subject, inspired by Tasso's *Gerusalemme liberata* has been treated by many artists, Bolognese as well as French. It was, for instance, the subject of Boucher's reception piece in 1734 (Louvre). It would, in fact, be interesting to know who first treated the subject: the future *Premier Peintre du Roi* or the older brother of his predecessor. Jean-Baptiste Van Loo shows here his inborn taste for elegance and rhythm. He surrounds his two heroes with graceful figures; he places them in an architectural landscape in a way which was then very much in fashion.

Angers, Musée des Beaux-Arts

LOUIS-MICHEL VAN LOO
Toulon 1707–Paris 1771

Older son of Jean-Baptiste Van Loo and his pupil, nephew of Carle, *Grand Prix* in 1725, Louis-Michel went to Italy between 1727 and 1733. Received by the Académie in 1733, he was recommended by Rigaud to occupy the position in the Spanish court left vacant by Ranc's death. First painter to Philip V and to Ferdinand VI in 1737, Louis-Michel, who had received the *Ordre de Saint-Michel* in 1748, returned to France only in 1752. He exhibited regularly at the Salon between 1753 and 1769 and occupied, after the death of his uncle Carle, the position of *gouverneur* of the Ecole Royale des Elèves Protégés.

A conscientious portraitist above all, Louis-Michel Van Loo, considered by Michael Levey as "perhaps the best artist of the family" (1973, p. 116), has been little studied with the exception of E. Dacier's research on the sale after his death (V and VI, 1911) and Yves Bottineau's study on his stay in Spain (1960).

109 *Portrait de Diderot, 1767* PL. 106

Oil on canvas, 81 x 65 cm / 32 x 25½ in.

Signed and dated in the center to the right: *L.M. Van Loo / 1767*

PROVENANCE: Salon of 1767, no. 8 — given by the artist to Diderot — bequeathed to the Louvre in 1911 by Albert Caroillon de Vandeul, descendant of the sitter.

BIBLIOGRAPHY: Seznec and Adhémar, 1957–1967, III (1963) pp. 17–18, 66–67, pl. 5.

This is the most famous portrait of Diderot, and also the most faithful, even if one prefers the slightly later one by Fragonard (Louvre since 1972). At the Salon of 1767, Louis-Michel Van Loo, whose name appears first in the *livret,* exhibited more than a dozen works which constituted some allegories, but mostly portraits: the portrait of Diderot was widely noticed. Bachaumont admired "this bare and smoking head onto which this author must occasionally throw some cold water to moderate the excess of a boiling genius."[1] Diderot, although not without some reservation, wrote the most interesting comment: "pretty like a woman, leering, smiling, cute, dainty and captivating in appearance . . . like an old coquette who still tries to look pleasant."[2]

Diderot, the great writer, probably wears the famous green and lilac robe offered to him by Mme Geoffrin. If the attitude, the movement and the look are somewhat frozen, the honest psychological analysis and the sobriety of composition make this portrait a good iconographic document. It places Louis-Michel Van Loo among the best portraitists of his generation.

Paris, Musée du Louvre

CLAUDE-JOSEPH VERNET
Avignon 1714–Paris 1789

Son of a modest coach painter from Avignon, father and grandfather of two great artists, Carle and Horace, Claude-Joseph Vernet was the pupil of Jacques Vialy in Aix-en-Provence. He was in Rome in 1734 and there received some training from Fergioni and the landscape painter from Lyons, Adrien Manglard (1695–1760). Vernet specialized in seascapes. He was famous as early as 1740 and painted for the artists, the French dignitaries (the Duc de Saint-Aignan, for example) and the English tourists. He exhibited at the Paris Salon from 1746 on. He met, in 1750, the Marquis de Vandières, later *Surintendant,* who played an important part in the artist's return to France in 1753. Received by the Académie, he began a series of *Ports de France* which kept him away from Paris for about ten years. Upon his return to the capital, he received lodging quarters at the Louvre and was unanimously admired: Diderot even preferred him to Claude, not only for his ability to paint, but also for the figures of his compositions.

Vernet's repertory is limited: views of ports or cities, some landscapes (mostly imaginary seascapes at dawn or sunset), shipwrecks, cloudy views, *tempêtes,* and moonlit scenes. Claude, Salvator Rosa, and the Dutch painters are his models; but Vernet quickly developed his own style, which was still realistic, already romantic and too often imitated.

Florence Ingersoll-Smouse's excellent research (1926) has not been replaced. Vernet, unfortunately, no longer has the reputation he had during his lifetime. The large number of works wrongly attributed to him is probably responsible for this: a real "Vernet", however, is often an authentic masterpiece which can only be compared to the most perfect Venetian, Roman or English accomplishments of the century.

[1] Seznec and Adhémar, 1957–1967, III, p. 18; "cette tête nue et fumante sur laquelle cet auteur est obligé de jeter de l'eau froide de temps à autre pour modérer les accès d'un génie bouillonnant."

[2] Seznec and Adhémar, 1957–1967, II, pp. 66–67; "joli comme une femme, lorgnant, souriant, mignard, faisant le petit-bec, la bouche en coeur . . . l'air d'une vieille coquette qui fait encore l'aimable."

110 *Vue du port de Naples,* 1748 — PL. 76

Oil on canvas, 100 x 197.5 cm / 39¼ x 77¾ in.

Signed and dated lower right: *Joseph Vernet f. Romae 1748*

PROVENANCE: Probably Besborodko (Grand Chancellor and Minister of Russian Foreign Affairs, died in 1800; the number 210, lower left, refers to this collection — Comtesse Koucheleff, St. Petersburg; her sale, Paris, March 27, 1877, no. 59 — Henri, and André Pereire — given to the Louvre with life tenancy in 1949; life tenancy renounced in 1974; at the Louvre since.

BIBLIOGRAPHY: Ingersoll-Smouse, 1926, II, p. 90, no. 1933.

Vernet went several times to Naples. His second trip took place in 1746, two years before the date of the Louvre picture, which was painted toward the end of his stay in Rome (1734–1753). In 1742, the Abbé de Canillac, Comte de Lyon, had already commissioned two views of Naples from the artist. They are identified, probably wrongly, with the pictures of the Boullongne and Dubois sales (Lord Elgin collection); they are noticeably smaller than the Canillac pictures. The composition of one of the Elgin pictures is very close to that of the Louvre, one of Vernet's most perfect paintings; only the foreground is somewhat modified. The rendering of the light, the fresh colors, the picturesque and amusing street scenes, and the fine and spontaneous observation show the degree of perfection attained by Vernet at that time. Rarely has any artist known how to ally precision of topographical description to the originality of a carefully considered composition.

Paris, Musée du Louvre

111 *L'après-midi,* 1753 — PL. 84

Oil on canvas, 99 x 137 cm / 39 x 54 in.

Signed and dated lower left: *Joseph Vernet f / 1753*

PROVENANCE: Ralph Howard, first Viscount Wicklow (died in 1789) — Count Wicklow at Shelton Abbey, Ireland — sale, Sotheby's, London, June 20, 1951, with its pendant, today in a private collection, Paris — Cailleux — acquired in 1951.

BIBLIOGRAPHY: Ingersoll-Smouse, 1926, I, p. 64, nos. 393–396 (?).

This painting can probably be identified with one of the *Quatre parties du jour* commissioned from Vernet in 1752 for "une année après" by a certain "chevalier Henry, Irlandais" (in fact, Howard). In spite of his Irish wife, Virginia Parker, Vernet was unable to record exactly the names of his English patrons in his account book from which this information is taken. The Toledo picture was executed (according to archival documents kept at Shelton Abbey) in Marseilles and in Aix-en-Provence on his return from Italy to France, where the King had called him to execute a series of *Ports de France* (today for the most part at the Musée de la Marine, Paris). It is a magnificent exercise of pure imagination, without any connection to any known place, as in Claude. The reflections of the sunset on the sea and the sails of the boats are rendered with great accuracy. Vernet plays with the contrasts among the foreground and its figures of fishermen; the light, the vastness of the sea and the sky mingle, as in the works of the seventeenth-century Dutch masters.

The Toledo Museum of Art, Gift of Edward Drummond Libbey

JOSEPH-MARIE VIEN
Montpellier 1716–Paris 1809

Vien arrived in Paris in 1740, received Natoire's advice and won the *Grand Prix* in 1743. He was in Rome between 1744 and 1750. Two of the works we show here date from this period, as well as the *Ermite endormi* which was warmly received at the Salon of 1753. Received by the Académie a year later, he, nevertheless, had to wait until 1763 and produce his *Marchande d'amour* (Fontainebleau) before being recognized as the first painter of his generation. This painting marks a radical departure, and a return to antiquity, not only in the subject "à la grecque" and its sources (*Les Antiquités d'Herculanum*), but also in its porcelain-like technique and its pure and voluntarily cold colors.

Vien was asked to paint, in 1773, a series of paintings for Louveciennes to replace the Fragonards Mme du Barry had refused. From 1775 until 1781, he directed the Académie de France à Rome. At the death of Pierre in 1789, he became *Premier Peintre du Roi*. Member of the Sénat in 1799, Comte d'Empire in 1808, he was, at the height of his career ("notre père a cessé de vivre" noted David), buried in the Panthéon, Paris.

To judge Vien globally is difficult: the first part of his career is that of a brilliant artist; he was passionate, vigorous and fluent in his style. The second part of it is more difficult to approach: its charm is somewhat bitter, colder and more intellectual. In importance and influence, it can be compared to that of Pompeo Batoni.

Thomas Gaehtgens is preparing the artist's monograph, the absence of which makes the understanding of a whole trend of French painting a delicate problem.

112 *"Sultane reine"*, 1748 — PL. 74

Oil on paper, 29.5 x 22.5 cm / 11½ x 8¾ in.

PROVENANCE: Formerly, Dutuit brothers — given to the Petit Palais in 1902.

BIBLIOGRAPHY: Volle in Rosenberg and Volle, 1974–1975, p. 40, no. 93, pl. XXXIII.

At the occasion of the carnival in 1748, the *pensionnaires* of the Académie de France à Rome and their friends dressed themselves up and organized, on the theme of the *Caravane du Sultan à La Mecque*, a large procession through the streets of Rome. Their director, Jean-François de Troy, wanted to keep a souvenir of this masquerade and commissioned from Barbault (see no. 4) a series of twenty small pictures, each representing a *pensionnaire* or one of their friends. Vien, Voiriot and others also engraved, drew or painted their comrades disguised as Turks. Vien, for instance, executed a series of admirable drawings which he engraved (Petit Palais), as well as three oils on paper. This one represents the painter and engraver Louis-Joseph Le Lorrain, disguised as "sultane reine". Le Lorrain (1715–1759) ended his brief but brilliant career as Director of the Académie des Beaux-Arts in Saint Petersburg.

The blue and yellow gamut of this invented costume (which almost recalls Vermeer) and the red spot of the pearl in the middle of the sitter's forehead add to the charm of this spirited rough sketch, which recalls one of the important aspects of life at the Académie de France à Rome. In addition to copying masterpieces of the past and executing studies after the antique or painting landscapes of the Roman *campagna*, the young artists did not mind festivities and occasions for diversion.

Paris, Musée du Petit Palais

113 *L'arrivée de sainte Marthe à Marseille* PL. 75

Oil on canvas, 312 x 202 cm / 123 x 79½ in.

Signed and dated lower left: *J.M. Vien 1748*

PROVENANCE: Painted for the cloister of the Capuchin Friars of Sainte-Marthe de Tarascon.

BIBLIOGRAPHY: Gaehtgens, 1974, pp. 64–69, with figure.

In 1746, after two years in Rome, Vien received through the Father Chérubin de Noves, the commission for six large paintings intended for the Church of Sainte-Marthe de Tarascon. For each painting the artist was to be paid 100 francs. This series, executed between 1747 and 1749 was completed, with a seventh painting, in 1751. All the pictures have subjects from the life of Saint Martha, sister of Mary-Magdalene and of Lazarus. All three were expelled from Palermo, and disembarked in Provence where they accomplished many miracles; Saint Martha, for instance, tamed a monster, the *tarasque*, which gave its name to the city of Tarascon where she died and was buried. This picture shows the Saint arriving in Marseilles with Saint Maximin, Saint Lazarus, first Bishop of Marseilles, and Mary-Magdalene.

The Saint thanks God for the happy conclusion of their journey; her white dress occupies the center of the composition. The four figures in the foreground are directly inspired by the Bolognese examples (principally Guercino) that Vien deeply admired. This composition has an undeniable feeling of magnitude and a breadth close to the research done in Rome at the time of Benefial, Subleyras and Batoni, all of whom had a tremendous influence on French painting.

Tarascon, Eglise Sainte-Marthe

This picture will not be shown in the exhibition.

114 *Vénus, blessée par Diomède, est sauvée par Iris,* 1775 PL. 127

Oil on canvas, 161 x 208 cm / 63¾ x 81¾ in.

Signed and dated lower left: *Vien 1775*

PROVENANCE: Salon of 1775, no. 4.

BIBLIOGRAPHY: Seznec and Adhémar, 1957–1967, IV (1967), pp. 234, 242, 276.

Diderot, usually very favorable toward Vien, found this painting "point du tout sans mérite." G. Bouquier in his review of the Salon (1975, p. 100) describes the subject: " 'Venus wounded during the siege of Troy.' The painter has chosen the moment when Iris has taken her away from the conflict and Mars helps her to climb into his chariot to carry her to Olympus." He adds: "This picture has pleasant colors, it is well painted and the light effect is well done, but the figures are chilly." A work like this one or like Vien's *Saint Thibault* (Versailles; see Paris, Grand Palais, no. 193, pl. 1), also shown at the Salon of 1775, are excellent examples of the most advanced research by French painters before the death of Louis XV and just before the Davidian revolution.

Paris, Private collection

JACQUES VIGOUROUX-DUPLESSIS
Known between 1700 and 1730

The biographical data on this artist is very scarce. It has been collected by Marvin Eisenberg in an article to be published in the *Walters Art Gallery Journal* (the author has kindly given us a typescript of his article).

In 1710, Vigouroux-Duplessis received a commission for the Paris Opera. In 1719, he was in Beauvais and two years later worked as a drawing teacher at the Manufacture Royale there. He regularly produced tapestry cartoons (in 1723 on the theme of the Island of Cythera for example) until 1726 when he was replaced by Oudry.

The Baltimore picture (1700), the two pictures in Chaalis (after 1715), the one in Glasgow (1719) and three others in French collections (two of which are dated 1730) constitute the *corpus* of this painter, according to M. Eisenberg.

Working for the Opera, the Manufacture de Beauvais, and painting fire screens, Vigouroux-Duplessis is more a decorator than a full-fledged painter. He is, however, a witness to the changes in decorative forms and to this curiosity for the "Orient", objects from China or visitors from Siam (Chaalis), which is typical of the time. His name should be associated with those of Gillot, Berain and even Watteau.

115 *Devant de cheminée montrant trois chinois soutenant un tableau rond sur lequel est représenté Jupiter et Danaë,* 1700 PL. I

Oil on canvas, 87 x 122 cm / 34¼ x 48⅛ in.

Signed and dated lower center: *Vigouroux Duplessis Invenit et pinxit 1700*

PROVENANCE: Formerly Jules Strauss; sale, Paris, Galerie Charpentier, May 1949, no. 40 — sale, Hôtel Drouot, February 6, 1970 — acquired from Galerie Pardo, Paris art market, by the Walters Art Gallery, 1972.

BIBLIOGRAPHY: Eisenberg, 1977 (to be published).

During the summer, it was the custom to close fireplace openings with painted *trompe-l'oeil.* The major artists of the seventeenth and eighteenth centuries executed such paintings (see Lastic, 1955). This picture by Vigouroux-Duplessis, about which there is a scholarly study by M. Eisenberg, is a delightful example of this type of work; it is useful, decorative, and, above all, an exercise of virtuosity.

On the left, a curtain reveals the scene which is supposed to take place on the hearth: three orientals support a round medallion held by a ribbon. A Jupiter and Danaë are painted on it in the form of a pastiche of mythological compositions then in vogue. To the right one sees an andiron in front of the fireplace; on the andiron is sculpted a bas-relief showing the story of Dibutade (an allusion to the invention of drawing) in which a woman engraves her own and her lover's initials on the wall.

Baltimore, The Walters Art Gallery

FRANÇOIS-ANDRÉ VINCENT
Paris 1746–Paris 1816

Son of a Genevan miniaturist established in Paris, Vincent is first the pupil of his father and then of Vien. *Grand Prix* in 1768, pupil at the Ecole Royale des Elèves Protégés, he stayed in Rome between 1771 and 1775, where he executed some extraordinary caricatures of other *pensionnaires,* and also painted some beautiful portraits. His *Président Molé et les factieux,* exhibited at the Salon of 1779, made him famous. His regular participation in the Salons instigated long commentaries which were often eulogizing (for instance, his *Combat des Romains et des Sabins,* 1781, Angers; *Zeuxis . . . ,* 1789, Louvre). *Académicien* in 1783, Vincent occupied a position of first rank in the history of French painting during the last quarter of the century: his "originality is evidenced in the precocious choice of subjects from French history, as well as in his choice of Roman subjects." A prolific artist, "caring for measure and distinction," Vincent is one of the great unknown artists of the time. It suffices to think of the many landscape drawings and portraits which are his, but which are still catalogued under Fragonard.

We impatiently await the monograph of Jean-Pierre Cuzin on this artist whose curious aspects are attractive, and who is more varied than one is led to believe by the few works reproduced until today.

116 *L'Assomption de la Vierge,* 1771 PL. 118

Oil on canvas, 65 x 43 cm / 25½ x 17 in.

Inscribed and dated on the back: *Fait et donné par F. A. Vincent à son ami D. H. Lemoine in 1771*

PROVENANCE: Paris art market

This is one of Vincent's first known works and probably the study for the lost painting (during World War I?), also dated and signed 1771, formerly in the Church of Saint Jean-Baptiste, Arras (Le Gentil, 1871). This sketch is a fully-mastered work by a promising artist before his departure for Rome. The colors are bold, even strong; the classical composition is sober, reduced to essentials; the stocky figures, with the ample folds of their dresses, seem stopped, and yet, do not look frozen. If we compare this sketch to that of David done two years later (no. 25), one can understand why the contemporaries of these two artists (who were born two years apart) hesitated, for some years at least, to give the palm to David.

Strasbourg, Private collection

NICOLAS VLEUGHELS
Paris 1668–Rome 1737

Son of a Flemish painter, second-place *Grand Prix* in 1696, Vleughels spent some time in Italy at the beginning of the century (between 1706 and 1713). *Académicien* in 1716, acquainted with Watteau (the question of the artistic relation between the two artists is an open one), he became Director of the Académie de France à Rome in 1724; one of his tasks was to transfer the

Académie to the Palazzo Mancini in 1725, the year of his election to the Accademia di San Luca. In 1731 he married Marie-Thérèse Gosset, sister-in-law of Panini. First among the great directors of the Académie de France in the eighteenth century, he was esteemed by the many *pensionnaires* he was in charge of (for example, Subleyras, Natoire, Carle Van Loo, Dandré-Bardon, and Boucher).

Vleughels is an excellent painter, particularly at ease with small pictures on copper. True, he gets his inspiration from the great masters, Veronese above all, whom he even imitates, (Mariette has already reproached him for this; 1851–1860, VI (1850), p. 90). His pictures, however, rich in lively details and in spirited notes, are "pleasant", their colors are natty, and generally speaking, well-turned. One easily understands the success he had in the eighteenth century among the most informed amateurs.

The studies of M. L. Bataille (1928) and of ourselves (1973) that are devoted to the painter will lose most of their interest after Bernard Hercenberg's monograph (to be published, 1975).

117 *Les noces de Cana,* 1728

Oil on copper, 37.5 x 51.5 cm / 14¾ x 20¼ in.

Monogrammed lower right, on the balustrade: *N.V.F.R.*, and dated on the tablecloth to the left: *1728*

PROVENANCE: Dupille de Saint-Séverin sale, February 1785, no. 288 — formerly, the Princes von Pfalz-Zweibrücken.

BIBLIOGRAPHY: Rosenberg, 1973, p. 144, fig. 16.

There are for this painting and its pendant, the *Repas chez Simon,* painted a year earlier, some beautiful studies (oil on paper as well as drawings at the Cabinet des Dessins, Louvre). As is usual with Vleughels, some of the figures (the man, seen in profile, standing to the right; the other in the background, seen from the back; the dog) are directly quoted from Veronese. Vleughels never ceased to get his inspiration from Veronese — even in a work like this — in which the format is unusual, and which was painted four years after he had arrived in Rome.

The charm and originality of the piece lie in the numerous details and in the spirited notes the artist places throughout his little painting, leaving us the pleasure of discovering and listing them all.

Bayerisches Staatsgemäldesammlungen, Munich (deposited in Bayreuth)

PIERRE-JACQUES VOLAIRE
Toulon 1729–Naples before 1802 or Lerici 1790

Grandson and son of painters from Toulon, Pierre-Jacques Volaire, called le chevalier Volaire, was trained locally. His career really began only with the arrival of Joseph Vernet in Toulon in 1754. Vernet was sent there by Louis XV to paint the various ports of France. Vernet took Volaire as his assistant and Volaire escorted him for eight years throughout France during his "pérégrinations portuaires". In 1763 Volaire was again in Toulon, and the next year in Italy; he never left the latter. He stayed in Rome until 1769 (became a member of the Accademia di San Luca in 1764) and in Naples. Volaire rapidly specialized in views of Vesuvius erupting in moonlight. This subject gave him a chance to contrast the flaming colors of the lava with both the cold shades of night and the reflections in the water.

Volaire exhibited in 1779, 1783 and 1786 at the *Salon de la Correspondance* in Paris. In 1784 he became a *membre correspondant* of the Académie de Marseille. Two years later he tried unsuccessfully to sell some of his paintings to Louis XVI. That the artist died in Naples before 1802 is usually advanced; one also has the more seductive theory that the "Voler peintre" who died in Lerici near Genoa in 1790 (see Montaiglon and Guiffrey, eds., XVI, 1907, p. 89 and p. 90 note 2), could well be the specialist of the volcanic eruptions. Volaire also executed a beautiful series of Italian views, some pastels and an ensemble of drawings today in San Francisco and Chicago.

Jacques Foucart's biographical entry in the catalogue of the exhibition *De David à Delacroix* (Paris, Grand Palais) adequately sums up what we know of the life and work of an artist otherwise seldom studied.

118 *L'éruption du Vésuve* PL. 125

Oil on canvas, 75 x 169 cm / 29½ x 66½ in.

Signed lower left: *Volaire p.*

PROVENANCE: Probably seized during the Revolution; the Marquis de Pestre de Senelle owned one painting of this kind; see *Nouvelles Archives de l'Art Français,* 1902, p. 336, no. 16 — transferred from the Louvre to Le Havre in 1876.

BIBLIOGRAPHY: Foucart in Paris, Grand Palais, pp. 666–69.

It would be impossible to make a list of all the paintings of this subject done by Volaire: every amateur cabinet included one. It is also impossible to establish firmly the date of this painting. Was it done before 1774, the limiting date of our exhibition? One should remember that a particularly spectacular eruption of this volcano took place in 1771. It was the subject of the painting owned by the Comte d'Orsay, shown at the *Salon de la Correspondance* in 1779 in Paris. In any case, the Havre painting is close, in format as well as in composition, to the pictures in Toulouse and Richmond, (recently shown in Paris). Only the attitudes of the silhouettes against the erupting volcano change from one painting to the next. The second part of the eighteenth century witnessed a growing scientific interest in natural phenomena, and artists enjoyed representing the picturesque or dramatic manifestations of nature: tempests or waterfalls. Volaire is only one among many representatives of this trend, which found followers in England (Wright of Derby was in Naples in 1774) as well as in Germany (C. D. Friedrich). Volaire's idea, too often repeated by himself, is, however, original: he plays with the contrast between the warm colors of the volcanic eruption and the cold shades of the moonlight over the bay of Naples.

Le Havre, Musée des Beaux-Arts

ANTOINE WATTEAU

Valenciennes 1684–Nogent-sur-Marne 1721

Watteau's father placed him in an apprenticeship in Valenciennes with Jacques-Albert Gérin. At the very beginning of the century, he went to Paris and worked in the studios of Gillot and Audran. In 1709 he tried unsuccessfully to obtain the *Prix de Rome* (an artist named Grison won it that year) and presented, three years later, several pictures to the Académie, after which he was *agréé*. In 1717, he was received by the Académie in the category of *fêtes galantes*, a category created especially for him. (*Pélerinage à l'île de Cythère*, Louvre). After a brief trip to England in 1720, he lived in the house of the dealer Gersaint for whom he painted the famous *Enseigne*. He died near Paris, in the arms of Gersaint, who described him as "restless and moody . . . obstinate in his whims, free in spirit but virtuous in his conduct, impatient and shy . . . always unhappy with himself and others."

It is certain that Watteau enjoyed, during the eighteenth century, a wide reputation through his paintings, his admirable drawings and the engravings Jullienne had done after his works. It is also certain that the importance given to him at that time was far from being the one he has had for a century in the history of European painting.

The French edition of Ettore Camesasca's *Watteau* (1970) lists all the books and articles devoted to the many aspects of his art.

119 *La perspective* PL. 13

Oil on canvas, 47 x 56 cm / 18½ x 22 in.

PROVENANCE: "Mr. Guenon", 1729 — Saint ("Painter of miniatures") sale, May 4, 1846, no. 56; 3805 francs — Sir Richard Wallace — Lady Wallace — Sir John Murray Scott — sale, Christie's, June 27, 1913, no. 138 — Agnew — A. Evans, as early as 1924.

BIBLIOGRAPHY: Adhémar and Huyghe, 1950, p. 3940, no. 111, pl. 56 — Camesasca and Rosenberg, 1970, no. 117 — Ferré, 1972, B. 52.

Unanimously accepted and usually dated 1715 (we believe it to be slightly later), this painting was engraved in 1729 by L. Crépy with an inversion in the dimensions. It then belonged to "Mr. Guenon" (probably one of the painters of ornaments). According to a note by Mariette (1851–1860, VI (1854–1856), p. 110) and the lettering of an engraving by Caylus, the painting was inspired by Crozat's garden in Montmorency and represents the façade of his château (on Crozat, see Stuffman, 1968). As rightly pointed out by the writer of the entry in the recent *Rubenism* exhibition (Brown University and Rhode Island School of Design, no. 45), it is Rubens from whom Watteau gets his inspiration in this painting, for both the figures and the landscape. As is often true of Watteau's paintings — incidentally, what is the subject of this one? — the protagonists turn their backs to us. They talk, the youngest play together, they listen to a guitar player under abundant autumnal foliage. With these few elements, Watteau is able to create an atmosphere of soft and nostalgic reverie.

Boston, Museum of Fine Arts, Maria Antoinette Evans Fund

120 *La rêveuse* PL. 17

Oil on panel, 24 x 16.5 cm / 9½ x 6½ in.

PROVENANCE: Comte du Barry; sale, November 21, 1774, no. 132 — Marquis de Montesquiou; sale, December 9, 1788, no. 214 — Morny — Jules Burat; sale, April 28, 1885, no. 109; as Lancret! — Laurent-Richard sale, May 28, 1886, no. 29; as Lancret — acquired then by Blumenthal, 6200 francs — acquired from Wildenstein in 1961.

BIBLIOGRAPHY: Adhémar and Huyghe, 1950, p. 219, no. 145 — Camesasca and Rosenberg, 1970, no. 165.

In spite of the engraving by P. Aveline (1729), this painting has not always been considered to be by Watteau. P. Mantz (in Paris, Galerie Petite, *Collection de feu M. Jules Burat,* 1885; followed by G. Wildenstein, 1924, no. 704, fig. 202) attributed it to Lancret. Today the work is unanimously recognized as one by Watteau, dated around 1717. Fragonard executed a drawing of this composition, probably after the engraving (Ananoff, 1963, II, no. 1123, fig. 325). The identification of the sitter is more difficult. I. S. Nemilova (1963) thinks it is *La Desmares.* The catalogue of the Montesquiou sale describes a figure in "Turkish costume".

In this small panel, Watteau shows an untroubled facility and a natural elegance for which he is so much admired today.

The Art Institute of Chicago, Mr. and Mrs. Lewis Larned Coburn Fund

121 *Le mezzetin* PL. 21

Oil on canvas, 55.5 x 43 cm / 21¾ x 17 in.

PROVENANCE: Probably Jean de Jullienne before 1735; his sale, March 30, 1767, no. 253 — Catherine II of Russia — Leningrad, Hermitage until 1931 — acquired from Wildenstein in 1934.

BIBLIOGRAPHY: Adhémar and Huyghe, 1950, pp. 28, 47, 102, 119, 152, 186, 230, no. 206, pl. 144 — Sterling, 1955, pp. 105–08, with figure — Camesasca and Rosenberg, 1970, no. 193 — Ferré, 1972, A 37.

Engraved by Benoît Audran and usually dated around 1718–1720, this painting, with its illustrious provenance, ranks among the most perfect accomplishments of Watteau. The Metropolitan Museum also owns an admirable preparatory study for this composition. The model is one of the character types common to the *Commedia dell'arte,* the sentimental servant in love. Some have tried to identify him with a famous Italian actor in Paris at the time, or with the art dealer Sirois, but unsuccessfully. "The disconsolate *mezzetin* is serenading a beautiful, insensitive woman, personified by the statue turning its back to the virtuoso . . . An aristocratic reserve covers the excess of expression," wrote Mirimonde in his study on Watteau's musical subjects (1961, p. 253).

Watteau adds, to the elegance of the nervous hands and to the delicate facial expression, a further refinement in the harmony of the greens and lilac roses which is reinforced by the black and yellow accents of the guitar.

New York, The Metropolitan Museum of Art, Munsey Fund

FRENCH SCHOOL, XVIIIth CENTURY

122 *La chapelle du calvaire à l'église Saint-Roch à Paris* PL. 107

Oil on canvas, 128 x 97 cm / 50½ x 38¼ in.

PROVENANCE: Gift of M. Bertil Orn, Consul General of Sweden, 1955.

This painting represents the *chapelle du Calvaire* in the Church of Saint-Roch, Paris (see Doyen, no. 30). Dézallier d'Argenville described the chapel: "It depicts the Christ on the Cross by Michel Anguier and a Magdalene, at the foot of the cross. On the mountain top, in the hollow of a niche, they are illuminated by a celestial light, set against a sky with banks of clouds, painted by M. Machy . . . At the bottom of the mountain, between two doors carved into the rocks, there is a deep blue marble altar with nothing but two urns as ornaments from which rises the smoke of the incense. In the middle of the altar, there is a tabernacle made of a broken column on top of which various implements of the Passion are grouped. The architecture of this altar and the sanctuary of the *chapelle de la Vierge* are by M. Boullée" (1778 edition, pp. 128–29). The *chapelle du calvaire,* one of the most innovative creations in Paris during the second half of the eighteenth century, was begun by Boullée in 1754 (see Pérouse de Montclos, 1969), modified under the Empire, and entirely remodeled in 1849.

Who actually executed the painting which represents it? It is usually attributed to Pierre-Antoine Demachy (1723–1807), the painter of the sky behind Christ and also the author of a view of the *chapelle de la Vierge à Saint-Roch,* exhibited at the Salon of 1771 (no. 57). In any case, the Salon picture cannot be confused with the Pau painting, which differs from it in size and subject. It is also clear that Demachy has never painted anything so vigorously, so strongly organized and so skillfully illusionistic. One could, but only on stylistic grounds and very cautiously, suggest Hubert Robert who, after his return from Italy in 1765, liked to execute monumental, almost monochromatic works, with this type of sepulchral light. In addition, the three worshipers seen from the back are firmly painted (looking almost like sculptures) in a manner characteristic of the artist.

In any case, the painter of this canvas has tried to do homage to one of the most audacious architectural realizations of the time, one which showed the pre-eminence of Paris in this field.

Pau, Musée des Beaux-Arts

FRENCH SCHOOL, XVIIIth CENTURY

123 *Morphée* PL. 117

Oil on canvas, 97 x 130 cm / 38¼ x 51⅛ in.

PROVENANCE: Sale, Paris, Hôtel Drouot, December 2, 1910, no. 13; attributed to Fragonard — formerly Octave Linet, Tours — sale, Paris, Palais Galliéra, March 23, 1963, no. 16; attributed to Boucher — Cailleux — acquired in 1963.

BIBLIOGRAPHY: Francis, 1966, pp. 66–73, with color plate.

Attributed to Fragonard, published as Brenet by F. Cummings (Paris, Grand Palais, 1974–1975, p. 38), we believe that this painting is by Jean-Bernard Restout (1732–1796), son of the great Restout. Jean-Bernard's portrait, dated 1736, is in Stockholm. He showed a *Sommeil figure d'étude* at the Salon of 1771 (no. 137), the dimensions of which are precisely those of the Cleveland picture. It is possibly the same picture as the *Morphée,* no. 144, shown at the *Salon de la Correspondance* (see Pahin de La Blancherie, 1783).

Two things make the attribution certain. First, while comparing it to Houdon's *Morphée,* which was shown at the same Salon (no. 279; Houdon's reception piece of the same subject, 1777; see Louvre, *Musées de France,* June 1950), Diderot's comments about the picture were severe ("mine de supplicié"). Second, one only has to compare this work with other attested compositions by J. B. Restout.[1]

In 1771 Restout had just been made professor at the Académie Royale. He was *agréé* and then received in 1769, but ceased to exhibit his pictures at the Salon after the Académie's decision to submit the works of the *académiciens* to a jury formed by them. He played an important political rôle during the Revolution.

If the picture has been perfectly well studied from the iconographical viewpoint (Francis, 1966; New York, Wildenstein, no. 15; should one see in this picture a *Morphée* or an allegorical study of sleep with the poppy, and bird wings replacing the traditional butterfly wings?), the date of it, however, remains to be established: was it painted in 1771 or in Rome several years earlier, in which case it would be one of those anatomical studies the *pensionnaires* were obliged to send to Paris so the *académiciens* could judge them? One should remember, for instance, that the painting by Brenet at the Worcester Art Museum (no. 12), where the artist transformed what was originally an anatomical study, into an *Endymion,* was probably another example of that sort of painting. Other examples are known, by David (Montpellier and Cherbourg) as well as by Ingres (Paris, Ecole des Beaux-Arts).

The Cleveland Museum of Art, Purchase, Leonard C. Hanna Jr. Bequest

[1] *Saint Bruno,* 1763, Louvre; *Les Saisons,* 1767; four pictures, Trianon; sketches in a private collection, Paris; *Anacréon,* several versions, see *Gazette des Beaux-Arts,* October 1968 and *Bulletin du musée national de Varsovie,* 1970, no. 1; *Saint Louis débarquant en Egypte,* 1774, Ecole Militaire, Paris; pictures in Quimper, 1777, Musée Magnin, Dijon (this one with a somewhat dubious attribution); churches of Brunoy and Cérilly; several portraits, Versailles, Dijon, A. Marie collection in Rouen. Furthermore, James Rubin has called our attention to an *Académie d'homme,* a study for this painting, in a private collection, Princeton, New Jersey. One should also note Cochin's remark to Marigny in a letter of July 15, 1766 (see *Nouvelles Archives de l'art français,* 1904, p. 51) which justifies the long-maintained attribution of this work to Fragonard: "Restout est coloriste harmonieux, fera de l'effet et sera, je pense, plus analogue avec la manière de Fragonard."

BIBLIOGRAPHY

Adhémar, H. and Huyghe, R., *Watteau, sa vie, son oeuvre,* Paris, 1950.

Ageville, M. d', *Eloge historique de Michel-François d'André-Bardon,* Marseilles, 1783.

Ananoff, A., *L'oeuvre dessiné de Jean-Honoré Fragonard, (1732–1806). Catalogue raisonné,* 4 vols., Paris, 1961–1970.

Argens, J. B. de Boyer d', *Réflexions critiques sur les différentes écoles de peinture,* Paris, 1752.

Arnaud, O., "Subleyras 1699 à 1749," in Louis Dimier, *Les peintres français du XVIIIème siècle,* Paris and Brussels, 1930, II, pp. 49–92.

Baré, "Edelinck (Nicolas-Etienne)," *Le Bulletin des Beaux-Arts,* II (1884–1885), pp. 37–39.

Bataille, M. L., "Tournières 1668 à 1752," in Louis Dimier, *Les peintres français du XVIIIème siècle,* Paris and Brussels, 1928, I, pp. 227–243.

———, "Vleughels 1668 à 1737," in Louis Dimier, *Les peintres français du XVIIIème siècle,* Paris and Brussels, 1928, I, pp. 245–260.

———, "Lajoue 1686 à 1761," in Louis Dimier, *Les peintres français du XVIIIème siècle,* Paris and Brussels, 1930, II, pp. 347–361.

Baudicour, P. de, *Le peintre-graveur français continué,* 2 vols., Paris, 1859.

Beau, M., *La collection des dessins d'Hubert Robert au musée de Valence,* Lyons, Audin, 1968.

Beaurepaire, Ch. de, "Notes historiques sur le musée de peinture de la ville de Rouen." *Précis analytique des travaux de l'Académie des Sciences, Belles Lettres et Arts de Rouen,* 1852–1853.

Bellier de la Chavignerie, E., "Notes pour servir l'histoire de l'Exposition de la Jeunesse," *Revue Universelle des Arts,* XIX (1864), pp. 38–67.

———, "Les artistes français du XVIIIème siècle oubliés et dédaignés. Pahin de la Blancherie et le Salon de la Correspondance," *Revue Universelle des Arts,* XIX (1864), pp. 203–224, 249–267, 354–367; XX (1865), pp. 46–58, 116–127, 189–195, 253–262, 320–329, 402–427; XXI (1865), pp. 34–48, 87–112, 175–190.

——— and Auvray, L., *Dictionnaire général des artistes de l'école française depuis l'origine des arts du dessin jusqu'à nos jours,* 2 vols., Paris, 1882–1885.

Belleudy, J., *J. S. Duplessis, peintre du roi (1725–1802),* Chartres, 1913.

Benisovich, M., "Sales of French Collections of Paintings in the United States during the first half of the nineteenth century," *The Art Quarterly,* XIX (1956), pp. 288–301.

Berckenhagen, E., Colombier, P. du, Kühn, M., and Poensgen, G., *Antoine Pesne,* Berlin, 1958.

Besançon, Musée des Beaux-Arts, *Collection Pierre-*

Adrian Pâris, Besançon, ("Inventaire Général des Dessins des Musées de Province," vol. I), Paris, 1957.

Billioud, J., "Un peintre de types populaires: Françoise Duparc, de Marseille (1726–1778)," *Gazette des Beaux-Arts,* XX (1938), pp. 173–184.

Blondel, J. F., *Architecture françoise, ou recueil des plans, élévations des églises, maisons royales, palais, hôtels et édifices les plus considérables de Paris, ainsi que les chateaux et maisons de plaisance situés aux environs de la France. . . ,* 4 vols., Paris, 1752–1756.

Bottineau, Y., *L'art de cour dans l'Espagne de Philippe V, 1700–1746,* Bordeaux, 1960.

Boucher, F., "A propos d'une récente acquisition du musée du Louvre. Gillot et Watteau," *Gazette des Beaux-Arts,* VIII (1923), pp. 165–178.

Bouquier, G., "Critique du Salon de 1775," *La Revue du Louvre et des Musées de France,* XXV (1975), pp. 95–104.

Bourin, H., "P. P. A. Robert (de Séry), peintre du cardinal de Rohan (1686–1733)," *Revue historique ardennaise,* 1907, pp. 129–193.

Boyer, F., "Catalogue raisonné de l'oeuvre de Charles Natoire," *Bulletin de la Société d'Histoire de l'Art Français, 1946–1949,* 1949, pp. 31–106.

Brière, G., "Remarques sur des portraits par Nicolas de Largillierre contenus dans la collection La Caze au Louvre," *Bulletin de la Société de l'Histoire de l'Art Français, 1918,* 1919, pp. 144–148.

———, "Detroy 1679 à 1752," in Louis Dimier, *Les peintres français du XVIIIème siècle,* Paris and Brussels, 1930, II, pp. 1–48.

Bronze, A., *Mémoire sur Simon Julien peintre d'histoire,* Toulon, 1862.

Brookner, A., *Greuze. The Rise and Fall of an Eighteenth Century Phenomenon,* London, 1972.

Caffieri, see Dussieux, L., . . .

Cailleux, J., "Personnages de Watteau dans l'oeuvre de Lajoue," *Bulletin de la Société de l'Histoire de l'Art Français, 1956,* 1957, pp. 101–111.

———, "Les artistes français du XVIIIème siècle et Rembrandt," in *Etudes d'Art français offertes à Charles Sterling,* Paris, 1975, pp. 287–305.

——— and Roland-Michel, M., *Hubert Robert, Louis Moreau,* [ex. cat.], Paris, 1958.

——— and Roland-Michel, M., *Watteau et sa génération,* [ex. cat.], Paris, 1968.

Caix de Saint-Aymour, Cte de, *Les Boullongne,* Paris, 1919.

Camesasca, E. and Rosenberg, P., *Watteau,* Paris, 1970.

Cantinelli, R., *Jacques-Louis David, 1748–1825,* Paris and Brussels, 1930.

Carritt, D., "Mr. Fouquier's Chardins," *The Burlington Magazine,* CXVI (1974), pp. 502–509.

Caylus, see Dussieux, L., . . .

Châtelet, A., 1964, see Thuillier, J., . . .

———, *Cent chefs d'oeuvre du musée de Lille,* Lille, 1970.

Chiego, W. J., "A boudoir scene by Le Prince," *The Toledo Museum of Art Museum News,* XVII, I (1974), pp. 11–14.

Colomer, Cl., *Hyacinthe Rigaud 1659–1743,* Perpignan, 1973.

Compiègne, Musée National de Compiègne, *Paysages de François Desportes (1661–1743): Etudes peintes d'après nature,* [ex.cat.], Compiègne, 1961.

Compin, I., "Un portrait de Charles-Antoine Coypel au musée du Louvre," *La Revue du Louvre et des Musées de France,* XIX (1969), pp. 93–97.

Courajod, L., *L'Ecole Royale des élèves protégés, précédé d'une étude sur le caractère de l'enseignement de l'art français aux différentes époques de son histoire,* Paris, 1874.

Cousin de la Contamine, *Mémoire pour servir à la vie de M. de Favanne, peintre ordinaire du Roi et Recteur de l'Académie royale de peinture et de sculpture,* Paris, 1753. Reprinted in *Revue Universelle des Arts,* XIV (1861), pp. 245–268.

Dacier, E., *Catalogues de ventes et livrets de Salons illustrés par Gabriel de Saint-Aubin,* 7 vols., Paris, 1909–1919.

———, "Gillot 1673 à 1722," in Louis Dimier, *Les peintres français du XVIIIème siècle,* Paris and Brussels, 1928, I, pp. 157–215.

———, *Gabriel de Saint-Aubin, peintre, dessinateur et graveur, 1724–1780,* 2 vols., Paris, 1929–1931.

——— and Vuaflart, A., *Jean de Jullienne et les gravures de Watteau au XVIIIème siècle,* Paris, 1922–1929.

Dandré-Bardon, *Vie de Carle Van Loo,* Paris, 1765.

David, J.-L.-J., *Le peintre Louis David 1748–1825. Souvenirs et documents inédits,* Paris, 1880. Plates: Paris, 1882.

Davies, M., *National Gallery Catalogues. French School,* 2nd. revised edition, London, 1957.

Detroy, P., "François de Troy 1645–1730," *Etudes d'Art publiées par le Musée National des Beaux-Arts d'Alger,* XI–XII (1955–1956), pp. 213–258.

Dézallier d'Argenville, A.-J., *Abrégé de la vie des plus fameux peintres avec leurs portraits gravés en taille-douce, les indications de leurs principaux ouvrages, quelques réflexions sur leurs caractères, et la manière de connoître les dessins et les tableaux des grands maîtres,* 4 vols., Paris, 1762 edition.

Dézallier d'Argenville, A.-N., *Voyage pittoresque de Paris; . . .* Paris, 1778 edition.

Didot, A. F., *Les Drevet (Pierre, Pierre-Imbert et Claude); Catalogue raisonné de leur oeuvre,* Paris, 1876.

Dimier, L., "Antoine Coypel 1661–1722," in Louis Dimier, *Les peintres français du XVIIIème siècle,* Paris and Brussels, 1928, I, pp. 93–155.

———, *Les peintres français du XVIIIème siècle,* 2 vols., Paris and Brussels, 1928–1930.

Doria, Cte A., *Louis Tocqué,* Paris, 1929.

Duplessis, G., *Catalogue de la collection de pièces sur les Beaux-Arts imprimées et manuscrites recueillies par Pierre-Jean Mariette, Charles-Nicolas Cochin et M. Deloynes. . . ,* Paris, 1881.

Dussieux, L., Soulié, E., Chennevières, Ph. de, Mantz P., and Montaiglon, A. de, *Mémoires inédits sur la vie et les ouvrages des membres de l'Académie Royale de peinture et de sculpture publiés d'après les manuscrits conservés à l'Ecole impériale des Beaux-Arts,* 2 vols., Paris, 1854–1856.

Ebbinge-Wubben, J. C., Salm, C., Sterling, Ch., and Heinemann, R., *The Thyssen-Bornemisza Collection,* 2 vols., Villa Favorita, Castagnola, and Ticono, 1969.

Edinburgh, National Gallery of Scotland, *Catalogue of Paintings and Sculpture,* Edinburgh, 1957.

Eidelberg, M., "Watteau's 'La Boudeuse'," *The Burlington Magazine,* CXI (1969), pp. 275–278.

Eisenberg, M., "A chinoiserie by Jacques Vigouroux-Duplessis," to be published in 1977 in *The Bulletin of the Walters Art Gallery.*

Engerand, F., *Inventaire des tableaux commandés et achetés par la Direction des Bâtiments du Roi (1709–1792),* Paris, 1901.

Ericksen, S., "Marigny and *Le Goût Grec,*" *The Burlington Magazine,* CIV, I (1962), pp. 96–101.

Estournet, O., "La famille des Hallé," *Réunion des Sociétés des Beaux-Arts des Départements,* XXIX (1905), pp. 71–236.

Faré M., *La nature morte en France. Son histoire et son évolution du XVIIème au XXème siècle,* Geneva, 1962.

———, "Un peintre indépendant: Jacques Courtin de l'Académie Royale (1672–1752)," *Gazette des Beaux-Arts,* LXVII (1966), pp. 293–320.

Ferré, J., and others, *Watteau,* 4 vols., Madrid, 1972.

Fierens, P., "Au Musée Carnavalet. La Deuxième Exposition de Chefs-d'Oeuvre des Musées de Province," *Bulletin des Musées de France,* V (1933), pp. 50–64.

Florisoone, M., see Paris, Orangerie des Tuileries, *David. . .*

Fontaine, A., *Les collections de l'Académie Royale de peinture et de sculpture,* Paris, 1910. Re-edited in 1930.

Fosca, F., *Liotard (1702–1789),* Paris, 1928.

———, *La vie, les voyages et les oeuvres de Jean-Etienne Liotard, citoyen de Genève, dit le peintre turc,* Lausanne and Paris, 1956.

Francis, H. S., "Two portraits by Aved and Gros," *The Cleveland Museum of Art Bulletin,* LI (1964), pp. 196–205.

———, "Jean-Honoré Fragonard *Morpheus,*" *The Cleveland Museum of Art Bulletin,* LIII (1966), pp. 66–73.

Gabillot, C., *Les Hüet,* Paris, 1892.

———, *Hubert Robert et son temps,* Paris, 1895.

———, "Les trois Drouais," *Gazette des Beaux-Arts,* XXXV (1906), pp. 246–258.

———, "Alexis Grimou peintre français 1678–1733," *Gazette des Beaux-Arts,* V (1911), pp. 157–172, 309–323, 412–426.

Gaehtgens, Th., "J. M. Vien et les peintures de la Légende de sainte Marthe à Tarascon," *Revue de l'Art,* XXIII (1974), pp. 64–69.

Gallet, M., "L'architecte Pierre de Vigny 1690–1722; ses constructions, son esthétique," *Gazette des Beaux-Arts,* LXXXII (1973), pp. 263–286.

Gaston-Dreyfus, Ph., "Catalogue raisonné de l'oeuvre de Nicolas-Bernard Lépicié," *Bulletin de la Société de l'Histoire de l'Art Français, 1922,* 1922, pp. 134–283.

Gauthier, J., "Le bisontin Donat Nonnotte, peintre de portraits (1708–1785)," *Réunion des Sociétés des Beaux-Arts des Départements,* XXVI (1902), pp. 510–540.

———, "Donat Nonnotte de Besançon peintre de portraits," *Mémoires de la Société d'Émulation du Doubs,* 1902, pp. 43–56.

Ghent, Museum voor Schone Kunsten, *Gent. Duizend Jaar Kunst en Cultuur,* [ex. cat.], Ghent, 1975.

Goncourt, E. and J. de, "Publication du livre de raison de Louis Lagrenée," *L'Art,* IV (1877), pp. 25–26, 136–141, 255–260. Reprinted in *Portraits intimes du XVIIIème siècle. Etudes nouvelles d'après les lettres autographes et les documents inédits,* Paris, 1878 edition, pp. 323–362.

———, *L'Art du XVIIIème siècle,* 3 vols., Paris, 1909 edition.

Gougenot, see Dussieux, L., . . .

Grimm, le Baron de, Diderot, Raynal and Meister, *Correspondance littéraire, philosophique et critique (1753–1790),* 16 vols., Paris, 1877–1882.

Guiffrey, J. J., *Notes et documents inédits sur les expositions du XVIIIème siècle recueillis et mis en ordre par. . . ,* Paris, 1873.

———, *Table générale des artistes ayant exposé aux salons du XVIIIème siècle,* Paris, 1873.

———, "Quittance d'un tableau du peintre Pierre Parrocel pour l'église de Cavaillon suivi d'un rapport de

Sabatier sur les monuments des sciences et arts de cette ville (1709–1794?)," *Nouvelles Archives de l'Art Français,* series 2, vol. I (1879), pp. 156–162.
———, "Histoire de l'Académie de Saint Luc," *Archives de l'Art Français,* IX (1915), pp. 1–516.
Halbout, M., *Jean-Baptiste-Marie Pierre,* mémoire de l'Ecole du Louvre, 1970.
Hautecoeur, L., *Greuze,* Paris, 1913.
———, *Louis David,* Paris, 1954.
Hédou, J., *Jean Leprince et son oeuvre, suive de nombreux documents inédits,* Paris, 1879.
Held, J. S., *Museo de Arte de Ponce. Catalogue I: Paintings of the European and American Schools,* Ponce, Puerto Rico, 1965.
Held, J., "Michel-Ange Houasse in Spanien," *Münchner Jahrbuch,* XIX (1968), pp. 185–206.
Hercenberg, B., *Nicolas Vleughels. L'artiste, le directeur de l'Académie de France à Rome,* to be published in 1975.
Hérold, M., "A propos du 'Miracle des Ardens' de Gabriel-François Doyen (1726–1806)," *La Revue du Louvre et des Musées de France,* XVIII (1968), pp. 65–72.
———, *G. F. Doyen. Peintre d'histoire 1726–1806,* 2 vols. and Plates, thèse de recherches IIIème cycle, University of Paris, 1973.
Hourticq, L., "L'Atelier de François Desportes," *Gazette des Beaux-Arts,* II (1920), pp. 117–136.
Huard, G., "Delyen. Env. 1684 à 1761," in Louis Dimier, *Les peintres français du XVIIIème siècle,* Paris and Brussels, 1928, I, pp. 261–266.
———,"Nattier 1685 à 1766," in Louis Dimier, *Les peintres français du XVIIIème siècle,* Paris and Brussels, 1930, II, pp. 93–133.
Ingersoll-Smouse, F., "Charles-Antoine Coypel (1694–1752)," *Revue de l'Art Ancien et Moderne,* XXXVII (1920), pp. 143–154, 285–292.
———, "Pièces inédites de collections particulières: trois portraits des enfants de Joseph Vernet par N.-B. Lépicié," *Revue de l'Art Ancien et Moderne,* XL (1921), pp. 323–329.
———, "Nicolas-Bernard Lépicié," *Revue de l'Art Ancien et Moderne,* XLIII (1923), pp. 39–43, 125–136, 365–378; XLVI (1924), pp. 122–130, 217–228; L (1926), pp. 253–276; LIV (1927), pp. 175–186.
———, *Joseph Vernet, peintre de marine, 1714–1789. Etude critique suivie d'un catalogue raisonné de son oeuvre peint,* 2 vols., Paris, 1926.
———, *Pater,* Paris, 1928.
Jamieson, I., *Charles-Antoine Coypel, Premier Peintre de Louis XV et Auteur Dramatique (1694–1752),* Paris, 1930.
Jamot, P., "Gillot and Watteau: a study of a new acquisition of the Louvre," *The Burlington Magazine,* XLIII (1923), pp. 130–136.
Jean-Richard, P., *François Boucher. Gravures et dessins provenant du Cabinet des dessins et de la Collection Edmond de Rothschild au Musée du Louvre* [ex. cat.], Paris, 1971.
Joppien, R., *Philippe-Jacques de Loutherbourg, RA, 1740–1812. Catalogue of an exhibition held at Kenwood, the Iveagh Bequest,* London, 1973.
Julien de Parme, "Histoire de Julien de Parme racontée par lui-même," *L'Artiste,* I (1862), pp. 80–88.
Kalnein, W. and Levey, M., *Art and Architecture of the Eighteenth century in France,* London, 1973.
Kansas City, William Rockhill Nelson Gallery of Art and Mary Atkins Museum of Fine Arts, *The Century of Mozart,* [ex. cat.], Kansas City, 1956.
Kircher, G., "Chardins Doppelgänger Roland de la Porte," *Der Cicerone,* XX (1928), pp. 95–101.
La Font de Saint-Yenne, *L'ombre du grand Colbert, le Louvre, et la ville de Paris, dialogue. Réflexions sur quelques causes de l'état présent de la peinture en France, avec quelques lettres de l'auteur à ce sujet,* n.p., 1752.
Lastic, G. de, "Des découvertes à faire. Les devants de cheminée," *Connaissance des Arts,* XXXIX (1955), pp. 26–31.
———, "Nicolas de Largillierre peintre de natures mortes," *La Revue du Louvre et des Musées de France,* XVIII (1968), pp. 233–240.
Le Blanc, J.-B., *Lettre sur l'exposition des ouvrages de peinture, sculpture, . . . de l'année 1747,* Paris, 1747. Reprinted: Geneva, 1970.
Leclair, A., *Louis-Jacques Durameau (1733–1796),* mémoire de maîtrise, 1970–1972.
Le Gentil, C., *Notice sur les tableaux des églises d'Arras,* Arras, 1871.
Lépicié, F. B., *Vies des premiers peintres du roi depuis M. Le Brun jusqu'à présent,* 2 vols., Paris, 1752.
Lespinasse, P., "L'art français et la Suède de 1688 à 1816 (suite.)," *Bulletin de la Société de l'Histoire de l'Art Français, 1912,* 1912, pp. 207–245.
"Lettres sur l'Académie royale de sculpture et de peinture et sur le salon de 1777. Deuxième Lettre. Suite coup d'oeil sur l'Ecole francaise," *Revue Universelle des Arts,* XXII (1865–1866), pp. 213–233.
Levey, see Kalnein, W., . . .
Levitine, G., "The Eighteenth-Century Rediscovery of Alexis Grimou and the Emergence of the Proto-Bohemian Image of the French Artist," *Eighteenth Century Studies,* II (1968–1969), pp. 58–76.
Lex, L., "Gabriel François Moreau, évêque de Mâcon

(1763–1790)," *Réunion des Sociétes des Beaux-Arts des Départements,* XXII (1898), pp. 606–639.

Locquin, J., *Catalogue raisonné de l'oeuvre de Jean-Baptiste Oudry peintre du roi (1686–1755),* Paris, 1912.

———, *La peinture d'histoire en France de 1747 à 1785. Etude sur l'évolution des idées artistiques dans la seconde moitié du XVIIIème siècle,* Paris, 1912.

London, Royal Academy of Arts, *French Art, an illustrated Souvenir of the exhibition of French art at the Royal Academy of Arts,* [ex. cat.], London, 1932.

———, *France in the Eighteenth Century,* [ex. cat.], London, 1968.

Lossky, B., *Inventaire des collections publiques françaises. Tours. Peintures du XVIIIème siècle,* Paris, 1962.

———, "Peintures peu connues du XVIIIème siècle au château de Fontainebleau," *Bulletin de la Société de l'Histoire de l'Art Français, 1966,* 1967, pp. 177–188.

"Louis XV à la chasse, ses trophées de chasse peints par Oudry et Bachelier," *Connaissance des Arts,* CLXXXVIII (1967), pp. 110–115.

Lugt, F., *Répertoire des Catalogues de Ventes Publiques,* 3 vols., The Hague, 1938–1964.

Luna, J. L., "M. A. Houasse," *Reales Sitos,* XLII (1974), pp. 170–176.

Lundberg, G. W., *Röslin Liv och Verk,* 2 vols., Malmö, 1957.

Mantz, P., see Paris, Galerie Georges Petit, . . .

Marandel, J. P., *French Oil Sketches from an English Private Collection,* [ex. cat.], Houston: The Museum of Fine Arts, 1973–1975.

Marcus, Cl.-G., "Alexis Grimou (1678–1733), peintre de portraits," *Art et Curiosité,* July-September, 1969, pp. 1–8, 21–26.

Mariette, P. J., *Abécédario de P. J. Mariette et autres notes inédits de cet amateur sur les arts et les artistes. Ouvrage publié d'après les manuscrits autographes conservés au cabinet des estampes de la Bibliothèque impériale, et annoté par mm. Ph. de Chennevières et A. de Montaiglon,* 6 vols., Paris, 1851–1860.

Marseilles, Musée des Beaux-Arts, *Catalogue des peintures, sculptures, pastels et dessins,* ed. Ph. Auquier, Marseilles, 1908.

Martin, J. and Masson, Ch., *Oeuvre de J.-B. Greuze. Catalogue raisonné suivi de la liste des gravures exécutées d'après ses ouvrages,* Paris, 1908.

[Maulay, L.-J.], *Notice des tableaux qui composent le museum du département de la Sarthe,* Le Mans, Vendémiaires, An VIII.

Messelet, J., "Belle 1674 à 1734," in Louis Dimier, *Les peintres français du XVIIIème siècle,* Paris and Brussels, 1930, II, pp. 283–290.

———, "Nicolas Coypel 1690 à 1734," in Louis Dimier, *Les peintres français du XVIIIème siècle,* Paris and Brussels, 1930, II, pp. 217–227.

———, "Jean Restout (1692–1768)," *Nouvelle Archives de l'Art Français,* XIX (1938), pp. 99–188.

Mesuret, R., *Les expositions de l'Académie Royale de Toulouse de 1751 à 1791,* Toulouse, 1972.

Michel, A., Soulié, L., and Masson, Ch., *François Boucher,* Paris, n.d.

Minneapolis, The Minneapolis Institute of Arts, *European Paintings from The Minneapolis Institute of Arts,* New York, 1971.

Mirimonde, A.-P. de, "Les sujets musicaux chez Antoine Watteau," *Gazette des Beaux-Arts,* LVIII (1961), pp. 249–288.

———, "Tableaux et documents retrouvés. Noël Gasselin. Watteau. Rigaud. Oudry. Mariège. Greuze. Brenet. Moreau le Jeune," *Bulletin de la Société de l'Histoire de l'Art Français, 1967,* 1968, pp. 97–107.

Montaiglon, A. de, *Procès-verbaux de l'Académie Royale de Peinture et de Sculpture, 1648–1793, publiés pour la Société d'Histoire de l'Art Français d'après les registres originaux conservés à l'Ecole des Beaux-Arts,* 10 vols., Paris, 1875–1892. Index: Paris, 1909.

——— and Guiffrey, J., eds., *Correspondance des Directeurs de l'Académie de France à Rome avec les Surintendants des Bâtiments,* 17 vols., Paris, 1887–1912. Published from the masuscripts in the Archives Nationales.

Montgolfier, B. de. "Trois esquisses peintes du XVIIIème siècle," *Bulletin du musée Carnavalet,* IX (1956), pp. 10–13.

Mouton-Gilles, C., *Jean-Baptiste Van Loo,* mémoire de maîtrise, 1970.

———, "Jean-Baptiste Van Loo," *L'Information d'Histoire de l'Art,* XVII (1972), pp. 187–191.

Munhall, E., "Greuze and the Protestant Spirit," *The Art Quarterly,* XXVII (1964), pp. 3–23.

———, "Les Dessins de Greuze pour 'Septime Sévère'," *L'Oeil,* CXXIV (April 1965), pp. 23–29, 59.

———, "Quelques Découvertes sur l'oeuvre de Greuze," *La Revue du Louvre et des Musées de France,* XVI (1966), pp. 85–92.

Nemilova, I. S., *Watteau et ses oeuvres à l'Ermitage,* Leningrad, 1963. In Russian.

New York, Columbia University and M. Knoedler and Company, *Masters of the Loaded Brush. Oil Sketches from Rubens to Tiepolo,* [ex. cat.], New York, 1967.

———, Finch College Museum of Art, *French Masters of the Eighteenth Century,* [ex. cat.], New York, 1963.

———, Wildenstein and Company, Inc., *Gods and*

Heroes. Baroque Images of Antiquity, [ex. cat.], New York, 1968.
Nîmes, Musée de Nîmes, *Catalogue du Musée de Nîmes, notice historique sur la maison-carrée. Biographie de Sigalon par Auguste Pelet, Nîmes,* 1853.
Nolhac, P. de, *Hubert Robert,* Paris, 1910.
———, *Nattier,* Paris, 1925.
Nonnotte, see Dussieux, L., . . .
Opperman, H. N., *Jean-Baptiste Oudry 1686–1755 with a sketch for a catalogue raisonné of his paintings, drawings and prints,* 4 vols., Ph.D. dissertation, Department of Art, The University of Chicago, Chicago, 1972.
Pahin de la Blancherie, *Essai d'un tableau historique des peintres de l'école française depuis Jean Cousin en 1500 jusqu'en 1783 inclusivement,* Paris, 1783. Reprinted: Geneva, 1972.
Paris, Archives Nationales, o[1] 1925. B, letter from J.-B.-M. Pierre to J.-B.-S. Chardin.
———, Bibliothèque Nationale, fonds Deloyne, "Entretiens de M. l'Abbé A*** avec Mylord B***."
———, Galerie Cailleux, *François Boucher, premier peintre du roi, 1703–1770,* [ex. cat.], Paris, 1964.
———, Galerie Cailleux, see also Cailleux, J. and Roland-Michel, M., . . .
———, Galerie Georges Petit, *Collection de feu M. Jules Burat,* [sale cat.], Paris, 1885.
———, Galerie Georges Petit, *Collection J. Doucet. Dessins, pastels, sculptures, tableaux, meubles et objets d'art du XVIIIème siècle,* [sale cat.], 3 vols., Paris, 1912.
———, Galerie Heim, *Le choix de l'amateur. Sélection de peintures et sculptures du XVème au XVIIIème siècle,* [ex. cat.], Paris, 1974.
———, Gazette des Beaux-Arts and Beaux-Arts, *Le Siècle de Louis XV vu par les artistes,* [ex. cat.], Paris, 1934.
———, Grand Palais, *De David à Delacroix. La peinture française de 1774 à 1830,* [ex. cat.], Paris, Detroit, and New York, 1974–1975.
———, Musée Carnavalet, *Les chefs-d'oeuvre des musées de Province. Deuxième exposition. Portraits et scènes de genre école française, 1650–1830,* Paris, 1933.
———, Musée de l'Orangerie, *Hubert Robert 1733–1808,* [ex. cat.], Paris, 1933.
———, Musée du Louvre, *Renaissance du Musée de Brest,* [ex. cat.], Paris, 1974–1975.
———, Musée du Louvre, Galerie Mollien, *Le Cabinet d'un Grand Amateur P. J. Mariette 1694–1774,* [ex. cat.], Paris, 1967.
———, Orangerie des Tuileries, *David. Exposition en l'honneur du deuxième centenaire de sa naissance,* [ex. cat.], Paris, 1948.
———, Orangerie des Tuileries, *Le portrait français de Watteau à David,* [ex. cat.], Paris, 1957.
———, Palais National des Arts, *Chefs-d'oeuvre de l'art français,* [ex. cat.], Paris, 1937.
Parker, K. T. and Mathey, J., *A. Watteau. Catalogue complet de son oeuvre dessiné,* 2 vols., Paris, 1957.
Pascal, G., *Largillierre,* Paris, 1928.
Pérez, M. F., "Tableaux de Nicolas-Guy Brenet (1728–1792) conservés dans la région lyonnaise," *Bulletin de la Société de l'Histoire de l'Art Français, 1973,* 1974, pp. 199–212.
Pericoli, C., "Un dipinto di Subleyras al Museo di Roma," *Bolletino dei Musei Comunali di Roma,* VIII, 1–4 (1961), pp. 37–43.
Pérouse de Montclos, J. M., *Etienne-Louis Boullée 1728–1799. De l'architecture classique à l'architecture révolutionnaire,* Paris, 1969.
Planchenault, R., "La collection du marquis de Livois. L'art français," *Gazette des Beaux-Arts,* X (1933), pp. 220–237.
Ponsonailhe, C., "Les deux Ranc," *Réunion des Sociétés des Beaux-Arts des Départements,* XI (1887), pp. 173–204.
Populus, B., *Claude Gillot (1673–1722). Catalogue de l'oeuvre gravé,* Paris, 1930.
Posner, D., *Watteau. A Lady at her Toilet,* London, 1973.
———, "Watteau mélancolique: la formation d'un mythe," *Bulletin de la Société de l'Histoire de l'Art Français, 1973,* 1974, pp. 345–361.
Procès-verbaux. . ., see Montaiglon, A. de, . . .
Providence, Brown University and Rhode Island School of Design, *Rubenism,* Providence, 1975.
Quarré, P., *Un paysagiste dijonnais du XVIIIème siècle, J.-B. Lallemand, 1716–1803,* [ex. cat.], Dijon, 1954.
———, "Dessins d'architecture de Colson," *Bulletin de la Société de l'Histoire de l'Art Français, 1970,* 1972, pp. 115–123.
——— and others, *Trois peintres bourguignons du XVIIIème siècle. Colson, Vestier, Trinquesse,* [ex. cat.], Dijon, 1969.
Réau, L., "Watteau 1684 à 1721," in Louis Dimier, *Les peintres français du XVIIIème siècle,* Paris and Brussels, 1928, I, pp. 1–59.
———, "Grimou 1678 à 1733," in Louis Dimier, *Les peintres français du XVIIIème siècle,* Paris and Brussels, 1930, II, pp. 195–216.
———, "Carle Van Loo," *Nouvelles Archives de l'Art Français,* XIX (1938), pp. 7–96.
Roland-Michel, M., *Anne Vallayer-Coster. 1774–1818,* Paris, 1970.

Roman, J., *Le Livre de raison du peintre Hyacinthe Rigaud,* Paris, 1919.

Rosenberg, P., *Inventaire des collections publiques françaises, Rouen, Tableaux français du XVIIème siècle et italiens des XVIIème et XVIIIème siècles,* Paris, 1966.

———, "Le XVIIIème siècle français à la Royal Academy," *Revue de l'Art,* III (1969), pp. 98–100.

———, "An Exhibition at the Barberini Gallery, Rome," *The Burlington Magazine,* CXII (1970), pp. 641–642.

———, *French Master Drawings of the 17th and 18th centuries in North American collections,* trans. C. Johnston, [ex. cat.], Toronto, Ottawa, San Francisco, and New York, 1972–1973.

———, "A propos de Nicolas Vleughels," *Pantheon,* XXXI (1973), pp. 143–153.

——— ,"Largilliere peintre d'histoire et de paysage," *La Revue du Louvre et des Musées de France,* XXIII (1973), pp. 89–94.

———, "Dandré-Barbon as a Draughtsman: A Group of Drawings at Stuttgart," *Master Drawings,* XII (1974), pp. 137–151.

———, "A propos d'un dessin d'Antoine Rivalz," *La Revue du Louvre et des Musées de France,* XXV (1975), pp. 182–185.

——— and Compin, I., "Quatre nouveaux Fragonard au Louvre. I," *La Revue du Louvre et des Musées de France,* XXIV (1974), pp. 184–192.

———, Compin, I., and Guilmard, L., in *Louis XV. Un moment de perfection de l'art français,* [ex. cat.], Paris, 1974–1975.

———, Méjanès, J. F., and Vilain, J., *P. C. Trémolières (Cholet, 1703–Paris, 1739),* [ex. cat.], Cholet, 1973.

———, Reynaud, N., and Compin, I., *Musée du Louvre. Catalogue illustré des Peintures. Ecole française XVIIème et XVIIIème siècles,* 2 vols., Paris, 1974.

——— and Schnapper, A., "Beaufort's Brutus," *The Burlington Magazine,* CXII (1970), p. 760.

——— and Schnapper, A., *Jean Restout (1692–1768),* [ex. cat.], Rouen, 1970.

——— and Volle, N., *Jean Barbault (1718–1762),* [ex. cat.], Beauvais, Angers, Valence, (Dijon), 1974–1975.

Rosenblum, R., *Transformations in Late Eighteenth Century Art,* Princeton, 1967.

———, "A Source for David's Horatii," *The Burlington Magazine,* CXII (1970), pp. 269–273.

Roux, M., *Bibliothèque Nationale. Département des Estampes. Inventaire du fonds français; graveurs du XVIIIème siècle,* Paris, 1930.

Sahut, M. C., *Le peintre Louis Galloche (1670–1761),* mémoire de maîtrise, 1972.

San Diego, Fine Arts Gallery of San Diego, *French Paintings from French Museums. XVII–XVIII centuries,* [ex. cat.], San Diego, San Francisco, Sacramento, and Santa Barbara, 1967–1968.

Sandoz, M., "Etudes et esquisses peintes ou dessinées de Jean-Baptiste Deshays (1721–1765)," *Gazette des Beaux-Arts,* XXXVIII, I (1951), pp. 129–146.

———, "Jean-Baptiste Deshays, peintre d'histoire (1721–1765)," *Bulletin de la Société de l'Histoire de l'Art Français, 1958,* 1959, pp. 7–21.

———, "Gabriel-François Doyen, peintre d'histoire (1726–1806)," *Bulletin de la Société de l'Histoire de l'Art Français, 1959,* 1960, pp. 75–88.

———, "Nicolas-Guy Brenet, peintre d'histoire (1728–1792)," *Bulletin de la Société de l'Histoire de l'Art Français, 1960,* 1961, pp. 33–50.

———, "Louis-Jean-François Lagrenée, dit l'Aîné (1725–1805), peintre d'histoire," *Bulletin de la Société de l'Histoire de l'Art Français, 1961,* 1962, pp. 115–136.

———, "Jean-Jacques Lagrenée, peintre d'histoire (1739–1821)," *Bulletin de la Société de l'Histoire de l'Art Français, 1962,* 1963, pp. 121–133.

———, "Tableaux retrouvés de Jean-Baptiste Deshays, Gabriel Doyen et Louis Lagrenée (l'Aîné)," *Bulletin de la Société de l'Histoire de l'Art Français, 1967,* 1968, pp. 109–122.

Saunier, Ch., "La Mort de Sénèque par Louis David," *Gazette des Beaux-Arts,* XXXIII (1905), pp. 233–236.

———, "Galloche 1670–1761," in Louis Dimier, *Les peintres français du XVIIIème siècle,* Paris and Brussels, 1928, I, pp. 217–226.

———, "Lemoine 1688 à 1737," in Louis Dimier, *Les peintres français du XVIIIème siècle,* Paris and Brussels, 1928, I, pp. 61–92.

Schnapper, A., "A propos de deux nouvelles acquisitions: 'le chef-d'oeuvre d'un muet' ou la tentative de Charles Coypel," *La Revue du Louvre et des Musées de France,* XVIII (1968), pp. 253–264.

———, *Au temps du Roi Soleil, Les peintres de Louis XIV (1660–1715),* [ex. cat.], Lille, 1968.

———, "Antoine Coypel: la Galerie d'Enée au Palais-Royal," *Revue de l'Art,* V (1969), pp. 33–42.

———, "Esquisses de Louis de Boullogne sur la vie de Saint Augustin," *Revue de l'Art,* IX (1970), pp. 58–64.

———, "A propos d'un tableau de N. Bertin," *La Revue du Louvre et des Musées de France,* XXII (1972), pp. 357–360.

———, "Deux tableaux de Henri de Favanne," *La Revue du Louvre et des Musées de France,* XXII (1972), pp. 361–364.

———, "A la recherche de Sébastien II Leclerc 1676–1763," *La Revue du Louvre et des Musées de France,* XXIII (1973), pp. 241–248.

———, *Jean Jouvenet 1646–1717 et la peinture d'histoire à Paris,* Paris, 1974.

Seznec, J. and Adhémar, J., *Diderot Salons,* 4 vols., Oxford, 1957–1967. Vol. 4, Seznec alone.

Slatkin, R. S., *François Boucher in North American Collections. 100 Drawings,* [ex. cat.], Washington and Chicago, 1973–1974.

Sterling, Ch., *François Boucher 1703–1770,* [ex. cat.], Paris, 1932.

———, *The Metropolitan Museum of Art. A Catalogue of French Paintings XV–XVIII Centuries,* Cambridge, 1955.

Stockholm, Nationalmuseum, *Catalogue descriptif des collection de peinture du Musée National. Maîtres étrangers,* Stockholm, 1928.

Stuffmann, M., "Charles de La Fosse et sa position dans la peinture française à la fin du XVIIIème siècle," *Gazette des Beaux-Arts,* LXIV (1964), pp. 1–121.

———, "Les tableaux de la collection de Pierre Crozat," *Gazette des Beaux-Arts,* LXXII (1968), pp. 1–144.

Sutton, D., *France in the Eighteenth Century,* [ex. cat.], London, 1968–1969.

Talbot, W. S., "Jean-François De Troy: Pan and Syrinx," *The Cleveland Museum of Art Bulletin,* LXI (1974), pp. 250–259.

Thuillier, J. and Châtelet, A., *La peinture française. De Le Nain à Fragonard,* Geneva, 1964.

Tzeutschler-Lurie A., "Hyacinthe Rigaud, Portrait of Cardinal Dubois," *The Cleveland Museum of Art Bulletin,* LIV (1967), pp. 230–239.

———, "Rigaud's Portrait of Cardinal Dubois," *The Burlington Magazine,* CXVI (1974), pp. 667–668.

Vaillat, A. and Ratouis de Limay, P., *J. B. Perronneau, sa vie et son oeuvre,* Paris, 1923. Editions also in 1909 and 1925.

Valory, see Dussieux, L., . . .

Vergnet-Ruiz, J., "Oudry 1686 à 1755," in Louis Dimier, *Les peintres français du XVIIIème siècle*, Paris and Brussels, 1930, II, pp. 135–194.

Vitet, L., *L'Académie Royale de Peinture et de Sculpture; étude historique,* Paris, 1861.

Volle, see Rosenberg, P., and Volle, N., . . .

Waterhouse, E. K., "English painting and France in the eighteenth century," *Journal of the Warburg and Courtauld Institutes,* XV (1952), pp. 122–135.

Watson, F., "The Missing Coronation Portrait of Louis XV?," *The Burlington Magazine,* CXVI (1974), pp. 534–537.

Welu, J. A., "Sleeping Endymion by Nicolas-Guy Brenet," *Worcester Art Museum Bulletin,* IV, I (1974), pp. 5–7.

Wescher, P., "Philippe Mercier and the French Artists in London," *The Art Quarterly,* XIV (1951), pp. 179–194.

Wildenstein, D., "L'oeuvre gravé des Coypel. II.," *Gazette des Beaux-Arts,* LXIV (1964), pp. 141–152.

———, "Sur le Verrou de Fragonard," *Gazette des Beaux-Arts,* Supplement to vol. LXXXV (1975), pp. 13–24.

——— and G., *Documents complémentaires au catalogue de l'oeuvre de Louis David,* Paris, 1973.

Wildenstein, G., *Le peintre Aved, sa vie et son oeuvre,* 2 vols., Paris, 1922.

———, *Un peintre de paysage au XVIIIème siècle; Louis Moreau,* Paris, 1923.

———, *Lancret,* Paris, 1924.

———, "Le Lever de Fanchon par Lépicié," *Pantheon,* I (1928), pp. 199–200.

———, *Chardin,* Paris, 1933.

———, "Premier supplément à la biographie et au catalogue de J. A. J. Aved (1922–1935)," *Gazette des Beaux-Arts,* XIII (1935), pp. 159–172.

———, "Les graveurs de Poussin au XVIIème siècle," *Gazette des Beaux-Arts,* XLVI (1955), pp. 77–371.

———, *The Paintings of Fragonard,* New York, 1960.

———, *Chardin,* Zurich, 1963.

Worcester, Massachusetts, Art Museum, *European Paintings in the Collection of the Worcester Art Museum,* 2 vols., Worcester, 1974.

York, City Art Museum and Kenwood (London), Iveagh Bequest, *Philippe Mercier,* [ex. cat.], York and Kenwood, 1969.

Zimmermann, X., *Watteau,* Stuttgart and Leipzig, 1911.

Zmijewska, H., "La Critique des Salons en France avant Diderot," *Gazette des Beaux-Arts,* LXXVI (1970), pp. 1–143.

PLATES

Pl. 1. Vigouroux-Duplessis, *Devant de cheminée montrant trois Chinois soutenant un tableau rond sur lequel est représenté Jupiter et Danaë*, 1700

Pl. 2. A. Coypel, *Adam et Eve sous le regard de Dieu après le péché*, 1704

Pl. 3. Boullongne, *Diane et ses compagnes se reposent après la chasse*, 1707

Pl. 4. Jouvenet, *La déposition de croix*, 1709

Pl. 5. La Fosse, *Le Christ au désert servi par les anges*

Pl. 6. Desportes, *Etude de nuages éclairés par le soleil couchant*

Pl. 7. Desportes, *Etude de paysage: coin d'étang dans lequel se reflète le ciel et les coteaux*

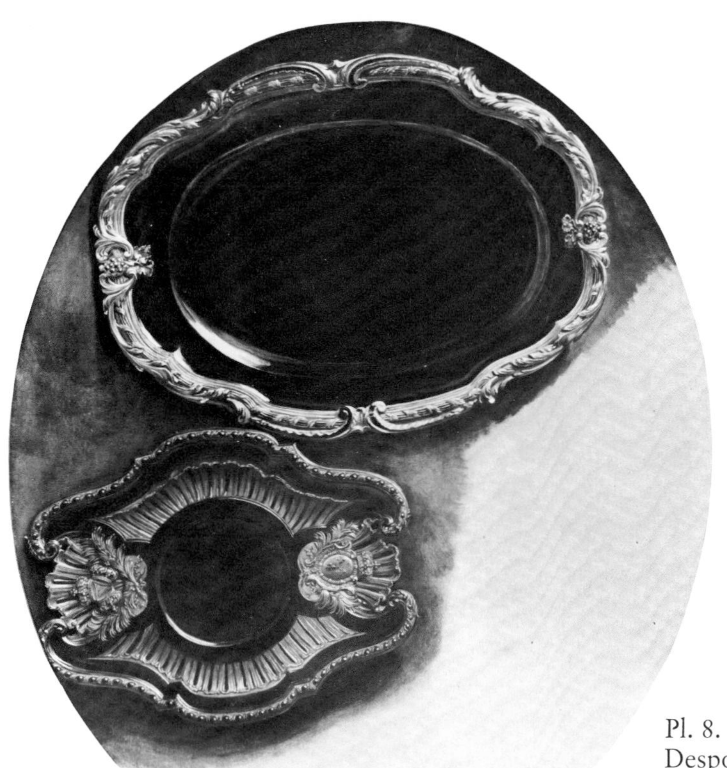

Pl. 8.
Desportes,
Etude de deux plats, l'un d'argent, l'autre de vermeil (dont l'un aux armes royales)

Pl. 9. Desportes, *Etude d'oiseaux: demoiselles de Numidie*

Pl. 10.
Allegrain,
Paysage au lac

Pl. 11.
Largillierre,
Nature morte au tapi

Pl. 12. F. de Troy, *La duchesse de La Force (?)*, 1714

Pl. 13. Watteau, *La perspective*

Pl. 14. Largillierre, *Paysage silvestre avec deux personnages*

Pl. 15. J.-F. de Troy, *L'éducation de Bacchus*, 1717

Pl. 16. Tournières, *Allégorie de l'été,* 1717

Pl. 17. Watteau, *La rêveuse*

Pl. 18. Le Clerc, *La mort de Saphire*, 1718

Pl. 19.
Nattier,
Persée, assisté par Minerve, pétrifie Phinée et ses compagnons en leur présentant la tête de Méduse, 1718

Pl. 20.
Gillot,
La scène dite des deux carrosses

Pl. 21. Watteau, *Le mezzetin*

Pl. 22. Bertin, *Anacréon et l' Amour*

Pl. 23. Robert de Séry, *Portrait de femme,* 1722

Pl. 24. Courtin, *Le jeu de bilboquet*

Pl. 25. Ranc, *Vertumne et Pomone*

Pl. 26. Rigaud, *Portrait du cardinal Dubois*, 1723

Pl. 27. Pesne, *Portrait du graveur Jean Mariette*, 1723

Pl. 28. Largillierre, *Portrait de François-Jules du Vaucel*, 1724

Pl. 29. Delyen, *Portrait du sculpteur Guillaume Coustou*, 1725

Pl. 30. Belle, *Mme de la Sablonnière (?) et sa fille*, 1724

Pl. 31. Favanne, *Coriolan quittant sa famille pour combattre sa patrie*, 1725

Pl. 32. Houasse, *Vue de l'Escurial*

Pl. 33. Rivalz, *Autoportrait,* 1726–1728 (?)

Pl. 34. Restout, *Portrait de l' architecte Pierre de Vigny*

Pl. 35. Grimou, *L'homme à la pipe*, 1726

Pl. 36. Ch.-A. Coypel, *Persée délivrant Andromède*, 1727

Pl. 37. N.-N. Coypel, *L'enlèvement d'Europe*, 1727

Pl. 38. Vleughels, *Les noces de Cana*, 1728

Pl. 39. Lemoine, *Pygmalion voyant sa statue animée*, 1729

Pl. 40. Restout, *La mort de sainte Scholastique*, 1730

Pl. 41. Lemoine, *Narcisse contemplant son reflet dans l'eau*

Pl. 42. Galloche, *Roland apprenant les amours d'Angélique et de Médor*, 1732

Pl. 43. Cazes, *La balançoire*, 1732

Pl. 44. Dandré-Bardon, *L'adoration des crânes*

Pl. 45. J.-B. Van Loo, *Renaud dans les bras d'Armide*

Pl. 46. Boucher, *Vénus demandant à Vulcain des armes pour Enée*, 1732

Pl. 47. Ch.-A. Coypel, *Portrait de Philippe Coypel, frère du peintre*, 1732

Pl. 48. Nattier, *Mme Crozat de Thiers et sa fille (?)*, 1733

Pl. 49. Pater, *La foire à Bezons*, 1733

Pl. 50. Tocqué, *Portrait du sculpteur Jean-Louis Lemoyne*, 1734

Pl. 51. Parrocel, *Jeune femme lisant devant une cheminée*, 173(5?)

Pl. 52. J.-F. de Troy, *La moissonneuse endormie*

Pl. 53. Domenchin de Chavannes, *Paysage au château,* 1737

Pl. 54. Trémolières, *Ulysse, sauvé du naufrage par Minerve, aborde à l'île de Calypso,* 1737

Pl. 55. Lancret, *La danse devant la tente*

Pl. 56. Chardin, *La gouvernante,* 1738

Pl. 57. Boucher, *Le déjeuner*, 1739

Pl. 58. Aved, *Portrait de Jean-Gabriel de La Porte du Theil*, 1740

Pl. 59. Oudry, "*Teste bizarre d'un Cerf pris par le Roy le 3 juillet 1741*", 1741

Pl. 60. Nonnotte, *Portrait du graveur Jean Moyreau*, 1742

Pl. 61. Rigaud, *La présentation au temple*, 1741–1743

Pl. 62. Liotard, *Dame franque et sa servante*

Pl. 63. Oudry, *Un vase de fleurs avec un parterre de tulipes, un perroquet et des papillons de nuit*

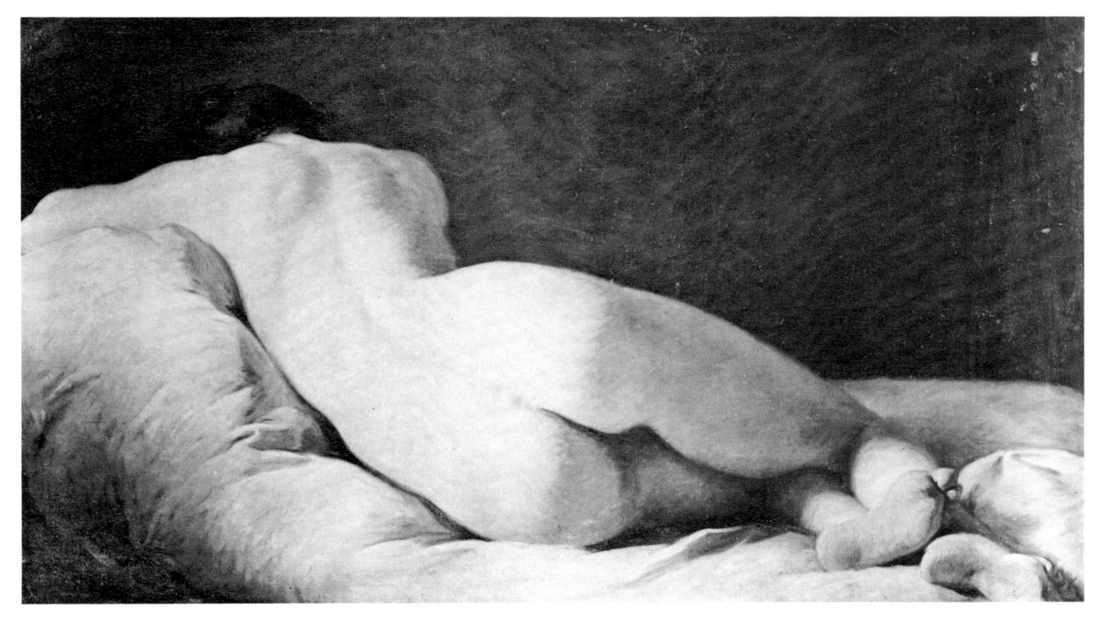

Pl. 64. Subleyras, *Nu de femme*

Pl. 65. Mercier, *L'éducation du chien*, 1744 (?)

Pl. 66. Subleyras, *Le bienheureux Jean d'Avila*

Pl. 67. Hallé, *Joseph accusé par la femme de Putiphar*, 1744

Pl. 68. Natoire, *La toilette de Psyché,* 1745

Pl. 69.
Natoire,
L'entrée solennelle de Monseigneur de Paris à Orléans en 1733

Pl. 70.
Pierre,
Bacchanale, 1747

Pl. 71. C. Van Loo, *Le voeu de Louis XIII au siège de La Rochelle*, 1746

Pl. 72.
Lajoue,
Paysage composé, au Neptune mutilé,
1746 (?)

Pl. 73.
Subleyras,
Saint Camille de Lellis sauvant des malades d'une inondation,
1746

Pl. 74. Vien, "*Sultane reine*", 1748

Pl. 75. Vien, *L'arrivée de sainte Marthe à Marseille*, 1748

Pl. 76. Vernet, *Vue du port de Naples,* 1748

Pl. 77. Lacroix, *Vue d'un port méditerranéen,* 1750

Pl. 78. Lallemand, *Vue du château Saint-Ange à Rome*

Pl. 79. Barbault, "*Fille dotée*"

Pl. 80. Barbault, "*Chevau-léger*"

Pl. 81. J.-F. de Troy, *Le marquis de Vandières*, 1751

Pl. 82. Fragonard, *Le colin-maillard*

Pl. 83. C. Van Loo, *Allégorie de la peinture*, 1753

Pl. 84. Vernet, *L'après-midi,* 1753

Pl. 85. Duparc, *Femme assise les bras croisés*

Pl. 86. Brenet, *Endymion endormi,* 1756

Pl. 87. Greuze, *La paresseuse italienne*, 1756

Pl. 88. Greuze, *Le geste napolitain*, 1757

Pl. 89. Boucher, *Le moulin dit de Charenton,* 1758

Pl. 90. Deshays, *L'Assomption de la Vierge*

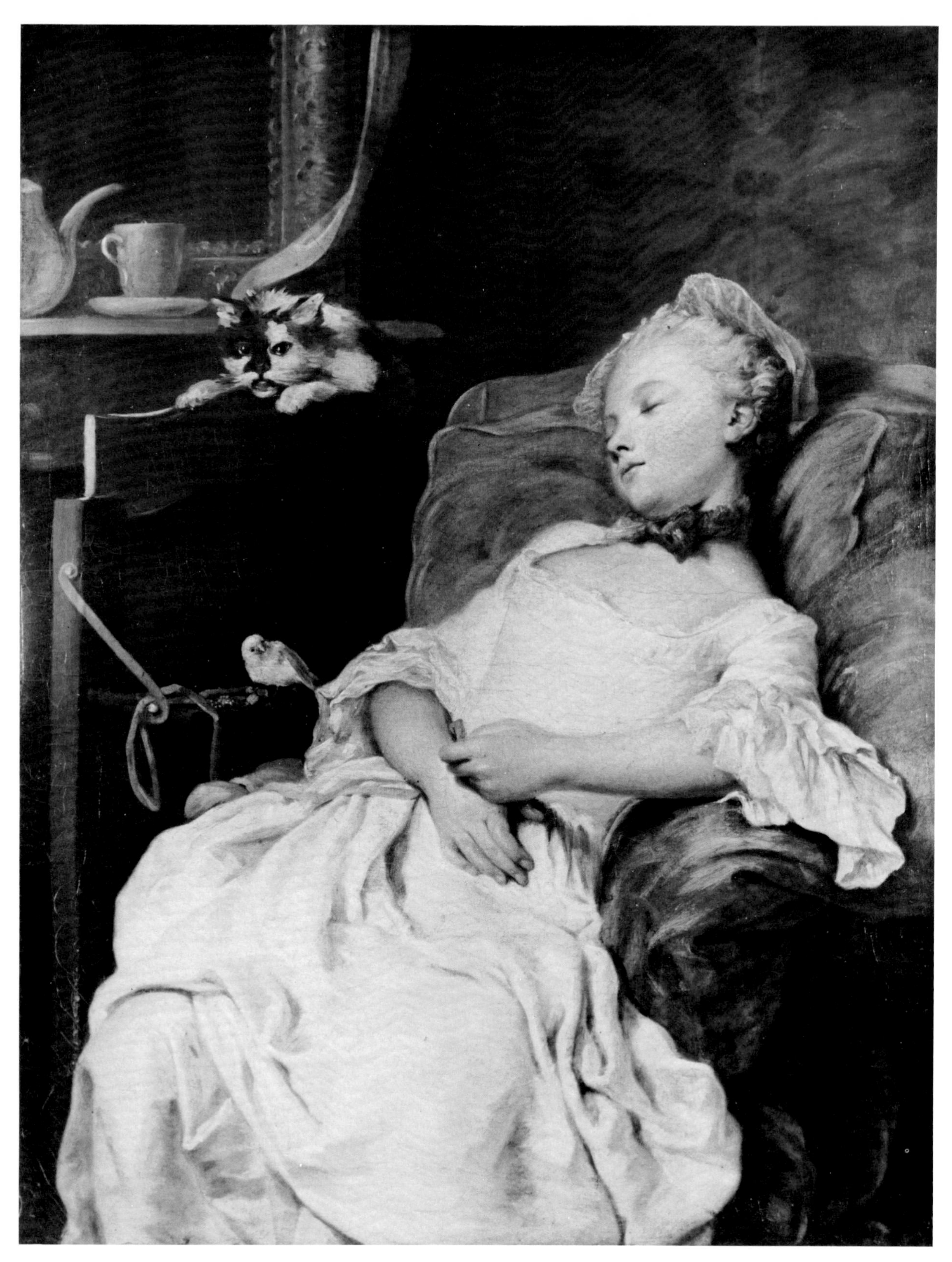

Pl. 91. Colson, *Le repos*, 1759

Pl. 92. Saint-Aubin, *La promenade,* 1760

Pl. 93. Fragonard, *Les cascatelles de Tivoli*

Pl. 94. Hallé, *Le colin-maillard*

Pl. 95. Julien, *Le sacrifice de Manué, père de Samson*, 1760

Pl. 96. Greuze, *Monseigneur de Valras*

Pl. 97. Drouais, *Le comte d'Artois et sa soeur, Madame Clotilde*, 1763

Pl. 98. Perronneau, *Portrait de Daniel Jousse*

Pl. 99.
Chardin,
Un dessert, ou la brioche,
1763

Pl. 100.
Bachelier,
"*Tête bizarre d'un cerf attaqué par le roi le 2 juin 1764 dans les taillis d'Épernon*",
1764

Pl. 101. Roland de la Porte, *"Les apprêts d'un déjeuner rustique"*, 1763

Pl. 102.
Robert,
L'escalier tournant du Palais Farnèse à Caprarola

Pl. 103.
Chardin,
Les Attributs des Arts, 1766

Pl. 104. Huet, *Un renard dans le poulailler*, 1766

Pl. 105. Lagrenée, *Allégorie à la mort du Dauphin*, 1767

Pl. 106. L.-M. Van Loo, *Portrait de Diderot*, 1767

Pl. 107. French School, XVIIIth Century, *La chapelle du calvaire à l'église Saint-Roch à Paris*

Pl. 108. Doyen, *Le Miracle des Ardents*, 1767

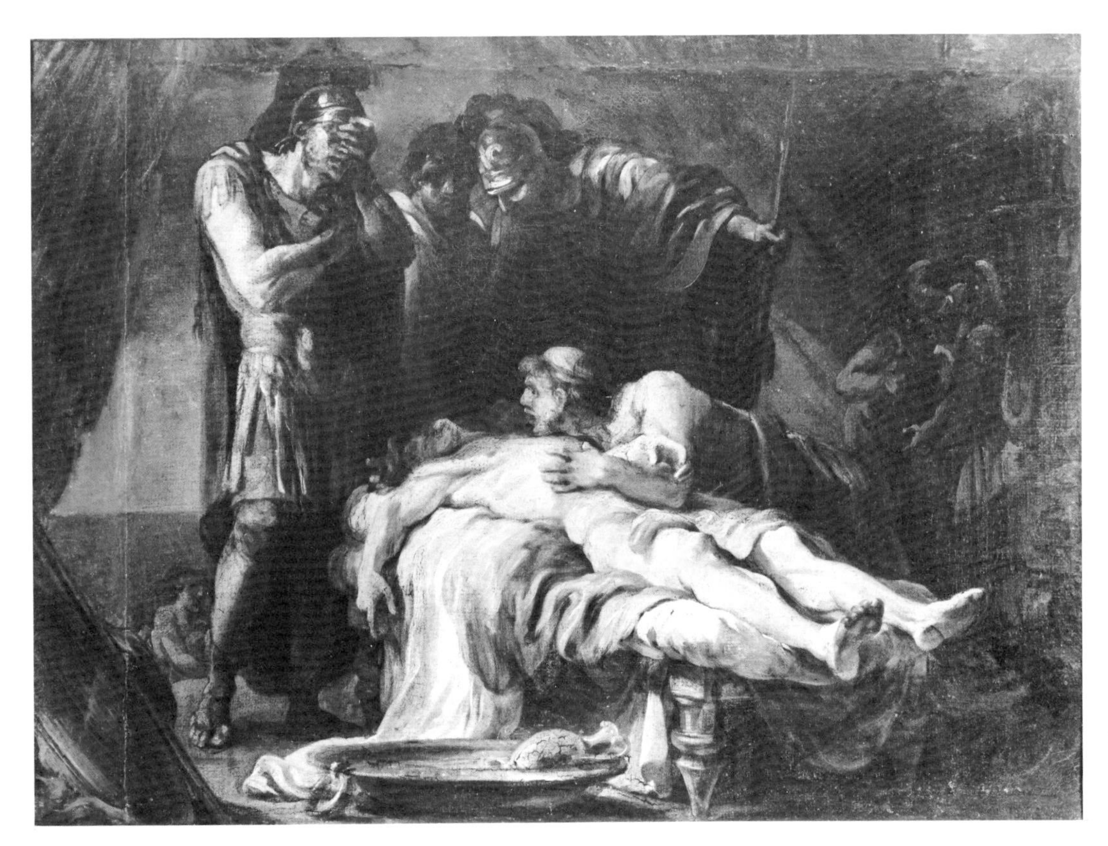

Pl. 109.
Durameau,
Achille pleurant Patrocle, 1767

Pl. 110.
Loutherbourg,
Combat sur mer, 1767

Pl. 111. Duplessis, *Portrait de Mme Freret-Déricour*, 1769

Pl. 112. Lépicié, *Portrait d'Emilie Vernet, future Madame Chalgrin*, 1769

Pl. 113. Fragonard, *Portrait de Marie-Madeleine Guimard*, 1769

Pl. 114. David, *Madame Buron*, 1769

Pl. 115. Leprince, *La crainte,* 1769

Pl. 116.
Vallayer-Coster,
Instruments de musique,
1770

Pl. 117.
French School,
XVIIIth Century,
Morphée

Pl. 118. Vincent, *L'Assomption de la Vierge,* 1771

Pl. 119. Beaufort, *Brutus, Lucretius, père de Lucrèce et Collatinus, son mari, jurent sur le poignard dont elle s'est tuée de venger sa mort et de chasser les Tarquins de Rome*, 1771

Pl. 120. Roslin, *Portrait de l'abbé Terray*, 1774.

Pl. 121. David, *La mort de Sénèque,* 1773

Pl. 122. Lagrenée, *"Une femme endormie sur un lit parsemé de roses"*, 1773

Pl. 123. Lépicié, *Le lever de Fanchon*, 1773

Pl. 124. Robert, *La découverte du Laocoön,* 1773

Pl. 125. Volaire, *L'éruption du Vésuve*

Pl. 126. Moreau, *Vue des coteaux de Bellevue, prise du parc de Saint-Cloud*

Pl. 127. Vien, *Vénus, blessée par Diomède, est sauvée par Iris*, 1775